TRUMAN

TRUMAN

ROY JENKINS

COLLINS
8 Grafton Street, London WI
1986

William Collins Sons & Co. Ltd
London · Glasgow · Sydney · Auckland
Toronto · Johannesburg

BRITISH LIBRARY CATALOGUING IN PUBLICATION DATA

Jenkins, Roy
Truman.
1. Truman, Harry S.   2. Presidents – United
States – Biography
I. Title
973.918′092′4   E814

ISBN 0 00 217584 3

Photoset in Linotron Bembo by
Rowland Phototypesetting Ltd,
Bury St Edmunds, Suffolk
Made and printed in Great Britain by
William Collins Sons & Co. Ltd, Glasgow

CONTENTS

PREFACE

This book was started in 1982, but mostly written in 1984 and early 1985. It arose out of a probably over-elaborate design which had interested me in the early 1970s. I then did some considerable work for a series of 'back to back' portraits of American presidents and British prime ministers – perhaps three of each – which were to be published in a single volume. It would have been a very big volume. However long books were already in fashion, and I was not then as sceptical of the value of setting the reader a solid thirty to forty hour course as I am now.

In the event only one of the British portraits was written before I again became too closely involved in other occupations to do any sustained writing. When I returned to the task I decided that less elaboration and more speed was necessary. One president would be enough to balance one prime minister. But who should it be? I had thought, for my original scheme, of covering Theodore Roosevelt, Hoover and Franklin Roosevelt. Of these F.D.R. was the most interesting, certainly to a British audience, and the one about whom I knew most. But the more I penetrated the subject the more I found that he suffered from one fatal disadvantage. There was nothing new in the compass of a short biography that I could say about him. The best that I could do would be a re-setting of old facts and familiar anecdotes. And while I was not attempting original re-search, this was clearly not good enough.

Truman, his successor, suffered from no such disadvantage. He did not have Roosevelt's refulgence and he was president for a little less than two-thirds of the time that Roosevelt was – but as Roosevelt was president for a third longer than anyone had ever been before this was not a disqualification. Truman presided over the creation of the Western world as it still broadly exists today. The creation of NATO, the Marshall Plan with its emphasis on European unity, the resistance to Soviet expansion, peacefully in Berlin, bloodily in Korea, all had long-lasting consequences. He was a president of great significance. He was an odd and in one central respect a paradoxical man, with whom, had I known him well (I met him once, for an hour) I would not, I suspect, have got along easily. He had an interesting and not over-known provenance. Although he has inspired biographies and other books about him running well into double figures (of which at least three are good) I did not have any of that sense of repleteness which had afflicted me with Roosevelt. I thought that there would be a good deal that was reasonably fresh to say about Truman, and found this in practice to be so.

I am indebted to a number of different groups of people for varying forms of assistance. Of those remaining who knew Truman well Mrs Clifton Daniels (Miss Margaret Truman) and her husband, Mr Averell Harriman and Mr Clark Clifford were particularly helpful. So, on this side of the Atlantic, was Lord Franks, British Ambassador in Washington from 1948 to 1952. Mr Robert Donovan, the most authoritative chronicler of the Truman presidency, answered several important questions. Mr and Mrs John Masterman of Kansas City gave me great assistance in visiting, in December 1983, the places of importance of Truman's early life.

My secretaries Miss Celia Beale and Miss Jenny Ross typed the manuscript. Miss Diana Fortescue, greatly assisted by the library of the United States Embassy in London, buttressed by that of the House of Commons, checked many facts and some interpretations.

The typescript was read and helpful suggestions were made by Professor Arthur M. Schlesinger (who made many invaluable points), Professor John Kenneth Galbraith, Mr Mark Bonham Carter, Sir Ian Gilmour, Lord Harris of Greenwich, Mr John Lyttle, and my wife. Mr Irwin Ross, whose *Loneliest Campaign* chronicles the 1948 election, read the chapter which covered that vital event in Truman's life. To all these and a number of others, I am very grateful.

October, 1985   R.H.J.

LIST OF ILLUSTRATIONS

I

THE TRANSITION

For twelve years and one month Franklin Roosevelt was President of the United States. It was the longest period of continuous elective power which had been seen anywhere in the world for a century or more. Moreover, this decade and a quarter coincided with the advance of America to world leadership.

Then, on April 12th, 1945, Roosevelt died, suddenly if not unexpectedly, at Warm Springs, Georgia. Three hours later Harry S. Truman was sworn in as the 33rd President.* He was nearly 61. It was the most intimidating succession in the English-speaking world since Addington succeeded William Pitt in 1801: 'Pitt is to Addington as London is to Paddington,' Canning wrote. And Paddington did not then even have a railway station. But Addington had been an intimate of Pitt's for years and enjoyed his continuing friendship until their quarrel of 1803. Truman knew the Senate, of which he had been a member since 1934, but his experience of the executive branch, with its expanded war-time complications, was minimal. He had been Vice-President for less than three months. During this period, except at Cabinet meetings, he saw Roosevelt twice. Also, as Truman recorded, 'Roosevelt never discussed anything important at his Cabinet meetings.'

Even more certainly Roosevelt never discussed anything important with his Vice-President. He looked to Truman to keep the Senate in order and to ensure that his peace treaty of the future did not meet the same fate as that which had befallen Woodrow Wilson's in 1919. He had encouraged him to do 'some campaign-

---

* He was only the 32nd person to hold the office. But as Grover Cleveland held it twice, the Truman presidency is normally counted as the 33rd.

ing' in 1944, adding rather incongruously 'I don't feel like going
everywhere.' (In fact he went only to New York, Chicago, Boston
and Philadelphia.) But there had been no question of treating
Truman as a deputy head of government. In accordance with the
American tradition, he regarded him as part of the legislative not
the executive branch. He treated him as he had treated Garner and
Wallace, and as indeed much as every previous president had treated
every previous vice-president. There was however an essential
difference between Truman and his two predecessors. They were
just vice-presidents, threatened with the obscurity which was
mostly the historic fate of those who had occupied that office.
Truman, from the moment of his nomination, was a likely president. But Roosevelt was the last man who wanted to recognize
that. He never thought of including him in the party of a hundred
or more Americans who went to the Yalta Conference in late
January 1945. He gave him no special account of the outcome.
Nor did he tell him about the Manhattan project, which was on
the threshold of creating the atomic bomb.

Roosevelt had indeed tossed the vice-presidential nomination to
him rather like a bone to a dog, except that Truman was not
hungry. But in so doing he had given almost his only indication
that he was concerned about the succession, and that a very faint
one. He was prevailed upon not to have Wallace again. This was
partly due to electoral considerations and threats from the South.
But he could have ridden these. He encouraged James Byrnes, but
eventually ditched him. Finally he committed something to paper,
although phrased in a manner well short of enthusiastic endorsement. He passed through Chicago on the opening morning of the
Democratic Convention, which he deliberately did not attend. He
had a conference in the railroad yards there, without getting out
of his train, with Robert E. Hannegan, the Chairman of the
Democratic National Committee, and Edwin Pauley, a Los
Angeles oilman who was a Democratic king-maker of the time.
They emerged with a note which expressed Roosevelt's willingness
to have either Truman or Justice (of the Supreme Court) William
O. Douglas on the ticket.★

As Douglas had no support in the Convention, and Roosevelt

★ But see pp. 59–60 *infra* for some exegesis on the uncertainty of the date
when this note was first composed and of the order in which Roosevelt placed
Truman and Douglas.

knew it, this effectively threw the President's endorsement to Truman. The only obstacle was that Truman genuinely did not want it. This was from a mixture of motives. He thought the vice-presidency itself was a grey and obscure job, and did not want it for that reason. 'I'll bet you can't name the names of half a dozen vice-presidents,' he told his sister during a discussion of the prospect. He apprehended however that in the circumstances of 1944 it might well lead to the presidency. And that he did not want for almost opposite reasons. He thought the responsibility was too great for him, and that in any event no man should seek the position. (Exactly how presidents were to emerge if this rule was followed was not clear.) Furthermore he was committed to nominating James Byrnes.

Although genuine, his reluctance was not unshakeable. After he had been present in the room (at the receiving end) when Roosevelt said to Hannegan on the telephone: 'You tell him that if he wants to break up the Democratic Party in the middle of a war that is his responsibility,' he gave in. He even made fairly strenuous efforts to find a proposer in the shape of his fellow Senator from Missouri. He was nominated on the second ballot. And so, nine months later, he found himself President of the United States. He was relatively old, more so than any new president since James Buchanan in 1857, although there have since been three older ones. Yet he was completely inexperienced in the executive side of government. He was unbriefed, and untravelled outside North America since 1919. The war against both Germany and Japan was still unwon, and he had succeeded the most charismatic figure in the world.

After the oath-taking ceremony in the White House he held a short, shocked Cabinet meeting, hurriedly asked everyone to stay in their posts, had a brief word with the Secretary of War, Stimson, who told him in the broadest terms about the atomic bomb project (he had, in fact, heard about it in even vaguer terms while he was vice-president, and then not from Roosevelt but from Byrnes) and then went home to his modest apartment on Connecticut Avenue. 'My wife and daughter and mother-in-law were at the apartment of our next door neighbor . . . They had a turkey dinner and they gave us something to eat. I had not had anything to eat since noon.' Then he telephoned his mother in Grandview, Missouri. Then he went to bed and to sleep, and 'did not worry any more.'[1]

The next morning he was up a little later than usual – at 6.30 – breakfasted with a 'crony',★ and was then driven to the White House, giving a lift to a rather derelict political reporter on the way. He had a series of mostly desultory meetings in the morning, and then went to the Capitol, for lunch with about 15 senators and congressmen. This, his diary suggests, he regarded as his most important meeting of the day, more so than briefing meetings with the Secretary of State and the Chiefs of Staff, or than exchanges of telegrams with Stalin. He also approved public arrangements for Roosevelt's funeral and made some private dispositions for his own living. These last were done so as to cause the minimum inconvenience, both to his neighbours, who in those days had not much noticed a vice-president but did not fancy the security upheaval of a president living alongside them, and to Mrs Roosevelt. He would remove his family to the subsidiary official residence of Blair House within a few days, but not to the White House for nearly a month. And, extraordinarily, all on that first day, he twice saw 'just to visit' a gentleman called Mr Duke Shoop, of the *Kansas City Star*.

So, one might have thought, the imperial presidency came to an end, within a few years of its beginning. Truman trailed none of Roosevelt's clouds of glory. He had none of his style, none of his prestige, none of his informal, patrician grandeur. A failed Missouri haberdasher had taken over from a Dutchess County country gentleman. Main Street had replaced the Hudson Valley. But the imperial presidency flowered with the change. Indeed in an important sense it developed only under Truman. Roosevelt had been the leader of the free world at war, when, after Pearl Harbor, the commitment of America was relatively easy to sustain, and the acceptance of its leadership automatic. Truman achieved the more difficult feat of being the leader of the free world at peace, or something fairly near to peace. He was the first president to

---

★ 'Cronies' always played a considerable part in Truman's life. They had to be male and possess at least some of the characteristics of being loyal, unpretentiously convivial, and adequately good at poker. Mostly they worked with or for Truman, although not necessarily so, and some of those with whom he worked most closely, and greatly liked and respected (notably General Marshall and Dean Acheson) were not cronies. This breakfast 'crony' of his first day as President was Hugh Fulton who had been counsel to the Senate committee over which Truman presided during the war. Fairly soon afterwards Truman cooled towards him. This was unusual: he was mostly very loyal to cronies.

preside over the *Pax Americana*. It was not immediately apparent that this would be so. There was considerable early faltering. But once he had got into his stride, his capacity for informal decision taking and for doing what he regarded as right, without regard to the personal consequence, became remarkable. '. . . his ego never came between him and his job,' Dean Acheson wrote. Acheson firmly believed that he was a better president than Roosevelt; but Acheson, for his own reasons, neither liked nor admired Roosevelt.

Truman did admire him, though he was instinctively very critical of the prominent. Of his successors in one form or another, he despised Nixon, was unforgiving of Eisenhower for his treatment of General Marshall, thought Stevenson effete, and believed that Kennedy's nomination, to which he was less entitled than Lyndon Johnson, had been bought for him by his father. But he admired Roosevelt as a great leader who was also a consummate politician. He tried to follow in his path without copying him. He would sometimes mock his grand voice and Harvard accent, and it is doubtful how much he liked him. But he was iron in his determination never to complain about the scant notice which Roosevelt had taken of him, and he had little of the resentment against the Eastern sophistication of his predecessor's White House which devoured Lyndon Johnson. 'I see red every time [the sabotage] press starts a ghoulish attack on the President (I can never think of anyone as the President but Mr Roosevelt)' he was writing, admittedly to Eleanor Roosevelt, nearly six months after he had taken office.

Truman was in some ways the superior of Roosevelt. He did not have his style, his resonance, his confidence, his occasional sweep of innovative imagination, or his tolerance and understanding of diverse human nature. But he was less vain, less devious and better to work for. He was more decisive, and quite apart from Roosevelt's physical disability, he had more sustained energy than the wartime Roosevelt. He could always be up at 6.00 or 6.30 in the morning and be consistently fresh and on the job until however late was required. He was mostly better briefed, and not only in an immediate and superficial sense. He was at least as well read in history and biography as was Roosevelt. He was steeped in the history of the Republic and particularly of the presidency, but he was also a considerable expert on the lives of the Roman emperors and of almost every great military commander in the history of the world. Yet his knowledge sat less easily on his shoulders. Mr Merle Miller, who published a so-called 'oral biography' of Truman after the death of his subject, made an interesting comment:

> 'He was a self-educated man, and he mispronounced a
> reasonable number of words, which in the beginning puzzled
> me. Then I realised that while he had often read them, he
> had seldom, if ever, spoken them aloud, not even in
> many cases heard them spoken aloud. It's like that if you
> are one of the few readers in town.'[2]

This gets close to the central paradox of Truman. His manner was that of a Midwestern machine politician, and he was intensely loyal to his background and to those who had helped him on the way up. His friends were mostly 'regular fellows', and he had many of the values of a member of a Rotary Club. But a few of those he most respected and liked – Dean Acheson and General Marshall – already mentioned – were very different from this and from each other. His affections were heavily concentrated upon his close relations, and he was not much at ease in female company outside his family.

It is tempting to say that he was an intellectual amongst political 'pros' and a political 'pro' amongst intellectuals. But that is much too easy an aphorism. As a boy and a young man he was more of a book-worm than an intellectual. He absorbed many facts, and he thought about them a good deal, but his conversation involved no spinning of general theories. He neither possessed nor aspired to intellectual or social sophistication. His speech and his writing – and he wrote a lot of unsent letters and undelivered speeches, even under the pressure of the presidency – were generally splendidly direct, but the choice of words was rarely distinguished, and the sentiments sometimes narrow and intolerant: 'Sissy' was one which he employed a good deal. He used it frequently, disparagingly and foolishly about Adlai Stevenson. But when once asked at a school question and answer session, after he had been President, whether he had been popular as a boy, he replied:

> 'Why no, I was never popular. The popular boys were the
> ones who were good at games and had big, tight fists. I was

never like that. Without my glasses I was blind as a bat,
and to tell the truth, I was kind of a sissy.'[3]

This interplay provided part of the formation of his personality
and character. He was an 'anti-sissy' sissy, a puritan from the poker
rooms, a backwoods politician who became a world statesman not
just because he was President of the United States in the plenitude
of its power but because he had an exceptional sense of duty and
power of decision, and because he could distinguish big issues
from little ones, and was as generally right on the big ones as he
was frequently wrong on the small ones.

2

JACKSON COUNTY

Truman's early life was wholly contained in the western part of the state of Missouri. There is no evidence that, as a young man, he ever went as far afield as Chicago, let alone to New York or Washington. Yet within this small perimeter his life was mobile. He changed houses, and later jobs, with almost excessive frequency. But there was also a strong undercurrent of stability, which came from the homogeneity of his stock, a close-knit family, and the continued existence of a fair-sized family farm at the impressively named Grandview.

His four grandparents were all Americans of several generations' standing who, coming from Kentucky, had settled in Missouri in the 1840s. The Truman side was of English origin. The origin of the Youngs, his mother's family, was Ulster, with a German infusion. The two families embraced various nonconformist sects: Presbyterians, Baptists, Methodists; no Episcopalians, and certainly no Catholics. In the literal meaning of the acronym, Harry Truman was as WASP as could be, although his style and outlook had little in common with the connotation for which the term was later contrived. This was not because of simple questions of geography or even wealth. The families, despite fluctuations and vicissitudes, had a certain underlying prosperity. Margaret Truman, the President's daughter, in no way a pretentious lady, stated in her biography of her father,* that the Youngs at least

* *Harry S. Truman*, published in 1973, a little more than a year after his death. It is the best 'daughter biography' that I know. It is also very near to being the best book on Truman. It is rightly partial and does not see everything in the round (otherwise there would be no point in writing this book). But it is both interesting and careful with facts.

were 'certainly upper-middle class' and that the Grandview farm, even when it had been reduced by one of these fluctuations, regularly earned $15,000 a year in the early 1900s, which would be the equivalent of a good $150,000 today.[1]

Western Missouri is obviously a long way from the Hudson Valley and the Hyde Park home of Truman's predecessor as president, who was born only two years before him. But it is barely 300 miles from Bloomington, Illinois, where Adlai Stevenson, his successor as leader of the Democratic Party and only 16 years his junior, grew up. The Stevensons, while substantially more prosperous than the Young/Trumans, were not rich by grand American turn of the century standards. Yet the chasm between Stevenson life and Truman life was immense. The Stevensons lived in a garrison town of American gentry; the Trumans were part of the countryside around them.

Both the Youngs and the Trumans arrived in Missouri by steamboat. They were part of the second or third wave of settlers, when the state was already more than twenty years old. Within a few years of each other they steamed down the Ohio River to Cairo, Illinois, and from there up first the Mississippi and then the Missouri to Westport Landing, so called because Westport, now a southern suburb of Kansas City, was there before the city itself. They moved back a few miles east and settled around Independence, which was a major staging point to the West and the South West. They each brought with them a few slaves. They established themselves, a little precariously, in ante-bellum Missouri, which was a border state but still, just, a part of the old South and very different from the territories to the west and north of it.

Solomon Young was the dominant figure of the four. He acquired more land and at one time had 5000 acres in Jackson County, as well as the title to much of what later became Sacramento, California. But he sold as well as bought, and did so somewhat haphazardly, so that he built up no great fortune. However, the few hundred acres of Grandview core remained in the family for many decades; it became a neon-lighted shopping centre in the late 1950s. As a younger man Solomon Young had run wagon trains from Independence through Salt Lake City to San Francisco, often being away for a year at a time. As a result he missed the Civil War depredations of the 'Red Legs' from across the Kansas border, which remained an abiding memory with Truman's mother. They slaughtered the hogs, removed the family silver and ruined a lovingly made quilt. Worse still, they tried, although not apparently very seriously, to hang her brother. Although more Missourians fought in the Union than in the Confederate armies, the Truman forbears and their neighbours were firmly for the South.

Solomon Young had an imposing presence, with a great white beard, and lived longer than Truman's other grandfather, Anderson Shippe Truman. He therefore had a greater impact upon Harry Truman. Anderson Truman lived most of his life as a smaller farmer a hundred or so miles to the south of the Youngs, in Cass County. He had about 200 acres. Of the two grandmothers, Mary Jane Truman died before Harry was born, but Louisa Young lived until 1905, when she was 91. This fortified the greater strength of the Young influence.

Truman's own parents were married in 1881. His father, John Anderson Truman, had been born in 1851, and survived only until 1914. He was the shortest-lived of the Truman tribe. His height was still more notably short. He was two inches below his wife. Her advantage in longevity was much greater. Born in 1853, she survived until the age of 95, well into Truman's presidency. She had a strong personality and very determined views. Again, there is an impression of the greater strength of the Young side of the family. But Truman, devoted though he was to his mother, was always determined to controvert any under-estimate of his father. 'He was just as great as she was,' he recorded, 'and had every bit as much influence on me . . .'[2]

John Truman, mostly known as 'Peanuts', pursued a variety of trades. In different stages or strands of his life he was a farmer, a cattle and horse dealer, a grain speculator, a night watchman, and an elected overseer of roads. Financial success always proved elusive, but he emerged from all these occupations, his son was insistent and uncontradicted, with his honour intact. He was also the first Truman to be an involved political militant. He held no notable offices, but he was a passionate Democrat. In 1892 he was excited by Grover Cleveland's victory. He had to wait until 1912 for another Democratic president to be elected, but he then welcomed Wilson's success, even though he would greatly have preferred Champ Clark, the only Missourian other than his son to come within striking distance of the presidency, to have secured the nomination. His politics were based on a simple, instinctive, loyal partisanship which he passed on to his elder son. He also took him to a greater number of political meetings, ensured he was made a page at the Kansas City Democratic Convention of 1900, when William Jennings Bryan was nominated for the second of his three unsuccessful candidatures, and, more surprisingly, introduced him to Plutarch's *Lives*, which became a major literary influence.

Harry S. Truman was born, and so registered, at Lamar, Barton County, Missouri on May 8th, 1884. The 'S' stood for nothing but 'S'.★ The choice of form by Truman's parents stemmed from a desire to balance between the competing claims of *Solomon* Young and Anderson *Shippe* Truman. Whether either was satisfied is not recorded. The subsequent two children of the marriage (John Vivian, born 1886, and Mary Jane, born 1889) were more normally named. Vivian passed his life as a moderately successful working farmer, until he retired on the proceeds of the land sale for the shopping centre. Mary remained a spinster, who lived with her mother. Truman remained fairly close to both.

The house in which he was born was more modest than anything in which he subsequently lived. It was not a share-cropper's shack, nor was it a solid farmhouse; it was between the two. It remained his home for little more than a year. Twice in 1885 his family moved to different houses in Cass County. Then in 1886 they removed themselves to the Young house at Grandview, nominally for 'Peanuts' Truman to manage the farm of the ageing Solomon. The management role must have been either nominal or unsuccessful, for in another three years they were off again, to Independence, without any apparent ill-effect upon the farm.

Independence was already a proper town, although with a population of only 6,000. Today it has 110,000 and is effectively a nine-mile-distant satellite of Kansas City. Then, Kansas City was an exploding place of 55,000. The inhabitants of Independence regarded it as a 'Yankee' city and themselves, with some residual Southern ways, as quite distinct. However, the presence of Kansas City was immanent. Both it and Independence were part of Jackson

★ Amongst earlier Presidents the 'S' in Ulysses S. Grant was equally sterile, although this arose accidentally from a confusion in Army records.

County, which was the political unit, and the encompassment of
Harry Truman's life until 1934.

The reason given for this move was that Harry needed 'graded'
schooling, as opposed to everyone being taught in one class at
Grandview. Maybe his father's desire to escape from too close a
Young dependence and to try some of his speculative ventures also
had something to do with it. They lived successively in two
substantial houses in Independence, each for six years. Then John
Anderson Truman had a disastrous year on the grain market and
they were forced to sell up and move in straightened circumstances
to the relative anonymity of Kansas City.

These twelve years, however, had seen Harry Truman through
his schooling in a compact community. He was a boy apart, for
his poor eyesight meant that he had to wear spectacles from the
age of six, which at that time was regarded as an oddity in the
mid-West and was held to preclude him from sports or rough
group pastimes. He became a voracious reader but this did not
lead to any outstanding brilliance in his school classes. A number
of good women teachers made a great impact upon him, but their
reminiscences give the impression that his impact upon them,
under the stimulus of his subsequent fame, was more retrospective
than actual. He learned to be a competent pianist, and for a time
went to special lessons in Kansas City, and practised for two hours
a day. There was a suggestion that he might aspire to be a
concert performer, but this was not pursued. His daughter says
straightforwardly that he was not good enough, even though he
was once given a private demonstration by Paderewski. He retained a tinkling talent throughout his life.

His more realistic ambition was to become an army officer. He
was fascinated by military history, and a military education would
have the advantage of being free, so he was specially taught, with
one other boy, for entry to West Point, or possibly the naval
academy at Annapolis. The other boy got to Annapolis, but did
not complete the course. Truman was turned down because of his
eyesight. Additionally, as a result of his father's *débâcle*, he could
not go to college. Instead he spent the summer of his eighteenth
year as a time-keeper for construction workers who were doubling
the Atcheson, Topeka and Santa Fé tracks from Chicago to Kansas
City. Then he went to work as a clerk in a Kansas City bank. He
was always insistent that he had had a happy childhood, and he

had more than enough buoyancy to survive this wave of vicissitudes. He was mostly uncomplaining.

He was also a good bank clerk (he got his salary up from $35 to $100 a month), but he had no vocation for banking. This was for the adequate reasons that he was not interested in money and did not like bankers. It was a persistent view. He was against usury. He was also suspicious of the East, where most banking power lay. And he was against pomposity and hypocrisy, which he associated with the power of wealth. 'High hats', who prayed too loud, were always in the forefront of his gallery of demonology. He was, I suppose, in favour of American 'free enterprise', but in a curious way, for his sympathy and even his respect was always at least as much with the failures as with the successes.

While in Kansas City he joined a new National Guard organization – bank clerks have always been good recruiting material for part-time armies – drilled once a week in the armoury, went to camp for six summers, was given charge of a gun in a troop of artillery, and was proud of a blue uniform with red trimmings.* He also did part-time work as an usher in a theatre, and saw most of the touring vaudeville acts free. He paid to go to classical concerts.

By 1906 the whole family was back in Grandview. The explanation given is that they were summoned home to run the family farm. But why? There was no obvious change in Young family circumstances. Solomon Young had been dead for thirteen years, and his son Harrison Young (the one the Union Red Legs had tried to hang) was still available and under 60 although probably developing a drink problem. In any event they returned. '. . . I became a real farmer,' Harry Truman recorded, 'plowed, sowed, reaped, milked cows, fed hogs, doctored horses, baled hay and did everything there was to do on a 600 acre farm with my father and brother. But we never did catch up with our debts. We always owed the bank something – sometimes more, sometimes less – but we always owed the bank.'†

---

* His grandmother was less impressed. When he appeared in it at Grandview she told him that it was the first time a 'blue [i.e. Union] uniform' had been seen in that house since 1863, and that he was not to bring it there again. (*Letters to Bess*, p. 219.)

† Biographical notes, written by Truman *circa* 1956, and quoted by William Hillman in *Mr President* (p. 135). There seems some discrepancy between this picture and Margaret Truman's statement that the farm earned $15,000 a year.

Truman stayed on the farm until 1917, from the age of 22 to 33.
This was the most static period of his life, not only geographically but in other ways too. Quite simply, not very much happened to him, at least until 1916: the farm was hard work. He
continued to read, although, to judge from his letters, more
novel serials in monthly magazines than political biography or
military history. He retained his connection with the National
Guard artillery unit, but did not go to summer camps. He
was too busy with the harvests. He had some, mainly cousinly,
social life. He became an active Mason. And he courted Miss
Bess Wallace.

This was one of the slowest courtships in history. It lasted in
some form or other for 29 years, and was then followed by 53
years of marriage. It was also one of the most time-consuming.
From 1910, when it entered its long home straight, to 1914, when
he rather adventurously acquired a Stafford motor car, it involved
him in the most appalling Saturday and Sunday journeys. Independence, although little more than 20 miles from Grandview, could
not be reached across country. It involved a railroad journey to
one of two junctions – Sheffield or the surprisingly named Air
Line – in the north of Kansas City and then an eight-mile street-car
stage to Independence. Still worse was the late night return. Any
idea that the pre-1914 years were the golden age of American
railroads is difficult to reconcile with Truman's experience. The
trains started late and arrived later. They were diverted by frequent
derailments and frozen in winter by heating breakdowns. Truman
often arrived back at Grandview at two in the morning and
sometimes at seven.

Miss Bess Wallace, on one side, came of the highest quality of
Independence. Her grandfather, George Porterfield Gates, made a
good deal of money out of milling and marketing 'Queen of
the Pantry' flour, which had many years of brand name success
throughout the Middle West. His daughter, Madge Gates Wallace,
as she was later to be known, played only too large a part in the
life of Harry Truman. She married a David W. Wallace, who
had some of the qualities of Eleanor Roosevelt's father. He was
handsome, charming, and drank. He shot himself in his bath in
1903. But Independence was not New York City, and David
Wallace, unlike Elliott Roosevelt, was not quite the social equal
of his wife. (No husband appeared to be in those democratic,

open-frontier Missouri days.) And Bess Wallace was certainly no Eleanor Roosevelt. In the first place, so far from being a shy, 'ugly duckling' of a child, she was the belle of her Sunday School class, where Truman first met her at the age of six, and of nearly every other class as well. Her 'golden curls' were what first struck Truman. Later she developed a considerable athleticism and became a locally outstanding tennis player, and was talented at most other games.

She floated in and out of Truman's life from the age of six to twenty-six. By the time they were about thirty (she was a year younger than he was) they were unofficially engaged. When he was 33 and she 32 they made it official. Two years later (World War I had intervened) they were actually married. The fact that this Independence belle married 'below her' to such a slow suitor was a sign of her outstanding good sense. Apart altogether from the chances of 1944–5, which led to Truman's propulsion to world fame, he must have been the strongest character of his generation in Jackson County. But she, in a quiet way, was still stronger than he: I think he was always more concerned about her good opinion than *vice versa*. He was also to prove about the most devoted husband in American presidential history. Not only did he 'not look at another woman': he was deeply embarrassed if they looked at him, which they mostly did not.

The question which remains is why others did not press harder to carry off earlier this prize bride. One reason may be that, after 1903, they realized they would have to take her mother with her, and that only Harry Truman had the uncomplaining devotion to accept this. The extent to which he did so turned out to be almost as unparalleled as was the length of his courtship. Mrs Wallace survived nearly 34 years after the marriage and she lived every single one of them as part of the Truman household. Not only was this so in Independence. It was also so in Washington. She removed herself faithfully with the family. At the time of Truman's accession to the presidency, Margaret Truman was sharing a bedroom with her in a small Connecticut Avenue apartment. She died in the White House a month after Eisenhower's election. It was no political loyalty which kept her so close: she was constantly critical of her son-in-law, thought it wrong of him to sack such a fine military gentleman as General MacArthur, and would have been a natural Dewey voter in 1948. Harry Truman, for her, always remained one of nature's 'dirt farmers'. Perhaps one of the reasons for his joyful return to Independence in January 1953, with the presidency behind him, was that he was at last entering his own house.

Towards the end of his eleven years on the farm Truman became more externally active. He was involved in oil, zinc and lead prospecting, first in Texas and then in south-western Missouri and the adjacent parts of Oklahoma. They were all relatively small-scale enterprises. In one he lost about $7,500. Like all prospectors he nearly struck big. Like most he did not. 'Maybe I wouldn't be President if we'd hit' he wrote to a partner forty years later. In the prospectus for an oil consortium of which he was Treasurer, he described himself a little vaguely as 'native of Jackson County, Missouri; widely known in Kansas City'. Both he and the investors came out about even. Although he had a touch of his father's speculative fever, he lacked the essential ingredient for making money, which is simply the overwhelming desire to do so. But he worked hard, dismally, and unsuccessfully to bring a lead and zinc enterprise at Commerce, Oklahoma to fruition through-out the spring and summer of 1916. He had no touch. He had no luck. The result was failure and the impression from his letters is that, while only just escaping his grasp, it was nevertheless almost totally inevitable. In business he snatched defeat out of the jaws of victory as consistently as in elections he was later to do the reverse.

The entry of the United States into World War I in April 1917 aroused his patriotism more than his idealism: '. . . I don't give a whoop (to put it mildly) whether there's a League of Nations or whether Russia has a Red government or a purple one . . .' he was writing a year or so later. 'We came out here to help whip the Hun. We helped a little, the Hun yowled for peace and he's getting it in large doses . . .'[3] Perhaps even more it offered him an honourable escape from the defeats of the preceding twelve months. He became immediately involved with the expansion of his National Guard battery into a regiment of field artillery. As part of the core he expected to become a sergeant, but found himself elected, under the system which prevailed in the early days of World War I recruitment, as in the Civil War, a first lieutenant instead. The regiment, the 129th Field Artillery as it had become, was sent to Camp Donihan in Oklahoma for training. It was the first time that Truman, at the age of 33, had been away from Western Missouri for more than a week or so. He enjoyed army life and was an efficient soldier. He was good with the men, learnt his gunnery proficiently, and ran an exceptionally successful regimental canteen. His assistant in this last was Sergeant Eddie Jacobson, a 26-year-old Kansas City Jew of New York City origin whose family were in the clothing business. Truman and Jacobson paid out vast percentage dividends on a small capital, and were commended for the most efficient canteen in the division. They congratulated each other on their complementary business acumen.

In the spring of 1918 Truman was sent to France as part of an advance party of the regiment. He saw New York,★ the ocean, and Europe for the first time. So far as Europe was concerned it was also the last time until he became President. He was overseas for almost exactly a year. As soon as he arrived he was promoted captain. He was sent on a command course for six weeks and returned as adjutant of one of the battalions into which the 129th was split. A month or so later he was made commander of Battery D, which had proved obstreperous, and too much for several predecessors. The men almost all came from an Irish Catholic district of Kansas City. Truman claimed that he was one of only six Protestants out of more than 180. He made a success of it. This was the most important achievement until then in Truman's life. It compensated for his inability to play games or get to West Point or strike oil. Thereafter the virtues of Battery D were given an unchallenged status in Truman's folklore.

The Battery's military exploits were respectable rather than remarkable. Between August 20th and November 11th it was three or four times in action near Verdun and in the Vosges. It was subjected to occasional bombardment and stood up well. But it was never in direct contact with the enemy infantry. It never lost a gun or a man. Neither the danger nor the privation was comparable with that suffered by most French or British artillery

★ Typically, he did not think much of it: 'New York is a very much over-rated burg', he wrote on March 26th, 1918. 'It merely keeps up its rep. by its press agents continually harping on the wonder of it. There isn't a town west of the Mississippi of any size that can't show you a better time.' (*Dear Bess*, p. 253.)

units. For Truman it was a short war which forged long-lasting friendships.

After the Armistice he stayed in France for another five months. He had periods of leave in Paris and in Nice and Monte Carlo, but life was mostly a series of poker games in muddy base camps, first behind Verdun and then near Le Mans. He landed in New York in late April 1919, and was discharged in Oklahoma four weeks later.

In June he was married, in an Episcopal church – the Wallace influence – and moved into Mrs Wallace's fourteen-roomed house on North Delaware Street, Independence, which old Porterfield Gates had built in 1867, and which was to remain Truman's Jackson County home for the rest of his life. In July he arranged with his old partner Eddie Jacobson that they should jointly open a men's outfitting business in the centre of Kansas City. They secured a good site on 12th Street, just opposite the new Muehlebach Hotel and close to the older Baltimore, and they paid a high rent. They traded up. With wheat at $2.15 a bushel it was possible to sell $15 shirts. They probably overtraded as well. They soon had $40,000's worth of stock. They had a good first year. Then the post-war boom began to crack. The main lesson Truman claimed to have learned from his retail experience was never to elect a Republican president, and particularly one who appointed such an epitome of an Eastern banker as Andrew Mellon as his Secretary of the Treasury. In any event this early dose of monetarism helped to reduce the price of wheat to 88 cents in 1922, though the Democrats had seen it fall to $1.44 even before the election. It also reduced the demand for silk shirts in Kansas City. The $40,000 stock became worth $10,000. Truman and Jacobson ceased trading in the spring of 1922. Jacobson later became bankrupt, but Truman, who had politics in view, declined to petition, and eventually managed to pay off all his debts. He later gave his total loss in the business at about $28,000. On his return from the war he had estimated that he had $15 to $20,000 in free capital, plus a small amount of land. The failure left him without assets, but in no way close to the breadline. He had too many relations and friends for that.

He also had fairly immediate political prospects. The outfitters had not only been a fluctuatingly successful sales outlet. It had in addition been a great political talking shop, particularly for demobilized veterans. Truman loved veterans. 'My whole political career is based on my war service and war associates,' he said with a little exaggeration 25 years later. Of course he could not love them all, not even those from Battery D, or the 129th Field Artillery. Some of them were Republicans, and this produced an awkward conflict of loyalties. But in 1920, for the only time in his life he crossed over party lines and voted for a Major Miles (of the 129th) as County Marshal. A few others of the battery played him false, either politically or financially, and his sense of shock and betrayal then made him unforgiving. But in general army reunion companionship was exactly to his taste. He always supported 'the bonus'.* It was one of the few issues on which he went against Roosevelt in the 1930s. The American Legion Convention in Kansas City in October 1921 was a brief uplift during his decline to insolvency.

Amongst the intermediate ring of his army acquaintanceships was Lieutenant James M. Pendergast. He was the son of Michael J. Pendergast, who was an older but less dynamic brother of Thomas J. Pendergast, one of the legendary city bosses of American politics in the first 40 years of this century. In 1911 Tom Pendergast had inherited from the eldest brother of the three, 'Alderman Jim', a traditional, poor neighbourhood, immigrant-based machine in the riverside areas of West Bottoms and North End. Within a few years he had extended this domain to include the new southern suburbs of Kansas City, as well as the more rural area to the east, and was endeavouring to control the state, although he was always subject to competition from St Louis, which was a bigger city.

Truman's relations in the early days were primarily with Mike Pendergast rather than with the 'Big Boss', Tom. He knew him better (through his son, the lieutenant). He liked him more. ('I loved him as I did my own daddy', he is recorded by

* 'The bonus' was an ex gratia payment to World War I veterans in the form of a twenty-year endowment insurance certificate due to mature in 1945. In the depression the American Legion demanded immediate cash payments. The issue was not resolved until January 1936. Hoover treated the 'Bonus Marchers', who camped in Washington in the summer of 1932, with cold legality. He sent the Army, under the command of General Douglas MacArthur, with his aide Colonel Eisenhower at his side, to disperse them. This was done with considerable roughness. Roosevelt gave them sympathy but not the money. Payment was eventually authorized by Congress over his veto.

Margaret Truman as saying after Mike Pendergast's death in 1929.) And while Truman's political arena was confined to the rural part of Jackson County, Mike was to him the more relevant figure. 'Tom didn't like the country,' he laconically and convincingly explained.

Later his relations with the greater Pendergast became a crucial and fluctuating factor in his career. He never 'loved him like his daddy,' but he was his awkward client. He could not have secured his Senate seat without him. He lived honestly and therefore uncomfortably alongside him, his reputation suffering as a result. As Vice-President, he insisted on flying 1000 miles to his funeral, after Tom Pendergast had collapsed into disgrace and a jail sentence.

But in 1922 it was Mike Pendergast who helped him to win the nomination for Eastern Judge. This mandarin-like title concealed a moderately significant executive local office. Its holder was in no sense a judge: he had no judicial functions; he was the elected assistant administrator of the eastern district of Jackson County; together with the Western Judge, he worked under the Presiding Judge who covered the whole county. The western district was Kansas City. The eastern part was Independence, Grandview, and five other small communities. Truman therefore fought his first election very much on his own doorstep. But it was certainly not a 'front-porch' campaign. He attempted to speak everywhere, but was frustrated not by the hostility of his audiences but his own tongue-tiedness.

There is complete agreement that he was at this stage an appalling speaker. At least it gave him the habit of never talking for more than 20 minutes, which he retained throughout his subsequent campaigns. He had the other advantages of a good local reputation and the enthusiastic support of the thick concentration of his army companions (the intensely local nature of the unit giving him a base which the dispersal policy of World War II would have made impossible). A claque from Battery D called for 'three cheers for Captain Harry' whenever his oratory broke down. And he had Mike Pendergast, who endorsed him enthusiastically for the office. 'Now I'm going to tell you who you are going to be for for county judge', Truman later recalled his saying to a Democratic Club meeting. 'It's Harry Truman. He's got a fine war record. He comes from a fine family. He'll make a fine judge.'[3]

Even so, Truman won with difficulty. The Democrats were split into two factions, mysteriously named Goats and Rabbits. Truman was an hereditary Goat. So were the Pendergasts, although the division pre-dated their sway. But the Rabbits were quite strong and made a determined attempt to get a local banker named Montgomery nominated. The Ku Klux Klan presented an additional complication. They began to erupt into Missouri at this stage, and torches were burnt near Grandview. Truman was at first inclined to join them, and offered a $10 subscription (the extent of their intolerance had not fully surfaced) but his Battery D loyalty came to his rescue. He was asked to give an assurance that, if elected, he would never give a job to a Catholic. That would have excluded 90% of his beloved associates. He firmly refused. The $10 were returned. That was the end of his flirtation with the Klan, but not of his embroilment with it.

The primary was on August 1st. Truman had a bare majority of 288, in a vote of over 11,000. The run-off was a formality. That autumn, at the age of thirty-eight, he was Eastern Judge for a two year spell, with a modest salary of $6,000, debts of well over that amount, considerable opportunities for graft, and his foot upon a rung of the political ladder.

Whatever else is in dispute about Truman's career, his repute, and relations with the Pendergasts, it is clear that he was totally untouched by personal monetary corruption. However great the temptation, with his debts and lack of financial prospects, however loose the surrounding practice, he was aggressively clean so far as anything approaching a bribe or even the free use of public expenses were concerned. He lived and died the poorest president of the past fifty years, probably of this century. (His closest rivals are Wilson and Coolidge.)

In this respect his administration of his new little office was therefore spotless. So far as jobs were concerned it was less immaculate, and this was to continue to be his pattern. But this fault stemmed from a mixture of instinctive partisanship and excessive loyalty to old friends rather than from paybacks for financial benefits. As county judge it took the simple form of appointing only Goats and never Rabbits.

When he came up for re-election two years later this made his basis of support too narrow. The Rabbits bolted the ticket. The

Klan, then near to its peak,⋆ was viciously against him. This accumulation of opposition counted for more than a good record of administration, particularly in relation to the re-funding of the county debt and the beginning of an efficient road building programme. An obscure Republican harness maker, who only got on the ballot paper by accident, was elected fairly easily. It was the only election which Truman ever lost. It left him once more without a job, and with only the most minor political achievement behind him.

He was out of office for two years. It was the height of the boom of the 1920s, and, although he certainly did not become rich, he had no difficulty in supporting his small family (Margaret Truman, his only child, had been born in 1924) in their habitual modest small-town prosperity. He became a minor Kansas City man of affairs. He established himself in an office in the Board of Trade building there. Successfully, and for a commission, he sold membership in the Kansas City Automobile Club. He became state president of the National Old Trails Association, but this, which remained an abiding interest, was a voluntary activity. And he had a business partnership with a gentleman crookster (as he subsequently turned out to be) from Independence, the suspiciously grandly named Spencer Salisbury. Salisbury had been a fellow captain from the 129th Artillery. They did housing finance business together, took over and then quickly withdrew from a tottering local bank. Jonathan Daniels, in his otherwise friendly life of Truman,† published during his presidency, suggested that Truman was lucky to escape from this association without serious damage not merely to his finances but to his integrity. But it was

⋆ It was a major issue at the Democratic National Convention in New York City that year. Even the exhaustion of 103 ballots to choose a 'neutral' candidate, John W. Davis, former Ambassador to London, rather than the Catholic 'wet' and therefore highly vulnerable Al Smith or William G. McAdoo, Woodrow Wilson's somewhat conservative son-in-law, did not prevent the delegates agonizing lengthily over whether or not to condemn the Klan in the platform, and only deciding not to do so by the splendid margin of $542^3/_{20}$ votes to $541^3/_{20}$.

† *The Man of Independence* (J. B. Lippincott, 1950). Daniels was the son of Josephus Daniels, Wilson's Secretary of the Navy to whom Franklin D. Roosevelt was Assistant Secretary from 1913 to 1919. Truman is reported as having said of it: 'That book is filled with a lot of bunk. He used to work for me when I was President and he worked for Roosevelt. But when he wrote that book he just seemed to go haywire in places [but] he got most things like that [facts & dates] right . . .' (Merle Miller, *Plain Speaking*, p. 60.)

Truman's birthplace at Lamar, Missouri. *(Harry S. Truman Library)*

The farm at Grandview, Missouri. *(Harry S. Truman Library)*

a decade and a half before Salisbury went to gaol, and long before that he and Truman had become implacable enemies, both politically and personally. There is no evidence that he and Truman did anything wrong together. They certainly made no substantial amount of money.

Truman's eyes were always on a return to political office. In 1926 he sought his one favour of Tom Pendergast. He proposed himself for the office of County Collector, which for some extraordinary reason carried a salary with fees of $25,000 a year, and which would have given him affluence. Pendergast refused. The office was bespoken. But later that year he promoted Truman for Presiding Judge of the whole county, the official to whom Truman had previously been subordinate. Truman accepted, and was elected with ease. It was to be his niche for the next eight years, and made his political reputation in Missouri. But it gave him no advance in salary. He was still on $6,000.

During these eight years he proved a sound, clean, constructive local administrator. He re-structured the County's debt and financed it at a much cheaper rate. He balanced the County's current books. But he was also a substantial builder, and one who was peculiarly successful in getting popular support (referenda were necessary) for bond issues to finance his projects. There was a local tradition of negative votes in these polls, based upon a well-founded cynical belief that a significant part of the proceeds would find its way into the pockets of the promoters. In Truman's time several Kansas City proposals were decisively rejected. But he got most of his County projects through, accomplished by barnstorming advocacy against a background of sound administration.

In his first term he built roads, 224 miles of them. With mass motor car ownership exploding in the boom of the late 1920s, they were an essential public service. He aimed to bring a metalled road within two and a half miles of every farmhouse, and broadly achieved it. In 1930 he claimed to have been told that, on some unspecified scale of measurement, Jackson County was throughout the nation second only to Westchester County, New York, in the quality of its roads. Also, although he had to obtain that gentleman's general approval for his bond issues, he built them without the aid of Tom Pendergast. This was a considerable feat, not

because Pendergast was a renowned civil engineer but because he
was the owner of the happily (if not wholly reassuringly) named
Ready Mixed Concrete Company, and was used to seeing a good
deal of the mixture spread on the highways of his domain.*
Apparently it was only used on three-quarters of a mile of Truman's
programme.

Even more provocatively, at a 1928 meeting in Pendergast's
office, which has subsequently found a place in almost every
biography of Truman, he declined to give any contracts to three
important clients of the Kansas City machine, and awarded a
substantial slice to an out-of-state low bidder instead. 'Didn't I tell
you boys,' Pendergast complacently summed up the meeting, 'he's
the contrariest cuss in Missouri?'³ Then he privately told Truman
to go ahead.

The story rings a little too good to be true. There is a feeling
that Pendergast was not trying to do business but was parading
Truman like a clergyman persuaded to visit a whore house (a form
of enterprise familiar to Pendergast) on a rest day when it was
disguised as a sewing class. However, the fact that he thought this
was temporarily the best use he could make of Truman is in itself
something of a tribute. Certainly the Judge's handling of public
money was impeccable, almost excessively so. He refused to allow
his far from affluent mother to be paid for two slices which were
taken off the Grandview land. She half-seriously complained for
the rest of her life.

In 1930 Truman was re-elected for a second term with a much
bigger majority than in 1926. The economic climate was very
different. Coolidge prosperity had given way to Hoover slump.
But Truman continued to build: additional roads but more spectacularly a 20-storey courthouse (administrative building) for
Jackson County in Kansas City, as well as re-fashioning its eastern
district off-shoot in Independence. This time the provision of jobs
was an essential part of the scheme. There could have been
no question of going for an out-of-state contractor. But he
was determined to get the best traditional design that he could
find. He toured the county looking at courthouses. He did 24,000

---

* And not only on the highways. Kansas City still has the rare distinction of
a suburban stream (Brush Creek) that runs for four miles or more along a wide
concrete bed.

miles in his own car, and at his own expense. He went to the old South, to New York State, to Illinois, Wisconsin, Nebraska, Colorado, Texas and into Canada. He saw more of North America than he ever had before. He was mostly accompanied by a villainous-looking courthouse custodian called Fred Canfil, who was no great judge of architecture, but intensely loyal to Truman.*

Truman found what he wanted in the improbable location of Shreveport, Louisiana. It had recently been built by an architect called Edward F. Neild. He was hired to come to Kansas City. It was a worthwhile assignment in itself and also a very good preparatory exercise for him. He was commissioned to do the internal reconstruction of the collapsing White House in 1948–52. The White House was a suitable job, for he was a highly conventional architect. Truman liked this; it was why he chose Neild. His taste in architecture, in music, in writing, was not bad but instinctively suspicious of the adventurous. He not only disliked but almost despised anything which sought to break new ground. It must be the work of city slickers, and probably 'sissy' as well. It was an extraordinary limitation for such a robust man with a sense, or at least a knowledge, of history. 'I don't understand fellows like Lloyd Wright,' he told Merle Miller in 1961, à propos of the Neild choice. 'I don't understand what gets into people like that. He started this whole business of chicken-coop and hen-house architecture, and I don't know why in the world he did it.'[4]

However, Truman got quite a good courthouse, and had it built far enough under the estimate (not too difficult a feat in those years of falling prices) to be able to afford an equally conventional equestrian statue of his hero, Andrew Jackson, after whom Jackson County was named, in the foreground. He at first wanted to put it on the roof but was persuaded that few would see it there, and that those who did would think it ridiculously placed. The complex was complete and inaugurated just after Christmas 1934, in the

* Fourteen years later Truman took Canfil to the Potsdam Conference as a sort of baggage master. He had recently appointed him US Marshal for the Western district of Missouri. This enabled Truman to introduce him to Stalin as 'Marshal Canfil'. Thereafter, Truman claimed, the Russian entourage treated him with immense respect. It became one of Truman's few enjoyable memories of Potsdam.

last days of his judgeship, with the ten-year-old Margaret Truman leading a troop of girls who unveiled the statue.*

Truman's extensive journeying in 1931 was probably not only a mark of his diligence in planning the new courthouse but also a sign that he was becoming bored with his routine county tasks. He wanted a change and wider horizons. In the reorganization of district boundaries which followed the census of 1930, he had worked hard to secure the creation of a new congressional seat comprised of the eastern wards of Kansas City and the western part of rural Jackson County. 'His dream was to represent that district in Congress,' his daughter tells us.[5] Pendergast however decided otherwise. He had his own candidate. Truman accepted the decision.

Then as the 1932 elections began to approach a substantial 'Truman for Governor' movement built up. His name had become fairly well known outside Jackson County. In 1930 he had been elected President of the Greater Kansas City Planning Association, which embraced three Missouri counties as well as another three across the state line in Kansas. He was also a familiar figure in the State House at Jefferson City, the Missouri capital. But St Louis, the metropolis to the east, remained alien territory to him. He would have been very much the candidate of the western part of the state. But, again, this did not fit in with Pendergast's ideas. He wanted to run his elderly candidate (Francis M. Wilson) of 1928. And once again Truman submitted and withdrew. The elderly candidate then died a month before polling day and a rushed replacement had to be found. Pendergast, even then, did not turn to Truman.

Altogether, during this period, Pendergast did not do much for Truman. Perhaps he was more resentful of Truman's stubbornness about the contracts than the latter realized. In the summer of 1932 there was a further irritant for Truman. He went to Chicago as

---

* Truman also placed a Jackson statue in front of the remodelled Independence courthouse. He would have been amazed to be told that a little over forty years later it would be complemented by a statue of himself, not on a horse, but walking at a vigorous pace – an unusual but appropriate portrayal. In Kansas City his courthouse was overshadowed within two years by a new City Hall of 26 floors, built across the street by his old rival Henry McElroy, who had become City Manager. The main contractors for both towers was the Sventon Construction Company, which must have had a good five years. McElroy died while awaiting trial after the Pendergast *débâcle* in 1939.

part of the Missouri delegation to the Democratic Convention. He was for Roosevelt. But Pendergast was playing a more complicated game. He persuaded James A. Farley, Roosevelt's man of business before the election, his Postmaster-General after it, and ultimately his dedicated enemy, that he wanted to see Roosevelt nominated. Probably he was realistically for Roosevelt. At the same time he was nostalgically committed to the candidature of James Reed, an old-style Missouri ex-senator, who had nominated Speaker Champ Clark against Woodrow Wilson as long ago as the Baltimore Convention of 1912. He kept Reed in until the third ballot, when he got him 27½ votes, and then did not so much deliver to Roosevelt the Missouri delegation, which had never been unanimous, as let it slip away to him. Truman had to vote for Reed. Worse still, he had to applaud a post-nomination speech of his which opposed every tenet of the New Deal, and would have seemed backward looking if delivered in 1900.

In spite of this 1932 was a good year for Pendergast. He got his second candidate for Governor elected. The re-districting had not gone through, so all the Missouri candidates for the House of Representatives had to run on a state list, which involved making their obeisance to the controller of the Kansas City vote. His only setback was that Bennett Clark, the former Speaker's son, was elected Senator against his wishes. Pendergast's disintegration did not come until later: in 1934 he was seized with a continuing and destructive gambling fever; in 1936 he stuffed the ballot box of Kansas City with false votes on a scale that was unacceptable even in that wide-open town; in that same year his bull-like body suddenly collapsed in New York; in 1939 he was indicted and gaoled.

Truman could sustain the personal vicissitudes of 1932 with reasonable equanimity. As a partisan Democrat and instinctive if not doctrinaire New Dealer, he rejoiced in his party's great national victory. He still had two years of his term to run, and he had his courthouse project to bring to fruition. And, a year later, he got a part time Federal appointment as Re-employment Director for Missouri, under Harry Hopkins.

1934 was necessarily to be the test year for him. He was 50 that May. He could not run for a third term as County Judge, even had he wished to do so. By early 1935 he would either have to return to one of his precarious business enterprises or find some other, preferably higher, political office. Although he always attached great importance to not looking eager for his own political advancement, there is no doubt about which alternative he wanted. But he could not command it. Whether another door was to be opened to him depended upon Pendergast.

There was a very grand door available. It was the Democratic nomination for the second Missouri seat in the US Senate. The Republican incumbent, Roscoe Patterson, was up for re-election. With the Roosevelt tide running so strongly across the nation there was not likely to be much difficulty about beating him. Pendergast's problem was the balance of Democratic power in Missouri. Bennett Clark of St Louis was installed in the other seat at least until 1938. In February 1934 Clark announced that he was supporting Congressman Jacob L. Milligan, of a rural county, to be his companion on Capitol Hill. Another congressman, John J. Cochran of St Louis itself, was also in the race. Neither was acceptable to Pendergast. They would have broken a rough convention that Missouri should have one senator from the Kansas City area. More important, they would have relegated him and his machine to a manifestly secondary position in the politics of the state. He had to beat Cochran and Milligan, and Cochran at least was a formidable challenger. This has led Truman apologists to claim that Pendergast needed Truman in this election at least as much as Truman needed Pendergast. Unfortunately for this theory, Pendergast did not appear to feel the need. He tried three other candidates before, as late as May, he came round to Truman. He then offered him the nomination and the promise of whole-hearted backing. Truman hesitated for a day or so, partly because he did not wish to appear too available, and partly because he feared that he did not command the money for a hard-fought primary. But there is no doubt that he greatly welcomed the opportunity.

He campaigned with vigour, but with small resources and decreasing enjoyment. His expenses amounted to $12,280. $1,400 came from the Pendergast family. There were a few other substantial donations, mostly from very respectable sources. There were debts of just over $3,000 at the end. Truman's disaffection stemmed from the increasing attacks upon him as a tool of Pendergast. Milligan claimed that in Washington Truman would get 'calluses on his ears listening on the long distance telephone to his boss'.

The head of the Missouri farmers' organization called him a 'bell-hop'. The *St Louis Post-Dispatch* stated retrospectively: 'County Judge Truman is the nominee of the Democratic Party for the United States Senate because Tom Pendergast willed it so.' Part of the trouble was that Pendergast was alleged (although Truman always refused to believe it) to have injudiciously boasted that he had decided to send his 'office boy' to the Senate. The jibe stuck.

Nevertheless Truman campaigned indefatigably if unjoyfully throughout one of the hottest Julys in the history of the Middle West. The temperature was over 100° F on 21 days. He visited 60 of the state's 114 counties, making around ten short speeches a day. He declared himself 'heart and soul for Roosevelt'. He survived a motor car accident and two broken ribs.

Polling was on August 9th. Milligan had faded, but Cochran remained a strong opponent. The result was remarkable, not so much for its overall out-turn as for the breakdown of the figures. Truman had a majority of about 40,000 in a vote of over half a million. In St Louis he polled only 3,742 against Cochran's 104,265 (Milligan got 6,670). Kansas City provided the mirror image. There Cochran got only 1,525, against Truman's 137,529 and Milligan's 8,912. The machines had shown their power, and not only Pendergast's. But his had the edge. The smaller city polled substantially more votes. Neither Truman nor Cochran would have had a chance without their machine backing. But equally either could have won or lost in the rural counties, where half of the votes were cast. And here Truman (and indeed Cochran) were largely on their own, with only the help of their records and their campaigning merits. In these 'outstate' areas they ran about equal, with Truman five thousand or so ahead.

The November election was easy. Truman overwhelmed Patterson. On January 2nd, 1935 (in a cutaway coat, which suited him ill, for he was always natty rather than elegant) and escorted, ironically but inevitably, by the senior Senator from Missouri, Bennett Clark, he took the oath of office before Vice-President Garner. He was nearly 51 years old. He was one of 96 members (69 of them Democrats) of what was on the way to becoming the most powerful elected chamber in the world. He was in a metropolis (if the Washington of those days, in uneasy transition between Southern swamp town and world capital, could be given such a name) which he had hardly visited before. He was a committed supporter of the Administration, but apart from Harry Hopkins, he hardly knew anyone in its inner circle. He had a modest record of local achievement behind him, but insofar as he had any national repute it was that of being thickly tarred with the Pendergast brush.

3

JUNIOR SENATOR
FROM MISSOURI

Truman came to Washington as one of thirteen new Democrats in the Senate. It was too many for any of them automatically to be the centre of attention. And, because of Pendergast, Truman started with about the lowest reputation of the lot. He was also inherently one of the least superficially adaptable, with an uxorious devotion but a wife for whom neither the political nor the social life of the capital was ever likely to have much attraction. He was in addition one of the poorest senators and self-consciously so. He had no profession on which to fall back, he was exceptionally unwilling to earn even the most honest of additional money, and he found the increase from his $6,000 as County Judge to the 1930s senatorial salary of $10,000 insufficient to compensate for his Washington expenses. The result was to put him in a complaining mood which was for him unusual.

It also locked him in to an unsatisfactory pattern of life. He could not afford to establish a house in Washington in which Bess Truman would have liked to live. As a result there was always a danger of her spending substantial chunks of congressional sessions in Independence. Their daughter alternated between schools in both places, private in Washington, public in Independence.

Truman, left alone in Washington, was lonely and often miserable. He had nowhere agreeable to live. Sometimes he was reduced to a hotel room. At first he knew few people, and had little to do in the evenings, except apply himself to the minutiae of senatorial business. He was good at such painstaking homework, and it was to be one of the foundations of his later Senate success; but at the time it did not do much to raise his spirits.

Although his income was nominally three times greater, he was worse provided for in two respects than a roughly comparable British provincial Member of Parliament of the period operating in similar straightened and alien circumstances. These were no habitual Senate sessions and therefore no habitual Senate life in the evenings and, more unfortunately, he could not afford to go home. This was partly a function of distance, with air services already possible but rudimentary and slow. Still more however was it a function of there then being no unlimited free travel for members of Congress. 'I almost came home . . .' he wrote to his wife in February 1937. 'I could have taken the train but the least I can do it for would be over one hundred dollars and we need those dollars too much.'[1]

When he went he mostly went by motor car. This was because it was cheaper. (The train was only seriously considered in 1937 because of a freeze-up in Missouri.) But it was a formidable journey. He could do it by leaving early one morning and getting to the other end late on the evening of the second day, but without pressing it had to be spread over three. It only began to be sensible for a week and not for a weekend. During his first Washington session, for instance, when Bess Truman left by June 15th and the Senate did not adjourn until the end of August, he only got home once during the intervening ten weeks. For the rest he spent his weekends as his weeks in the Washington summer (fortunately he was always almost totally impervious to heat), occasionally going to New York, sometimes being asked out of town to parties with people he did not know very well, but mostly working, or searching for an apartment which would make the District slightly more enticing to his wife during the next session.

It was principally for this that he needed 'too much' the dollars that he was reluctant to spend on the train fare home. It was an almost impossible dilemma. If he was to afford an apartment which might induce his wife and daughter to spend more time in Washington he could not afford to go and see them often when they were in Independence. Even with this abstinence he could not afford to pay more than about $150 a month. And nearly all available apartments under this price were either too small (there was always his mother-in-law to be accommodated) or too disagreeable.

It was a problem which he never solved, at least throughout his first term. He changed apartments every session, and sometimes more often, but it was mostly a change without a difference. Tilden Gardens, Warwick Apartments, Sedgwick Gardens, the castellated and Tudorized eight to ten storey 1920s apartment houses of the most anonymous part of north-west Washington were tried one after the other. None was much worse than the other, but none was much better either. 'I knew every block of Connecticut Avenue before Dad's senatorial career ended', Margaret Truman wrote with more resignation than enthusiasm.[2]

The only significant changes were that in 1937 they were in the Carroll Arms, which presumably had apartments as well as rooms for 'transients' but which, on First Street, NE, was almost the 'local' of the Capitol and must have made for rather claustrophobic living, and that in 1941, at the beginning of his second term, he decided there was no point in movement without variety and settled in 1401, Connecticut Avenue, where, four years less eleven days later, he slept his first night as President of the United States.

It seemed about as likely in 1935 and 1936 that he would be Roosevelt's successor as that he should be offered the Presidency of Harvard (or 'Há vŭd' as he liked to call it when imitating F.D.R.). Certainly Roosevelt did nothing to help him settle down as a new senator. Mostly, I suppose, he never thought about Truman, just knew his name and had difficulty attaching a face to it. He had him once to the White House after he had been in Washington for about six weeks, but Truman said that the meeting was not a success as he was so overawed as to be almost inarticulate; and there is no record of any further direct contact for nearly a year. Of more public importance was the fact that Roosevelt froze Truman out of Federal patronage in Missouri. He paid much more attention to Bennett Clark, who was admittedly the senior senator but who, apart from being lazy and often drunk, was a very doubtful supporter of the New Deal; Truman, on the other hand, continued to vote the ticket, on every issue except 'the bonus', with conviction and loyalty.

Worst of all was the only occasion when Roosevelt had to seek Truman's support in a vote, and did it, not by a direct approach, but by getting Pendergast to telephone Truman. The occasion was the choice of a new majority leader in the Senate after the sudden death in July 1937, of Joseph T. Robinson of Arkansas. Roosevelt wanted Alben Barkley of Kentucky, and got him, but by the somewhat slender margin of 38 votes to 37. Truman was in the

minority, for Pat Harrison of Mississippi. He had no difficulty in
fending off Pendergast and sticking to his commitment to Harrison. But he was rightly insulted by Roosevelt's method of
approach, sent a message saying so to the White House (perhaps
he, too, ought to have telephoned direct) and also muttered to the
press. There were several ironies in the incident. Barkley was to
be Truman's own choice as running mate in 1948. Pendergast was
already in decline in the summer of 1937. Truman was already off
the floor of his low period as a senator. And the elementary and
obviously offensive *bêtise* was committed by the most elegantly
skilled politician in the world, who, in general, used direct charm
with great effect, particularly on those not of his own background.
The best excuse for Roosevelt is that, although only eight months
after his annihilating 1936 triumph, it all occurred against the
background of his greatest domestic political setback, the impending defeat of his plan for the expansion (or reform, or packing,
according to perspective) of the Supreme Court.

Although Truman was eager to vote as he thought right, and
free in particular of any behests from Pendergast, he was far from
having severed connection with the old Kansas City boss. In the
1935 session he had signalled his independence by voting for the
Public Utility Holding Company Bill. This was designed to restrict
the grip of financial trusts on electric power supply. It was favoured
by the Administration. It was opposed by Pendergast, by the
Kansas City Journal-Post, the only major newspaper to have supported Truman in the 1934 campaigns, and by at least 40,000
Missouri electors who were organized to write or telegraph to him
on the issue. It was not an awful lot of electors in relation to the
total, but it was an awful lot of mail. Truman, however, shrugged
it off very well. So he did the violent editorial attacks which
followed. His old enemies, the *Kansas City Star* and the *St Louis
Post-Dispatch*, were not converted by the defection of the *Journal-
Post*. When they could not accuse him of being a tool of Pendergast
they accused him of being a tool of Roosevelt. At this stage no
newspaper would allow that he might be his own man.

This vote under his belt, Truman was delighted to keep in close
touch with Pendergast. He saw him several times in New York in
the late summer of 1935. On one occasion he went with Bennett
Clark to discuss the 1936 Democrat candidate for the Missouri
governorship. The man at issue was a rich nurseryman or fruit

farmer of obsessive ambition called Lloyd Stark. Clark was wiser than Truman. He urged caution. Truman urged Stark. A hesitant Pendergast was persuaded. Stark ran, and won. He was then taken up by Roosevelt, and invited on presidential boat trips down the Potomac, a favour which not even Clark, let alone Truman, ever received. In 1939 Stark led the pack against Pendergast and destroyed him totally. In 1940, not discouraged by Roosevelt, he ran against Truman in the Democrat primary, and came within an ace of destroying him. This visit was therefore a disaster for all the participants except Clark, the lucky one of the trio whose advice was not taken. On the train back to Washington Truman was able to enjoy himself telling Stark that he had triumphed on his behalf with Pendergast.

Another visit was only two weeks later. It appears to have been more social and less destructive. It was certainly warm. 'We then (after breakfast) walked up to the Waldorf and I had a most pleasant visit with T.J.P.,' Truman wrote to his wife.* 'He was as pleased to see me as a ten-year-old kid to see his lost pal. I found that [he] had been on my side in everything he talked about and it looks as if everything is going to come out all right. I talked about county affairs too, and he's going to straighten them out along the lines I suggested.'[2]

The following summer, with the 1936 election impending, the Democratic Convention met in Philadelphia. There was not much to do there, except re-nominate Roosevelt (and Vice-President Garner) and generate some enthusiasm. Truman, although accorded no significant role, duly put in four or five days. Pendergast, who had again been installed in the Waldorf-Astoria since his late May arrival from Europe on the maiden voyage of the *Queen Mary*, came down to take charge of the Missouri delegation. There is a beaming photograph of him, accompanied by Truman and a fine collection of political 'pros', including Farley. It was almost his last self-confident beam. His illness began that week, and he had to face many weeks, not of the Waldorf but of hospital in

---

* What Pendergast was doing spending weeks of high summer in a Waldorf-Astoria suite is not clear. He had returned from Europe during July, almost immediately after having sailed there on the much-publicized first eastward trip of the *Normandie*. It sounds as though a paranoia which could be assuaged only by the protection of vast caravanserai, whether floating or static, had already set in, even though he did not become physically ill until the next year.

New York before he could go home to Kansas City. And soon after his return there began the harrying investigations into both his ballot-rigging and his acceptance of a massive bribe from the insurance industry.

For Truman, on the other hand, it was the beginning of a better period. Jonathan Daniels considered that 'his effective senatorial career began in the fall of 1936'.* The improvement was based on two props. First his committee work became more purposeful and began to bear some fruit. Previously his hard work had been somewhat undirected. He just read whatever document came to hand, rather as, when a boy, he had read almost any book which he picked up in the Independence public library. The second prop was that he began to be accepted as a sort of junior member of the core of the Senate. This came from a combination of straight-dealing, willingness to work, and 'regular guy' folksiness. In itself it had little to do with the highest qualities of statesmanship. Few of the most lastingly well-known senators of the past 150 years qualified: not Clay, Calhoun, Webster, Benton, neither La Follette, Wagner, Fulbright, Lehman, nor any Kennedy, with the possible but doubtful exception of Edward. To try to recollect those over a century or more who it did include would be a contradiction in terms.

In the thirties, the core centred around John Nance Garner (never a member of the Senate as such but its presiding officer as Vice-President after 30 years as a Congressman from Texas), Barkley of Kentucky, Harrison of Mississippi, Wheeler of Montana and Vandenberg of Michigan (a Republican), with Sam Rayburn of Texas, already a Congressman of 24 years' standing and later to be Speaker, providing a buttress from the House of Representatives. All of these, and as a result, a number of others too, approved of Truman. So, a different and perhaps more astringent test, did most of his freshmen contemporaries of the 1934 election: certainly Minton of Indiana, Schwellenbach of Washington State and Hatch of New Mexico, who were amongst the best of them, did so. By the autumn of 1936 he had developed a base of friendly acquaintances and potential allies. They nearly all came from west of the Alleghenies. They would nearly all have been surprised,

---

* Daniels *op cit* p. 183. Daniels' judgments, in my view and despite Truman's own disparagement of the work (see p. 22 *supra*), remain perceptive after 34 years.

two years earlier, to have been told how good they would find Truman to be.

His committee success was partly luck and partly work. From the beginning he was pleased with his major committee assignments – Appropriations (under Glass of Virginia) and Interstate Commerce (under Wheeler). The latter, with Wheeler's encouragement, he was able to make into something substantial. Wheeler put him on a sub-committee of three to enquire into civil aviation. The other and senior Democrat hardly attended. Truman conducted the hearings with acumen and energy, and from them there emerged the Civil Aeronautics Act of 1937.

Wheeler set up another sub-committee to investigate railroad finances. The prosperity of the system was already past its peak, but financial interests were still taking a lot of money out of the companies. Wheeler himself took the chair of this sub-committee and began hearings in December 1936. Truman at first was not even a member. But he sat in at meetings assiduously, out of interest. When a member fell out, he was added. He quickly showed himself the best briefed. Then, after Roosevelt's defeat on the Supreme Court issue, Wheeler, who had been one of the President's most determined opponents,* decided that he needed an autumn rest in Montana. Truman took over as chairman for some of the most crucial hearings. The first company on which he led the investigation was right in his back yard, the Missouri Pacific. Indeed its tracks had literally run at the bottom of one of his childhood gardens, in South Crysler Street, where he lived from 1890 to 1896. There were fears that he would pull his punches against such an intimate *vis-à-vis*. They were misplaced. Truman resisted a lot of home state pressure in a way that surprised and impressed the staff of the sub-committee. He also played the dominant role throughout 1938 and 1939 in preparing what, after several setbacks, became the Transportation Act of 1940 and is sometimes known as the Wheeler-Truman Act. He therefore ended his first Senate term with a good record of legislative achievement.

His Senate floor speeches were less distinguished. For the first two years they were almost non-existent. For the next two they

* Truman firmly supported the President but this did not seem to impair his relations with Wheeler.

were infrequent, strident and often ill-judged. They were populist
in tone and a little out of date, William Jennings Bryan without
the oratory or the imagery. The railroad companies in the early
years of the century, he claimed, had been far bigger robbers than
Jesse James and his hold-up gang who occasionally got away with
a few tens of thousands of dollars from express cars. The Carnegie
libraries were 'steeped in the blood of the Homestead steel
workers'. The Rockefeller Foundation was built 'on the dead
miners of the Colorado Fuel and Iron Company, and a dozen other
similar performances'. More interestingly, and under the influence
of Justice Brandeis,* who had taken him up, he launched an attack
on bigness: 'I believe that a thousand insurance companies, with
$4 million each in assets would be a thousand times better for the
country than the Metropolitan Life, with $4,000 million in assets
. . . I also say that a thousand county seat towns of 7,000 people
each are a thousand times more important to this Republic than
one city of 7 million people.'

The occasion of remarkable ill-judgment came in February 1938.
Maurice Milligan, the brother of the Milligan who had opposed
Truman in the 1934 primary, was at the end of his first term as
District Attorney for the Kansas City area. Roosevelt, supported
by his Attorney-General, was resolved to re-appoint him. This
commanded the strong support of Governor Stark and the agreement of Senator Clark. It did not however command the agreement
of Senator Truman, whose acquiescence might have been considered essential, on grounds of senatorial courtesy, in view of the
location in the state of Milligan's field of operation and the fact
that Truman had previously done badly for patronage in compari-
son with Clark. The issue was now however not one of simple
senatorial courtesy. Milligan, with Stark's encouragement, was
deeply involved in an investigation into Kansas City vote frauds
at the 1936 elections. Pendergast was not directly involved for he
had been ill in New York City at the time, but his machine most
certainly was, and 259 over-eager supporters of it were convicted.
It was also thought to be Truman's machine. In addition, Federal

---

* Louis Dembitz Brandeis, 1856–1941, associate justice of the Supreme Court,
1916–1939, the first Jew to be appointed to that body. Mostly his judgments
(often in a minority) supported the New Deal, although he was a little suspicious
of Roosevelt's centralizing tendencies and was against him on the constitutionality
of the National Recovery Act and on the Court-packing issue.

A late marriage, June 1919. *(Harry S. Truman Library)*

Haberdashery and politics: the Truman/Jacobson shop in Kansas City c.1921.
(Kansas City Star)

219 North Delaware Street, Mrs Truman's home throughout her life. Truman's Independence, Missouri house from 1919 to 1972. *(Kansas City Star)*

agents, working with Milligan's knowledge, were investigating Pendergast's non-payment of income tax on his $750,000 insurance companies' bribe.

In these circumstances Roosevelt's circumnavigation of Truman was understandable. Truman could have taken one of two courses, either of which, without being glorious, would have had something to be said for it. He could have rolled with the punch and quietly accepted Milligan, hoping that Roosevelt would compensate him on some future occasion. Or he could simply have blocked Milligan in the Senate, by saying, without reasons, that his re-appointment was unacceptable to him. The Senate would have drawn its own conclusions but it would almost certainly, for the sake of the prerogatives of other senators, not have overruled him.

He did neither. He waived his right to formal objection, but launched a most violent attack on the whole administration of justice in Jackson County. Of course, he said, he did not defend voting frauds. (He could hardly have said otherwise.) Those responsible should be prosecuted. But not by the methods employed. Milligan was corrupt because he accepted bankruptcy fees outside his salary. His witch hunting made him the cheap hero of the *Kansas City Star* and the *St Louis Post-Dispatch*. He was supported both in his corruption and in his prosecutions by two Republican judges, the strength of who's impartiality could be deduced from the facts that one was appointed by President Harding and the other by President Coolidge. Milligan and they could only get convictions by excluding inhabitants of Jackson County from juries in federal cases in the district. His conclusion was as extreme as it could be: 'I say to this Senate that a Jackson County Missouri Democrat has as much chance of a fair trial in the Federal District Court of Western Missouri as a Jew would have in a Hitler court or a Trotsky follower before Stalin.'

Truman's speech was hardly designed to make friends, either in Missouri or on Capitol Hill. It did not. It was heard with impatience by his opponents and with embarrassment by his normal allies. No one voted with him. He cast a single 'nay' vote. What was his motive? To support Pendergast, most people said. To revive the humiliating label of being his 'office boy' after three years of working to rub it off? And to do so at a time when Pendergast was manifestly no longer in a position to do anything more for Truman? The explanation does not begin to make sense.

Was it then just spleen against Roosevelt's disregard of him? Probably he was offended at the time. But nineteen months later he was writing to his wife with a remarkable calm wisdom about his relations with the President on exactly this type of issue. And this was when it was becoming depressingly clear to him that F.D.R. was probably for Stark, and certainly not ringingly for Truman, for renomination in 1940. 'I am most happy you are back in line,' he wrote on September 24th, 1939. 'You should not have gotten out seriously. [Presumably Mrs Truman had not unnaturally gone a little cool on Roosevelt.] My patronage troubles were the result of the rotten situation in Kansas City and also the jealous disposition of my colleague. While the President is unreliable, the things he's stood for are, in my opinion, best for the country, and jobs should not interfere with general principles. With most people they do.'[3]

More probably Truman just acted almost on impulse, although he must have prepared his speech over at least a few hours, without advice or any clearly worked-out objective. He was irritated, he was frustrated, he hated to trim, he could stand isolation and disapproval, so he lashed out without much thought of the consequences. It was a similar reaction to that which he exhibited in the letters of expostulation, a few privately posted but the majority fortunately not sent, with which he relieved his feelings during his presidency. However this speech was neither suppressed nor privately posted, but indelibly inscribed in the records of the Senate and impressed, although fortunately not indelibly, upon the memories of many of those who heard it. If the qualities he exhibited on this occasion, rashness, ill-judgment, pig-headed lack of concern for his own immediate interest, had to be weighed against each other and the balance measured as a test of fitness for the highest office the result would have been an almost unanimous adverse view.

However, in the second part of his first Senate term, the last thing that Truman himself, or anyone else, was thinking about was his fitness for the highest office. It began to seem increasingly unlikely that he would be able to continue in the Senate. The indictment of Pendergast in April 1939 was a major blow. Although Truman had slowly shaken off the slur of being the boss's office boy, the gain was substantially offset by the boss turning out to be not merely a boss but a crook, who was sent to serve 15 months in Leavenworth, which had one of the most symbolic names of the Federal penitentiaries, as well as the disadvantage of sitting on the doorstep of Kansas City. There was no question of Truman being directly involved in the scandals, but apart from inevitable guilt by association the collapse of the Kansas City machine threatened him with a substantial loss of votes in any primary contest.

From the early summer of 1939 it was obvious that there was going to be such a contest. Governor Stark previously had alerted Truman, so the latter always subsequently asserted, by assuring him that, although he might be pressed, he would never run against him. Soon after the Pendergast *débâcle*, Stark declared himself a candidate. (Later Milligan, the disputed US Attorney, came into the contest too.) A year or so before Truman had been doubtful about how much he wanted to continue in the Senate, with the dreary Washington apartment life that it involved for him. Stark's emergence concentrated his mind. 'I'm going to lick that double-crossing, lying governor if I can keep my health,' he wrote to his wife from Washington on July 5th.* 'If I do then I can really do something here for Missouri. I know I could if old Jack or Wheeler should happen to be the fair-haired boy.'[4]

The interesting sentence is the third one. Truman, not unreasonably at that stage, two months before the outbreak of the war in Europe, was not contemplating a third term for Roosevelt. Retrospectively, however, his idea of possible successors does suggest a remarkable inwardness of senatorial approach. 'Old Jack' was Garner, already 71 and about to retire from the strains of the vice-presidency to his Texas ranch, from which he hardly ever subsequently emerged, and, perhaps for this reason, lived to the

* Truman's health was of some continuing concern throughout the late 1930s. In September 1937 he went to an army hospital (he was a lieutenant-colonel in the reserve) at Hot Springs, Arkansas for two weeks of intensive check-up and tests, and returned there on several subsequent occasions. He was concerned about a whole variety of complaints: erratic sleeping, tiredness by day, lack of appetite, headaches. The picture of Truman as a man of unblemished health, robust appetite for simple food, assured sleep, effortless ability to rise every morning at 6.00 and walk a brisk four miles before breakfast, all adding up to a predictably long life to the age of 88, was something which came with his presidency and not long before. In his early fifties (as when he was a much younger man on the farm) there was a good deal of complaint about the difficulty of getting out of bed, accompanied by occasional bursts of 12 or 15 hours of sleep, and some touches of hypochondria.

age of 99. Wheeler became one of the most isolationist of senators. Truman was not an early prophet of the imperial presidency.

Indeed, even when the European War had started and Roosevelt had begun to nibble at staying on, Truman remained opposed to a break with tradition. So was Bennett Clark, who even thought of himself for the nomination, an idea to which Truman gave some support. This had the unfortunate effect of further improving the position with Roosevelt of Governor Stark, who was unequivocally for a third term from the beginning. Quite how well the President thought of Stark is not clear. He delivered some disparaging *non sequiturs* ('I do not think your governor is a real liberal . . . He has no sense of humour . . . He has a large ego . . .') about him to Truman in August 1939, which the latter gratefully recorded to his wife. But this may just have been playing a little politics with Truman. He certainly did not discourage Stark, he blandly declined to endorse Truman, and by January 1940, he regarded him as sufficiently unlikely to win that he offered him a well-paid appointment to the Interstate Commerce Commission.

Truman himself at this stage probably took little better a view of his own chances than did Roosevelt. His daughter recorded: 'Never before or since can I recall my father being so gloomy as he was in those latter months of 1939, after Tom Pendergast went to prison. Nothing seemed to be going right.'[5] Nevertheless he became determined to run. It was not particularly his love of the Senate. Much more it was his contrariness, his good appetite for a fight against the odds, and an inherent optimism in adversity. When things were going well he was sceptical and self-critical. His good opinion of himself mostly surfaced when he was up against a wall. Life could not be as bad as it looked. Apart from anything else he deserved that it should be better. An almost equal resistance to both euphoria and despair was one of his most considerable qualities. He was not particularly magnanimous in victory, but he was certainly defiant in the face of defeat. It was the spirit which had given him control over D Battery in 1918, and which was to get him through in 1948. Perhaps, as has been ingeniously suggested by one of his later biographers, it was due to his abnormally slow heart-beat.[6] It sounds as good an explanation as any other.

The early stages of the 1940 campaign were about as discouraging as it is possible to imagine. There was practically no money, little apparent support on the ground, and a nearly universal conviction that the fight was hopeless. The Jackson County machine, his base in 1934, was in ruins. The press was not merely hostile but often derisory. Milligan declared as a third candidate in March, and while this somewhat weakened Stark it also made Truman's base seem even more exiguous, and in particular gave Bennett Clark, whose half-promised support Truman desperately wanted, a reason for further equivocation. Clark by this time was bitterly hostile to Stark, but really preferred Milligan to Truman.

There were only a few people in Missouri who remained wholly loyal and worked devotedly from the beginning, but even they did so without any conviction of victory. One was Jim Pendergast, but the name had become useless. Others were John Snyder, a St Louis banker, whom Truman was to make an undistinguished Secretary of the Treasury, and Colonel (of the reserve) Harry Vaughan, who as General Vaughan was to become Truman's not wholly impeccable military aide, and a core crony in the White House. Truman's gratitude to those who were staunch during the months of apparent hopelessness remained intense.

How, out of this impossible beginning, did he snatch victory? His dogged determination was an essential basis. He also had good pockets of hidden support, which responded well to his vigorous, hard hitting but intimate, face-to-face campaigning. And the luck suddenly began to run with him. Stark, who was far enough ahead to prevent the more effective Milligan looking a serious challenger, began to defeat himself.

Truman's campaign opened officially at the mid-state town of Sedalia on June 15th, 1940, the day after German troops entered Paris. He was supported on the platform by Senator Schwellenbach of Washington State. Aid from other senators became a strong feature of his campaign. Alben Barkley of Kentucky and Carl Hatch of New Mexico came to speak for him in St Louis (unfortunately attracting an audience of only 300 in a hall for 3,500, which at least gave great pleasure to the *Post-Dispatch*), as, elsewhere, did one or two others. And public messages of support poured in from a wide span of leading Democrats: Wagner of New York, Connally of Texas, Byrnes of South Carolina, Harrison of Mississippi, Wheeler of Montana.

In addition Truman got massive labour union support, particularly from the railroad brotherhoods, who remembered with favour his work on the Wheeler sub-committee. A. F. Whitney, the president of the trainmen, with whom Truman was to have a very rough joust in 1946, was much to the fore. 'Truman for Senator' clubs were set up at the main depôts, and half a million copies of a special union produced newspaper were distributed throughout the state. These were careful to stress his support for agriculture as well as his labour relations record.

Truman also did well with blacks: there were still relatively few in Kansas City, but more in St Louis, and a quarter of a million in the state as a whole. At Sedalia he made a firm civil rights pronouncement, certainly the strongest of his career until then. There has been some suggestion that this stemmed more from opportunism than from principle. He needed the votes. Stark was weak in the black constituency. And he therefore cast aside his traditional Missouri prejudices in a blatant piece of political angling.

The main argument for this view is that as a young man he had been full of racial prejudice, although no doubt no more so than most Missouri Democrats of his time. 'I think one man is just as good as another so long as he's honest and decent and not a nigger or a Chinaman', he had written to Bess Wallace in June 1911. 'Uncle Will says that the Lord made a white man from dust, a nigger from mud, then threw up what was left and it came down a Chinaman. He does hate Chinese and Japs. So do I. It is race prejudice I guess. But I am strongly of the opinion that negroes ought to be in Africa, yellow men in Asia, and white men in Europe and America.'[7] And for several decades after that he used the word nigger without embarrassment both in private writing and speech. The arguments the other way are first that at Sedalia he desperately needed a warm response to the start to his campaign and that there were probably more in that summer's day country town audience to be alienated than won on the issue; and more significantly, that the line he there laid down was one to which he adhered increasingly strongly in his years power.

However the main force working on Truman's side during the campaign was Stark's humourless, megalomaniac ambition. It led him to alienate too many people, both amongst politicians and the public. He strutted around Missouri surrounded by uniformed colonels from the state troopers, which display, Margaret Truman wrote, 'made him look like a South American dictator'. He mis-judged the mood of audiences. But above all he ran for too many offices at the same time. In April he was being talked about as Secretary of the Navy. In July, less than a month before the primary vote, he suddenly threw his hat into the vice-presidential ring, only to see it contemptuously thrown out within a day or so, both by Roosevelt, who wanted Henry Wallace, and by his own Missouri delegation which, under Clark's control, was for Bankhead, the Speaker of the House. Clark was not much good at positive support for Truman, a cause in which he never had his heart, but he was good at opposing Stark, who was threatening his own power base, and particularly at ridiculing his pretensions.

Truman also had the luck to achieve a last minute alliance of opportunism in St Louis, the city in which he had been annihilated in the 1934 primary. The Democratic machine there had been for Stark, but they were more committed to their own candidate to succeed Stark as Governor (under Missouri law he was ineligible for a second term or he might have run for that as well), and discovered late that they needed Truman's support for this candidate. Dickmann, the Mayor, probably remained with Stark, but the up and coming figure in St Louis politics, Robert Hannegan, switched and worked hard for Truman. Hannegan's efforts, even if late, were crucial. Truman beat Stark by 8,411 in St Louis, which was within 500 votes of his bare and unexpected majority throughout the state. Hannegan was to become Democratic National Chairman within four years.

The victory, while it had ceased to seem impossible during the campaign, remained unexpected up to the night of counting. Truman went to bed on August 6th with those around him still believing he had lost. He woke up to find he had probably won, but the needle flickered until 11.00 a.m. when it finally settled. He had overcome not merely a severe crisis of morale but the specific handicap of a major collapse of his Jackson County position. His majority there was down from 128,000 in 1934 to 20,000 and the total vote had shrunk to two-thirds of the nominally recorded 1934 figures. Pendergast's old strength was even more vividly displayed by his absence than it had been by his presence. In the outstate counties Truman ran just enough behind Stark to dissipate his Jackson County lead. This left the result to be settled by St Louis, where the favourable turn round in his position was as spectacular as the unfavourable one in Kansas City.

It was a famous victory given his starting point, and the buoyancy and determination which were required to pull out of that valley of hopelessness. In that sense it was a foretaste of the qualities he was to show in 1948. But in other respects it was not a foretaste of the Truman presidency. It was fought during two of the most critical months in the history of the Western world. But it was not won because the Democrats of Missouri looked to Truman as a potential world figure who might help steer them through the shoals of international danger. As Hitler swept to victory, as France surrendered, as Britain prepared for invasion, Truman was pre-occupied containing the Pendergast curse and sundering the alliance between Stark and Hannegan.

Nor was it a ringing endorsement of a senator of six years' standing against a governor who had neither judgment nor sparkle. Truman had polled little more than 35% of the total vote. It was however a result which gave great pleasure on Capitol Hill. 'It certainly is gratifying (to put it mildly),' Truman wrote from Washington on August 9th, 'when every employee in the building – elevator boys, policemen, waiters, cooks, negro cleanup women, and all – were interested in what would happen to me. Biffle, (Clerk to the Senate) told me last night . . . that no race in his stay here had created such universal interest in the Senate. He's having lunch for me today. I guess it will be a dandy. It almost gives me the swell head – but I mustn't get that disease at this late date.' The senators themselves were no less enthusiastic. 'You should have been in the Senate yesterday,' he wrote the next day, 'when I slipped in at the back door. Hiram Johnson was making a speech and he had to call for order. Both floor leaders and all the Democrats made a great rush . . . I thought Wheeler and Jim Byrnes were going to kiss me. Barkley and Pat Harrison were almost as effusive. Schwellenbach, Hatch, Lister Hill, and Tom Stodart, and Harry Swartz almost beat me to death.'

In the White House there was less enthusiasm but a full recognition of reality. Henceforward Truman was treated as the plenipotentiary of Missouri. Stark wrote to Roosevelt complaining that he had been defeated by a low vote occasioned by the drought. Roosevelt replied with political elegance. 'Pure Roosevelt' was how Jonathan Daniels described it:

'Dear Lloyd,
  Your letter enclosing the clipping has been received and
I was interested to hear the analysis of the recent Primary
fight. I am sure you understand my personal feeling
towards you. I can only say that we will all have to get
behind the ticket and work for a Democrat victory.
    With all good wishes.
      Your friend,
        Franklin D. Roosevelt.'[9]

At the beginning of 1941 Roosevelt proposed giving Stark a
Federal appointment on a new Labor Mediation Board. Truman
was not pleased, but not anxious to block the move himself.
Instead ex-Senator Minton of Indiana wrote on his behalf. Roosevelt promptly desisted. On the other hand Truman himself wrote
to Roosevelt in September urging that Milligan, who had had to
resign to contend the primary, should be re-instated as District
Attorney. He even went so far as to say 'he has made a good
District Attorney'. This however was a matter of politics and not
of conviction, as he made clear in two letters to his wife.[10] Five
years later, as President, he reverted to his earlier position and
declined to give him a further term.

Unlike 1934, the 1940 election proper (as opposed to the primary) was not a walk-over for Truman. He won satisfactorily,
but only by about 40,000 votes, which was less than half the
majority by which Roosevelt carried Missouri. However, the
Democratic candidate for Governor, whose needs had been crucial
to the primary outcome in St Louis, lost to a Republican, so that
Truman could not be held to have got a notably bad result.

In the three months between the primary and the general election
Truman received one agreeable accolade and suffered one major
(and somewhat mysterious) family misfortune. The accolade was
his election as Grand Master of the Grand Lodge of the Masons of
Missouri. He had been an active Mason since his pre-World War
I days on the farm at Grandview, and was a natural member of
the 'brotherhood'. But it was an odd time for his installation in
the Scottish Rite Temple in St Louis. Most of those involved in
inducting him were Republicans, it was in the middle of a fairly
vicious campaign, and it marginally helped his re-election.

The other event was much odder and wholly disagreeable. The

Grandview house and farms had a mortgage of $35,000 upon them. The money had somewhat mysteriously been advanced not by a bank or other financial institution but by the Jackson County School Board. Interest payments had got into arrears. On August 22nd, 16 days after the primary triumph, the County moved in, got a court order for default, sold up the whole property, deprived Truman's brother of his occupation, and forced his mother (then aged 88) and his sister to move out and set up a new house in the town of Grandview. No sooner had they done this than his mother fell and broke her hip, largely due to the disagreeable unfamiliarity of the new surroundings, so Truman always maintained.

It is very difficult to understand why Truman could not stop the foreclosure. $35,000 was a substantial amount of money in those days, but it was not vast, even if, which seems an unlikely assumption, he had to raise the whole sum to resist the process. Before the primary, certainly in the slough of despair at the beginning of the campaign, it might have been impossible. But in the flush of victory, particularly in view of his reception in the Senate, it is almost inconceivable that the money or any necessary part of it could not have been raised in Washington or Missouri. John Snyder, for instance, an almost constant companion of Truman's at this stage, was moving up to be the President of the First National Bank of St Louis.

Yet Truman took it all curiously casually. Of course he minded greatly about his mother. But Merle Miller recorded him as saying: 'Had an old squint-eyed guy that was head of the county government, and he thought that would be a good way to help in my defeat, but nearly everybody in Missouri had a mortgage, so it didn't do me a bit of harm.'[11]

To complete the bizarreness of the incident there was the fact that Charles Ross, an old class-mate of Truman's and a staff writer with the *St Louis Post-Dispatch* had probably sparked off the whole process by writing an article about the alleged impropriety of the mortgage. It was the sort of behaviour which could easily have led Truman to bear one of his relatively few but unrelenting grudges. On the contrary he made Ross his press secretary when he became President, in which office Ross matched his loyalty with the quality of his service, which was not always so in the Truman entourage, until he died at his desk in December 1950.

Eventually the Grandview house and two parcels of farm land

returned to the ownership of the Trumans in 1946. It was arranged through the intervention and to some extent the generosity of a Kansas City real estate dealer who was an old acquaintance and was happy to have nothing more than a few White House invitations in return. Nevertheless, Truman's acceptance of the assistance is inconsistent with a view that it was over-scrupulousness about any form of outside help which accounted for his paralysis in 1940. The mystery remains.

So did Truman's money troubles as he began his second term. He assuaged them by taking Bess Truman on to his Senate office payroll, at a salary of $4,500 and in the capacity of a mixture of mail sorter and political advisor. Neither much liked the arrangement; at least it was public and unconcealed.

Truman's work, during the three and a half years which he served as a second term senator, was almost wholly concentrated upon his chairmanship of the Special Committee to Investigate the National Defense Program. Mostly it was known as the Truman Committee. In consequence it gave him a national reputation and for the first time made his name known outside Missouri and the Senate. *Time* magazine put him on its cover in March 1943. About the same time *Look* conducted a poll of political correspondents which put him among the ten men in Washington most valuable to the war effort; no other member of the Congress was in the list.

It was loosely estimated that the Committee saved the nation $15 billion. It did so by methods that were non-partisan – all the reports were unanimous – and undemagogic because they were designed to achieve results and not to pillory individuals or create sensation. It also steered firmly away from trying to influence strategy or to make or unmake commanders. It investigated contracts and not battles. As a result it was tolerably acceptable to the White House. Roosevelt and those around him would probably have preferred no committee, but if they had to have one the Truman Committee was about the best for which they could have hoped. It operated (and consciously so in Truman's case) in sharp contrast with the 1860's Congressional Committee on the Conduct of the War, which tried to sack General McClellan, investigated the alleged anti-Union activities of Mrs Lincoln, and generally infuriated the President. Except on one occasion when Truman put his name to an ill-judged article which he had not properly read and allowed it to appear close to the 1942 mid-term elections

– which were very bad for the Democrats – he became popular
with the public without quarrelling with the President. Without
the Committee he would not have been a possibility for the
vice-presidential nomination in 1944.

The Committee was not only Truman's vehicle. It was also his
creation. During his election campaign he had been struck by
Missouri examples of wasteful contracting for the rapid creation
of new camps and munition plants made necessary by the greatly
enlarged army which the United States was building up. He also
believed that the contracts were stuffed too fast into the open
mouths of too few large companies for efficient digestion. It was
partly a re-surfacing of the anti-bigness *motif* which had drawn
him to Brandeis three or four years before; and it was partly
empirical observation.

Immediately after he was sworn in for his second term he decided
to widen his field for such observation. He did it in a form which
was typically direct and informed. He got into his Dodge coupé
and spent the month of January 1941 on another vast tour, comparable with the one he had made ten years before looking for a
courthouse he liked. This time he was looking for contracting
practices which he disliked, and he found them in abundance from
Florida to Michigan.

On February 10th he reported what he had seen in a speech to
the Senate. In its long-term effect it was by far the most important
that he had made. Its immediate impact was less dramatic, partly
because there were only sixteen senators on the floor to hear it.
This however had its advantages. It meant that his accompanying
resolution for a solution could slip by fairly easily. He was also
fortunate that the bitterly anti-Roosevelt Congressman Cox from
Georgia had a similar resolution before the House. The White
House realized that it could not block both, and that the best course
was to forestall Cox with Truman. Byrnes, as chairman of the
Audit and Costs Committee and very close to Roosevelt at
the time, was the key man. He neatly expressed the view of the
administration by supporting the ideas of a committee but offering
it only $10,000 for expenses, which would have meant no staff.

Truman successfully avoided this obstacle. First he got a good
committee: Connally of Texas, who as chairman of the Foreign
Relations Committee carried high prestige, and Mead of New
York, both of whom were influential with the administration;

Wallgren of Washington and Hatch of New Mexico, who were his own friends; and Ball of Minnesota with Brewster of Maine, who were internationalist and relatively non-partisan Republicans. Then he got the appropriation up to $15,000, and later, by stages, to $300,000. More importantly he assembled effective assistance by the expedient of using the influence of his fellow committee members to get the staff kept on the payroll of the different Government departments and agencies from which they came. The principal ones were Hugh Fulton, who was from the Justice Department and had just convicted a Federal judge for fraud; Matthew J. Connelly, who went on to serve with Truman throughout his White House years; and William M. Boyle, a former Kansas City director of police, who much later was to be Democratic National Chairman. They proved to be the core of an extremely effective investigating team (gradually the numbers of the investigators went up to twelve, and of senators to ten) and they worked well with Truman throughout his chairmanship.*

Despite its shoe-string beginning the Committee does not appear to have been restricted in its ability to do its work, either in Washington or about the country. Truman was constantly travelling, by train, by commercial airline, by army plane. He spent many nights in hotels, some small some grand, across the nation, and indeed in Missouri, for he effectively removed his family to the still small apartment in Washington in the autumn of 1941, with the house in Independence closed for long periods. The poverty-induced immobility of his first term disappeared during his second. The Committee and the more open-handed habits of wartime enabled him to travel free almost anywhere. His letters to his wife, instead of being rather plaintively sent from Washing-

---

* A few days after he became President, Truman was embarrassed and offended by Fulton sending out business cards for his entry into private practice which stressed his closeness to the new President. Connelly served as appointments secretary throughout Truman's presidency, and was in charge of the campaign train during the 1948 campaign. In 1955, when working in public relations in New York, he was charged, jointly with Truman's assistant Attorney-General, of conspiring to prevent an income tax suit being brought against a St Louis shoe manufacturer, and sentenced to two years' imprisonment. There was however considerable suggestion of Republican vindictiveness in the process, and Connelly was given a full pardon by President Kennedy in 1962. Boyle retained both his friendship with Truman and his liberty. Nevertheless the pattern confirms a feeling that Truman had an uncertain touch, both as a picker of staff and in his relations with them.

ton to Independence were mostly sent from all over the continent
to Washington. They were no less constant, no less full, fluent and
vivid, not often elegant, but no longer plaintive.

In Washington he was mostly engaged in hearings and the
preparation and presentation of reports. He was throughout both
firm and thorough. He had sub-committees under other senators,
but he never allowed their reports to go out without having himself
been carefully through them. He almost invariably presided over
the hearings of the full Committee, and insisted that they be
conducted in a calm, quasi-judicial atmosphere, although that was
hardly his natural style. 'And another thing I'm proud of,' he told
Merle Miller, 'we didn't give a hoot in hell about publicity.'[12]
They were not, of course, subject to the temptations of television
cameras, but his claim was true so far as the raw material of the
proceedings, as opposed to the finished product of the reports,
was concerned. As a result there were no confrontations for the
sake of headlines. But there were notable jousts with Jesse Jones,
Secretary of Commerce and head of the Reconstruction Finance
Corporation, as well as with two labour leaders: John L. Lewis,
who although rough in controversy was relatively safe to take on
because he was maverick and unpopular; and Sidney Hillman, who
was much more redoubtable, because he was highly responsible and central to the administration's relations with organized
labour.

Only in rare cases did the committee seek retribution. Its aims
were essentially that lessons should be learned for the future and
that economy and honesty should be encouraged by the fear of
exposure. No more than three or four people went to gaol as a
result of its activities. But neither this continence nor the eschewal
of deliberate publicity-seeking prevented the Committee, and
particularly Truman himself, from gaining speedily in both the
awareness and the esteem of the public.

As the 1944 election began to loom so thoughts turned to the
composition of the Democratic ticket. The prospect of a fourth
term for Roosevelt was much more easily accepted than had been
the idea of a third term. The country was at war, as opposed to
being buffeted by a European conflict, and once the 150-year-old
convention of a maximum of eight years had been breached there
was no great excitement in favour of erecting a new limit. Truman
did not repeat his reluctance of 1939/40. At a 1944 Jackson Day

(February 17th) dinner in Florida he came out firmly and early in favour of electing F.D.R. to see the war through.

There was much more doubt as to whether Henry Wallace should be asked to do it with him. And some of those who doubted began to think of Truman as a possible substitute. The first reference to the matter in his letters to his wife came as early as July 12th, 1943:

> 'The Senator from Pennsylvania [Guffey] took me out into his beautiful back yard [garden in the capital] and *very confidentially* wanted to know what I thought of Henry Wallace. I told him that Henry is the best Secretary of Agriculture we ever did have. He laughed and said that is what he thinks. Then he wanted to know if I would help out the ticket of it became necessary by accepting the nomination for Vice-President. I told him in words of one syllable that I would not – that I had only recently become a Senator and that I wanted to work at it for about ten years.'[13]

There is no reason to doubt the genuineness of Truman's reluctance at this stage. In fact it persisted and strengthened over the ensuing year. But this was the oddest possible way of putting it. At the time he had been a senator for eight and a half years, and on the day he was sworn in as vice-president he had been one for exactly ten years and seventeen days.

4

HEIR TO A
DYING PRESIDENT

'The truth is that . . . the last year and a half of the President's life
was a time when his superb machine . . . was slowly but inexorably
running down, because of the long and taxing use that he had
made of it.'[1] So in 1981 wrote Joseph Alsop in his penetrating
and succinct centenary evocation of Franklin Roosevelt. Eighteen
months back from April 12th, 1945 takes us to October 12th,
1943, a few weeks after the second Quebec meeting between
Churchill and the President, a few weeks before the Teheran
Conference, the first meeting of Roosevelt, Stalin and
Churchill.

If, as I believe it to be, Alsop's judgment is true, it means that
during the whole period when Roosevelt was contemplating a
fourth term, deciding upon it, influencing the choice of a vice-
presidential running-mate, campaigning for re-election, winning,
being re-inaugurated, seeing, if he happened to look that way, his
third vice-president in operation, he had no surplus energy and
probably knew, if he cared to contemplate it, which he mostly did
not, that he had not long to live.

There were a substantial number of other people who knew this
too, including the possible vice-presidential nominees and the
would-be king makers in the Democratic Party organization. Apart
from favourite sons, of whom there were many, there were at
least eight, who, with varying degrees of seriousness were at one
time or another discussed as possible vice-presidents by Roosevelt
himself. There was obviously Wallace, the incumbent. There
was Byrnes, ex-senator from South Carolina, then (very briefly)
associate justice of the Supreme Court before becoming Director
of the Office of War Mobilisation and, as some dubbed him, not

to his displeasure, 'assistant President' and future Secretary of State under Truman. There was Barkley, majority leader in the Senate; and there was Rayburn, Speaker of the House. There were Winant, ambassador to London and ex-Governor (Republican) of New Hampshire, Supreme Court Justice William O. Douglas, and Henry Kaiser, the man who, it was currently thought, could build anything from ships to motor cars to aircraft, quick, plentiful and cheap. And there was Truman.

Winant, Douglas and Kaiser in vice-presidential terms, were little more than figments over whom Roosevelt allowed his imagination to flicker. Whether or not any of them wanted the job is therefore not known; they may not even have posed the question to themselves. All the others except for Truman did, stimulated or at least undisturbed by the prospect of the succession and therefore by the unusually ambiguous nature of the nomination they were seeking.* Truman, by no means wholly out of modesty, was unattracted either way. So far as the vice-presidency *per se* was concerned he stressed the obscurity in which nearly every vice-president in the history of the Republic had lived and died. He liked asking those who pressed him if they could remember who was vice-president to Fillmore or Polk or some other nineteenth-century president who had survived his term, and even on one occasion over-reached himself by asking it in relation to McKinley and still getting a negative response.

Additionally, however, he fully apprehended the probability of Roosevelt dying without four years, and liked that prospect no more. '1600 Pennsylvania is a nice address,' he wrote to his daughter twelve days before he was nominated, 'but I'd rather not move in through the back door – or any other door at sixty.'[2] He also answered a *St Louis Post-Dispatch* reporter: 'Do you remember your American history well enough to recall what happened to most vice-presidents who succeeded to the presidency? Usually

---

* Cordell Hull, on the other hand, declined it flatly when Roosevelt dangled it before him. And Speaker Rayburn, Truman's first preferred candidate, in no way allowed himself to become obsessive. When Truman had proposed him at a San Francisco banquet in March he returned the compliment by proposing Truman at St Louis one week later. And when he found himself effectively eliminated by being judged insufficiently conservative to carry his own Texas delegation he took the setback calmly.

they were ridiculed in office, had their hearts broken, lost any
vestige of respect they had had before. I don't want that to happen
to me.'[3]

The hand that Roosevelt played in the approach to the choice
was enigmatic at the time, remains puzzling, and now seems
unlikely ever to become clear. The earlier statements about his
health should not be taken as meaning that a persistent pall of
indifference had settled over him. He was convinced that it was
his duty to run, and that being so, he was determined to win. This
was not something which could be taken for granted. Dewey,
Governor of New York and the youngest presidential candidate
of this century (a year younger than John F. Kennedy) had been
smoothly nominated on the first ballot at the Republican Convention in mid-June. In retrospect the 'little man on the wedding cake'
looks an easy candidate to beat. But this was not obvious at the
time. Indeed Dewey's reputation as a loser only came four years
later with his amazing defeat by Truman. In early July 1944 the
main poll showed Roosevelt leading him by a margin of only 51
to 49. And the actual outcome in November was not very different.
Roosevelt secured a strong electoral college result – 432 to 99 –
but this was due to the luck of all the big states except Ohio just
slipping his way. His lead in votes cast was only 53½% to 46½%,
the narrowest popular majority since Wilson's second election in
1916.

It was not magnificent for the leader of the free world against a
man who two years before had been only a District Attorney,
although a very successful one. What is significant however is that
Roosevelt could not afford to think that he could stroll to victory.
Nor did he attempt to do so. He made very few speeches – in
effect only five – and for the rest of the time sheltered behind an
Olympian commander-in-chief role. But this was probably sound
tactics as well as a necessary conservation of energy. Of these five
speeches at least three showed most of his old campaigning verve.
His 'my little dog Fala' speech in Washington in September contained some of the most daring and brilliant political raillery in
which he had ever indulged, and the orations at Soldiers' Field,
Chicago (before 100,000) and in the Boston Bowl were both
memorable. In New York he subjected himself to the ordeal of a
50-mile 4-hour waving drive in pouring rain and an open motor-
car, and did a near repeat in Philadelphia. He was of course battling

against the rumours of his ill-health as much or more than against Dewey, but the fact that he felt he had to fight so hard against either meant that he could not be indifferent to the identity of his running-mate. Nor was he beyond making shrewd political judgments about this identity.

There is a widespread view that he was persuaded by the spring that Wallace, with whom he would have been personally happy to continue and who was strongly backed by many Democratic enthusiasts, including Eleanor Roosevelt, would not do, both because Wallace would alienate votes across the nation and because he would be ineffective in the new term at delivering two-thirds of the Senate for the peace treaties and American adherence to the United Nations, and that of the other possibilities the President wanted Truman for the converse of these two reasons. If Roosevelt was as clear as this his convolutions ran great risks of frustrating his purposes.

It is understandable that he did not wish to impose a candidate on the Convention. He was vulnerable to the charge of being monarchical. And he had to give the assembled delegates something to do. He was not going to attend himself, even though he passed through Chicago while they were assembling. All he gave them by way of an acceptance speech was a somewhat flat radio link-up from San Diego before he embarked on a Pacific bases trip. If he was going to show them any respect it had to be over the vice-presidential choice.

There was also his endemic dislike of telling people to their faces that they were not his choice. This was fortified by a more rational political desire not to make unnecessary enemies, and embellished by a slightly sadistic enjoyment of a teasing, ambivalent approach to appointments. In mid-May he sent Wallace off on a seven-week trip to China, from where he re-emerged only on July 9th. That cut him off from canvassing his support and did him no good for publicity as the journey had to be secret. When he returned he was told by intermediaries that he was to be dropped. He insisted on seeing Roosevelt and stressed his strength in the polls and with delegates. Roosevelt, we are told, appeared 'surprised and impressed'. He concluded the interview by saying: 'I hope it's the same team again, Henry.'[4] This is necessarily hearsay. What is documented is the letter of exquisitely qualified endorsement which he

wrote for Wallace. It was addressed to the probable Permanent
Chairman of the Convention and signed at Hyde Park on Friday,
July 14th:

> '. . . because I know that many rumours accompany annual
> [sic] conventions, I am wholly willing to give you my own
> personal thought in regard to the selection of a candidate
> for Vice-President . . . The easiest way of putting it is this:
> I have been associated with Henry Wallace during his past
> four years as Vice-President, for eight years earlier while
> he was Secretary of Agriculture, and well before that. I
> like him and I respect him, and he is my personal friend. For
> these reasons, I personally would vote for his renomination
> if I was a delegate to the Convention.
>
> At the same time I do not wish to appear in any way as
> dictating to the Convention. Obviously the Convention
> must do the deciding. And it should – and I am sure it will
> – give great consideration of the pros and cons of its
> choice.
>   Very sincerely yours,
>   Franklin D. Roosevelt.'[5]

Three days earlier, in the White House, Roosevelt had caused
Ed Flynn, the boss of the Bronx and his closest persistent friend
and ally amongst the 'pros' to summon the core of the Democratic
Party organization to dinner. The main participants, apart from
Flynn, were Hannegan, the National Chairman and Truman's St
Louis ally of 1940, who had taken on this post when Truman
himself refused it at the end of 1943, Edwin Pauley, a Los Angeles
oil man who was National Treasurer and powerful at this stage,
Frank Walker, the Postmaster-General, Ed Kelly, Mayor of
Chicago, and George Allen, the Secretary of the Democratic
National Committee.

They were all against Wallace, not only as a vote loser (although
Flynn had previously reported to Roosevelt, surely with a touch
of hyperbole, that his presence on the ticket would cost the party
New York, Pennsylvania, Illinois, New Jersey and California) but
also because they were terrified of the prospect of having him as
President of the United States. Roosevelt was well informed of
their opposition beforehand. If he had really wanted Wallace, he

would have asked a different group to dinner. Wallace's name was hardly seriously discussed.

Others were fairly quickly discarded: Rayburn with regret because he could not carry the Texas delegation, and Barkley nominally on grounds of age (which did not prevent his being elected four years later) but perhaps more because he and Roosevelt had fallen out over the President's veto of a tax bill. Winant and Kaiser did not get off the ground. Nor did Douglas, except that Roosevelt chose to keep him in play. That left Byrnes and Truman. The President had undoubtedly been recently and actively encouraging Byrnes, while there is no evidence that he had made any sort of direct approach to Truman. Nonetheless he easily accepted the ditching of Byrnes, on the grounds that he was too Southern and that being a renegade Catholic gave him the worst of two religious constituencies.*

That left Truman. Hannegan and Pauley were determinedly for him. The others with the possible exception of Kelly of Chicago, who wanted to keep Senator Lucas of Illinois in with a chance, were somewhere between content and enthusiastic. Truman 'just dropped into the slot,' Flynn wrote. Roosevelt spoke appreciatively of him on a number of grounds, said that he did not know him very well (which was indeed the truth), in particular did not know his age (just 60), but allowed those present who must have known it perfectly well to remain silent while not causing it to be looked up, and is variously reported as having summed up by saying 'Let's make it Truman' (Jonathan Daniels) and 'Everybody seems to want Truman' (James Macgregor Burns).

They filed out in satisfaction. Then they remembered Roosevelt's capacity for changing his mind, and Hannegan was sent back to try to get something in writing. Roosevelt does not appear to have resented this slightly suspicious precaution, and there is a unanimity of testimony that Hannegan did get something. But there is no unanimity about what he got. Truman believed that he got a pencilled note on the back of an envelope saying 'Bob, I think Truman is the right man, F.D.R.,' and that this is what he

---

* Neither fact could have been new to Roosevelt, particularly as he is reported as having been told by Cardinal Spellman of New York in 1940 how damaging the second would be. Spellman subsequently denied that he made any such statement. The Cardinal however was notable neither as an ally of Roosevelt nor as a witness of the truth.

(Truman) was shown in Chicago. No trace of that note remains. The alternative view is that he got the first version of a famous letter, a copy of which is in the Roosevelt archives:

> 'Dear Bob:
>   You have written me about Harry Truman and Bill Douglas.* I should of course be very glad to run with either of them and believe that either one of them would bring real strength to the ticket.
>   Always sincerely,
>   Franklin D. Roosevelt.'

The complications do not however end here. First Grace Tully, the President's principal secretary of this time, stated in her memoir of F.D.R. that the letter she typed in Washington put Douglas's name first and the order was only reversed in a second version, written under pressure from Hannegan and Pauley when they again met the President in his train in the Chicago yards on Saturday, July 15th. Again there is no trace of such a first version, and Hannegan specifically denied its existence a few weeks before his death in 1949. But Miss Tully had no motive for making it up. Second, the letter in the archives is dated July 19th, when the President was already on the West Coast, although it was certainly in Hannegan's hands by July 15th, if not on July 11th.

So the extraordinary story unrolled itself. But this was not the limit of the *opéra bouffe*. There was a Byrnes sub-plot. That adroit and ambitious gentleman from South Carolina was not going to give up merely because Hannegan and Walker told him that the President had switched to Truman. He had the good sense to realize that the President's 'switch' might not be as firm as these two wished it to be. He insisted on telephoning Roosevelt at Hyde Park. The call was well worth the toll. When asked why he was reported as having turned against him and as favouring Truman and/or Douglas, Byrnes recorded the President as saying: 'Jimmy, that is all wrong. That is not what I told them. It is what they told me . . . They asked if I would object to Truman and Douglas and I said no. That is different from using the word "prefer".' He ended by 'virtually urging Byrnes to run'.[6]

---

* Hannegan almost certainly had not. The last thing he wanted to do was to confuse the issue by bringing in Douglas's name.

Byrnes responded to these ambiguities with boldness and skill. At eight o'clock the next morning (Friday, July 14th) he telephoned Truman in Independence, said that he was still the President's choice and asked Truman to make the nominating speech for him at the Convention. As no one seemed to have bothered to tell Truman about the July 11th dinner, as Truman was in any event a reluctant candidate, and as at this stage he was fond of Byrnes, he readily agreed. Byrnes caught him at a characteristic moment: he was packing up the family car in order to drive to Chicago with his wife and daughter. Before he could complete the job he was summoned back into the house to take another call, this time from Alben Barkley, with the same request on his own behalf. He was bespoken to Byrnes, Truman said. And in this conviction he drove the 350 miles.

When he got to Chicago he encountered a horrified Hannegan and Pauley, and was then forced to a gradual realization that just as the political establishment of the Democratic Party would not have Wallace, so the labour union leadership, Sidney Hillman, Whitney, Murray, Green, with whom Truman ate a lot of breakfasts, would not have Byrnes. Both groups would have him. And there was mounting evidence too that Byrnes was misrepresenting his position with Roosevelt. Eventually on the Wednesday (July 19th) Truman confronted Byrnes and made him try to corner the President in his own presence. Byrnes failed. Roosevelt would not return his call. This made Truman disengage and Byrnes withdraw without his name being placed before the delegates. He had no strength on his own.

Truman still needed to be persuaded that he himself should be a candidate. This second stage of persuasion was accomplished by the now famous Hannegan-Roosevelt telephone conversation in Truman's presence: 'He's the contrariest Missouri Mule I've ever dealt with' was Hannegan's opening line: 'Tell him that if he wants to break up the Democratic Party in the middle of the war, that is his responsibility' was Roosevelt's response. Obviously there was a substantial element of contrived theatre about it; but it at least showed that Hannegan's lines of communication with Roosevelt were at this stage better than Byrnes's. Obviously, too, Truman was already prepared to move when it took place. The words attributed to him by his daughter after Roosevelt clicked his telephone down are both plausible and reasonable: 'Well, if that's the situation, I'll have to say yes. But why the hell didn't he tell me in the first place?'[7]

Apart from anything else, Wallace, who unlike Byrnes had real strength without official backing, was well on the way to stampeding the convention. He had the galleries packed although Mayor Kelly was not for him; but he was not for Truman either. He wanted a deadlock, with Senator Lucas coming through as a compromise. Wallace had acquired an organist who would play nothing but 'Iowa, that's where the tall corn grows,' to such an extent that Pauley had to threaten to chop the wires unless the tune were changed. Most important he had genuine enthusiasm and the support of a large number of delegates. Pauley and Hannegan decided that they could not risk nominations and balloting that (Thursday) night, and managed to get a fire hazard declared in the overcrowded hall and the Convention adjourned until the next day.

The Friday session did not begin well. For some inexplicable reason Truman, once persuaded of his duty, had decided that he must get his Missouri colleague, Bennett Clark, to nominate him. Clark was neither his friend nor his ally, and distinctly shop-soiled by this stage: he lost his Senate primary in that same year. Furthermore he was extremely difficult to find. Truman himself eventually ran him to ground, asleep and rather the worse for wear in a hotel other than the one in which he was supposed to be staying.

Not surprisingly in these circumstances Clark made a limp nominating address. Wallace, by contrast, was brilliantly proposed and enthusiastically carried along by five supporting speeches. On the first ballot he did extremely well. He was ahead throughout and finished with 419½ votes to Truman's 319½. Bankhead had 98, Lucas 61, and Barkley 49½. Eleven favourite sons polled handfuls of votes.

Hannegan then took the risk of a second ballot rather than an adjournment. It improved Truman's position substantially, mainly because of shifts from Oklahoma, Maryland, and within the New York delegation. He finished just ahead but in no way decisively so: 477½ to 473. A deadlock and a move away from both Wallace and Truman after an adjournment could easily have been the outcome. Then, after a brief pause, there began a growing wave of vote changing. Within a few minutes, without any formal third ballot, Truman went to a final score of 1031 to 105. That was overwhelming, but it had been a very close run thing at times.

Truman made one of the shortest acceptance speeches on record – less than 200 words – and then fought his way through a hysterical mob of photographers, police, delegates and public, first to a box to collect his family, and then out of the stadium, 'Are we going to have to go through this for all the rest of our lives?' Mrs Truman quietly but percipiently asked as they drove to the hotel.

In fact Truman was then eased rather gently into his new position and exposure. He drove himself home to Independence and stayed there for ten days. Then he went to Washington, wound up his committee chairmanship, and had his only meeting of any note with Roosevelt before election day. They lunched together in their shirt sleeves on the White House terrace on August 18th.

Even this meeting was more for the newsreels and the photographers than for any serious business. The President's daughter, Anna Boettiger, was present, and Mrs Truman was expected, but Truman did not understand this and in any event she was in Independence. Furthermore it was an off day for Roosevelt. He looked terrible, his hand shook so much that he could not get the cream into his coffee, he talked with difficulty, and Truman thought that 'physically he's just going to pieces'. They hardly discussed the tactics of the campaign let alone the strategy of the war. Roosevelt merely encouraged Truman to get on with it and get around the country, although forbidding him to travel by air on the unusually unguarded ground that 'one of us have to stay alive'.[8] The main things that Truman found to record about the meeting were what they had to eat (which was not much) and the White House china, silver and butlers. It was almost certainly the first time he had ever lunched or dined there. It was also the last as well as the first time that Truman had an intimate meal with Roosevelt.

Not notably fortified by this encounter, at once intimidating and dispiriting, Truman set about working out his schedule with his allies of the Democratic national machine. They planned a medium-profile campaign, which Truman faithfully carried out: no oratorical fireworks, but no major gaffes either. He began with a big rally at Lamar, his birthplace, which he had not visited for many years, supported by nine other senators and by too large a crowd for the facilities of the small town. He then went twice across the continent, to the Pacific, to the Atlantic and then back to Missouri. He mostly campaigned in the northern industrial states. He travelled by two special Pullman cars, one for himself and his staff, the other for the press, hooked on to ordinary trains. He was at best a semi-star, oratorically always in danger of being outclassed, by Tom Connally at Lamar, by Henry Wallace in New York, by Orson Welles in Pittsburgh. But on the whole he drew good and friendly crowds. There were attempts to portray him as being a weak almost hysterical incompetent, totally out of his depth even in a vice-presidential role, and the old Ku Klux Klan *canard* was revived towards the end. These attacks did not greatly stick. The truth was that Truman, like Senator Bricker, his Republican opposite number from Ohio, was not a big factor in the campaign. He neither harmed nor much helped the ticket. He had the advantage for most places of not being Wallace, but beyond that it was the fourth Roosevelt-dominated election. The issue of the succession was one for the pundits not for the public.

For the poll and the result the Trumans went back, which was wholly traditional, to Jackson County. For some unexplained reason it was not to Independence, where the house, open in August and September, was closed, but to a suite or series of suites in the Muehlebach Hotel, Kansas City. There emerges an odd impression of the less reputable part of Truman's Battery D and Masonic friends having been allowed to take over. Unlike previous election nights, and still more his only subsequent one, when he showed iron will by going to sleep with the result in total doubt, Truman stayed up, playing the piano and no doubt consuming a good deal of bourbon, until Dewey conceded at 3.45 a.m. One difference was that, unlike 1940 or 1948, it was Roosevelt and not he who was at test. His friends mostly got drunk. He himself got rather maudlin about the terrible responsibilities which would fall upon him when Roosevelt died. His wife and daughter, although present in the hotel, seem for once to have been excluded from the centre of his stage.

Whatever happened, he had plenty of time to recover, because between election day on November 5th, 1944 and inauguration day on January 20th, 1945, he had practically nothing to do. He saw Roosevelt only once. He did not even have a new house into which to move. There was then, as for nearly 30 years subsequently, no official vice-presidential residence. He just stayed in his old five-room apartment on Connecticut Avenue. He was vicariously victorious, highly likely to be President within a year or two, unbriefed but untroubled by any attempt to brief him, and probably less occupied than he had been at any time in the previous five years.

Roosevelt decided to have his fourth inauguration ceremony on the south porch of the White House rather than on Capitol Hill. The war provided the excuse. It was a bleak ceremony on a day of driving rain and sleet. Roosevelt had done it too often before to be much interested. He made a fairly perfunctory address to the 7,800, a high proportion from Missouri (one of his few signs of consideration for Truman) who were given the privilege of standing on a squelching lawn, and then quickly disappeared upstairs, leaving Mrs Roosevelt and the Trumans to receive these guests in their damp shoes and somewhat lowered spirits.

In spite of this inauspicious beginning, Truman rather enjoyed being Vice-President. He only held the job for eleven weeks and five days (both Tyler and Andrew Johnson had held it even more briefly), which hardly gave him time to become bored. Of these 82 days, Roosevelt spent only 30 in Washington. His absences did not of course mean that Truman took over the government of the United States. The power of executive decision remained wholly with the Cabinet officers and with the White House staff left in Washington, subject to such instructions as they received from the other members of the staff who were travelling with the President. But it at least meant that Truman, who had not been considered for inclusion in the Yalta party, could not feel resentment at not seeing Roosevelt, who was mostly 6,000 miles away. He got on with presiding over the Senate, cultivating his congressional relationships, and, rather surprisingly, being the most social Vice-President for many years. 'For a while,' Margaret Truman wrote, 'scarcely a night went by without him and mother departing from our Connecticut Avenue apartment, looking tremendously regal in evening dress.'9

The main task, at once ironical and disparaging, which Roosevelt set him was that of getting Henry Wallace confirmed by the Senate as Jesse Jones's replacement as Secretary of Commerce. He achieved it with great difficulty and at the price of Wallace losing a substantial part of the powers that Jones had exercised.

The main initiative that he took was to requisition a US Army bomber to attend Tom Pendergast's funeral in Kansas City.

Pendergast died on January 26th. He was long since out of gaol, but was without influence and left only $13,000. It was six days after the inauguration and Roosevelt had already departed for Yalta. So Truman had to make his own decision about both the funeral (which he would no doubt have done in any event) and the bomber (which alone made his attendance compatible with an important Philadelphia speaking engagement). He was much criticized, but his presence meant a great deal to the Pendergast family. He had no doubt that it was a proper discharge of an old debt of political friendship.

Roosevelt got back at the end of February. A week before Washington had been swept by a rumour that he had died at sea, but it was General 'Pa' Watson, his long-standing military aide, and not the President himself who had gone. March was a month of continuing allied military success, but also of gravely deteriorating relations with the Russians, with the exchange of messages of mounting complaint and acerbity between Stalin and Roosevelt. There were also several disagreeable edges to the relationship between the President and Congress. Truman had two meetings at the White House during the month, but it was only Congressional difficulties and not global problems which were even perfunctorily discussed. Truman was given no special account of the Yalta Conference. It became abundantly clear that the President had neither the energy nor the desire to bring a new face into the inner core of government.

At the end of March Roosevelt left for Warm Springs, Georgia. There, two weeks later, at the beginning of a sunny afternoon he had his massive stroke and was dead in a couple of hours. Truman received the news in Washington in the rain. After a desultory day presiding over a desultory session of the Senate he was having a restorative drink in Sam Rayburn's office when he was hurriedly summoned to the White House. He made the journey only half fearing the worst. When he got there he was shown to Mrs Roosevelt's upstairs study, where she was with her daughter and son-in-law and the White House press secretary. She told him what had happened. He was sworn in at 7.09 p.m. just over three hours after President Roosevelt had been pronounced dead. So, as the news rang around the world, there began the transition described at the beginning of this book.

5

THE NEW PRESIDENT

Almost all Truman's early views about how he should handle the Roosevelt inheritance, at once splendid and frightening, turned out to be wrong.

His initial ideas, I believe, were roughly these. First, his perceived inferiority would be greater than he himself thought it to be. (His real view of Roosevelt stood well short of idolatry; in view of the treatment he had received it would have been a miracle had this not been so.) He would therefore respond by exaggerating his own very considerable modesty. This reflected itself in his early statements to the press: 'I don't know whether you fellows ever had a load of hay or a tree fall on you. But last night the house, the stars and all the planets fell on me. If you fellows ever pray, pray for me.' The trouble with this was that he was in danger of publicly under-valuing himself.

Second, on policy issues, particularly in the, to him, largely hidden fields of strategy and inter-Allied relations, he would discover Roosevelt's designs and continue to execute them. The trouble with this was that Roosevelt had at the end very few designs. He had always relied heavily on improvisation. This tendency became still greater as he grew more tired, and in any event the circumstances were changing so fast as the strains with Russia increased and the discipline of the single objective of victory was removed.

At the same time Truman believed that he should exploit his few obvious areas of greater strength: notably his natural accessibility, and the fact that (Harding, who hardly counted, apart), he would be the first president from the Congress since McKinley. He symbolized both by going to lunch on Capitol Hill almost as 'one of the boys' on his first day in office. The trouble with this was that it was very time consuming, and combined with his self-deprecation looked as though he was putting the presidency into commission. There was more real danger of time loss than of making himself a cipher of the legislature. In domestic policy he turned out to have more battles with the Congress than any president since Andrew Johnson. But his appointment sheets were full of 'Judge X – to pay respects' and 'Representative Y – just to visit'.

This combined with the development of an almost obsessive desire to leave no decision untaken – another area where he believed he could improve upon Roosevelt – meant that he left himself inadequate time for reflection and discussion. It was not that he was ill-briefed. He read his papers meticulously and impressed those around him with the thoroughness with which he mastered facts. But he was so determined to be decisive on the issues of the day, and then to have an untroubled night's sleep before awakening fresh and early for the separate decisions of the next day, that he was in danger of not fully considering the options, and not seeing one decision's impact upon another, or indeed its relation with a coherent general policy. A classic early example was his acceptance of a recommendation to cut off Lend-lease within a few days of the end of the war in Europe.

There was also a risk of his losing the advantages of the remarkable quality of many of the people who were assembled in wartime Washington. First he lurched towards continuity by asking all the members of the Roosevelt Cabinet to stay in office. The trouble with this was that it was not where Roosevelt had assembled his most useful talent. He took scant notice of his Cabinet. After Pearl Harbor it rarely met. In accordance with American practice it did not engage in serious collective discussion. And by 1945 the older members were becoming played out. This was true of Frances Perkins at Labor and even of Harold Ickes at the Interior. Stettinius, who as the holder of the most senior post should have been the most important of the newer ones, was a handsome nonentity. Morgenthau, the Secretary of the Treasury since 1934, was in a separate position. He was intellectually vigorous, but the author of a singularly silly plan for the post-war treatment of Germany. Wallace was Wallace. Forrestal, Secretary of the Navy for the past year, had more brio than balance.* The Cabinet officer with the most authority was probably Henry L. Stimson, the Secretary of War since 1940, but as a 78-year-old Republican† he was certain not to stay long in a post-war Democrat Cabinet.

Truman balanced this temporary obeisance to continuity at Cabinet level by the replacement (with only one senior exception, old Admiral Leahy) of Roosevelt's staff with his own in the White House. Probably no one would have expected him to have done otherwise, although nearly twenty years later Lyndon Johnson, for all his Texan chips, was to keep far more Kennedy men.

There were far more to keep, and this White House change was not as important in 1945 as it would have been in 1963 or still more so 1985. Truman's own White House staff was never more than thirteen, compared with the many times that number who served President Johnson in the 1960s and the more than 300 who serve President Reagan today. The biggest growth was under President Nixon. Quality did not however make up for quantity. Truman liked cronies immediately around him, and there was mostly a strong whiff of the second-rate about the immediate entourage. Poker players from Missouri got too many places. For a number of reasons this did not do as much harm as might have been expected. First there were exceptions, most notably Clark Clifford, who although a Missourian arrived by accident as an assistant naval aide, and emerged after a year as an outstanding top staff man, who effectively ran Truman's White House until 1950.

Second the Missouri poker players were neither vicious nor over-ambitious. They were a little easy-going. General Vaughan was a typical example. Unlike some of their successors they did not pursue dedicated feuds either amongst themselves or with the rest of official Washington. Above all they did not try to make the President their creature or to cut him off from other advice.

Truman did not stick long to Roosevelt's Cabinet. By July 1945, he had replaced the Secretary of State, the Secretary of the Treasury, the Attorney-General, the Secretary of Agriculture, the Secretary of Labour, and the Postmaster-General. Only four remained, and of these Stimson went in September and Ickes in the following

* He committed suicide in 1949.
† He had been Hoover's Secretary of State in 1929–33, as well as Taft's Secretary of War in 1911–13.

February. One of the changes had been arranged under Roosevelt, two or three of them were wholly voluntary, and at least one (the removal of Stettinius) was highly desirable. But on balance Truman probably reduced the quality of the Cabinet, while at the same time considerably elevating its importance. He stopped well short of turning it into a collective decision-making body. His vote, following the Lincoln aphorism, counted for more than all the rest put together. Nevertheless he assembled them, in principle at least, twice a week, once in formal session and once at lunch.

Stettinius's replacement was Byrnes. He was one of Truman's two most mistaken appointments. (The other, much later, was Louis Johnson, Secretary of Defense, 1949–50). Byrnes was quick-footed, self-confident, politically astute, but at once know-all and ill-informed about foreign affairs. Above all, however, his disadvantage was that he thought he and not Truman ought to be President,* and so behaved. As a result their relations quickly declined. This neutralized what should have been the big gain of getting someone more able than Stettinius.

Biddle, a distinguished Attorney-General, was replaced by one of his less good assistants, Tom Clark. For the rest, as with Byrnes, Truman leant heavily upon former members of Congress, which Roosevelt had never done. Anderson, the new Secretary of Agriculture, Schwellenbach, the new Secretary of Labour, and Vinson, the new Secretary of the Treasury, were all in this category. Schwellenbach was a near disaster. Vinson was the best, certainly the one Truman most respected. Unfortunately, from the point of view of the quality of the Cabinet, Truman added friendly consideration to respect and appointed Vinson Chief Justice of the Supreme Court when Stone died in the spring of 1946. He was then succeeded by Snyder, Truman's old St Louis banker friend, who was already in the government, and who made a thoroughly second-rate finance minister.

Little of this either sounds inspiring or gives an adequate picture of the quality of mid-1940s Washington. This is largely because of

* He would indeed have become so, despite his rout at the Chicago Convention, had Truman died. Until 1947 the Secretary of State, in the absence of a vice-president was first in line for the succession. He was then replaced by the Speaker of the House of Representatives, on the ground that an elected officer was more appropriate than an appointed one. The previous position of the Secretary of State was however one reason why Truman was so eager to replace Stettinius.

Roosevelt's fondness for operating outside structures. Many of the most talented officials whom he bequeathed to Truman were in neither the Cabinet nor the White House staff. They operated from somewhere between the two, and became a feature of the Washington scene which has never been wholly paralleled elsewhere. Hopkins, Harriman, McCloy, Lovett were quintessential figures of this *demi-monde*. When he could Truman kept them on (Hopkins was dead in nine months but Truman had probably got more hard information about what Roosevelt had done or intended out of him in the first three months than from any more formal source), often gradually drafting them and others into more structured positions. He was also extremely lucky to have General Marshall available, first for a special mission to China, then as Secretary of State after Byrnes, and finally, after a gap, as Secretary of Defense during the Korean War. He, with Dean Acheson, Under-Secretary of State from 1945 to 1947, Secretary of State from 1949 until January 1953, were the twin pillars of Truman's international reputation.

In the spring and early summer of 1945 all this lay well ahead. Truman floundered. But as is frequently the case in comparable circumstances the nation either did not notice or it decided, after twelve years of Roosevelt and with the initial shock over, that what they would most enjoy was a little presidential floundering. By mid-May Truman's approval rating in the Gallup poll rose to 87%, three points higher than Roosevelt had ever achieved. It compensated for the frustrations of dealing with Stalin, and indeed with Churchill too. '. . . I was having as much difficulty with Prime Minister Churchill as I was having with Stalin,' he recorded on May 19th.[1]

This was broadly the mood in which he set off on July 6th for the Potsdam Conference. He was temporarily popular beyond belief. He had the sense to realize how temporary this was likely to be. He had been fully (although for the first time) informed about the atomic development and knew that there was a good chance that the bomb would be shown to work in the next couple of months. He was willing to be conciliatory with the Russians – much more so than he had been at a Washington meeting with Molotov on April 23rd, which he had handled so roughly as to be in danger of giving the impression of a big shift of policy from Roosevelt. But he was equally prepared to be tough and felt fortified for this by the news about the bomb. He approached the expedition – his first outside the Western hemisphere since 1919 – with distaste and in no over-generous mood. 'How I hate this trip!' he wrote in his diary on the first day out in his battle cruiser. 'But I have to make it – win, lose or draw – and we must win. I'm not working for any interest but the Republic of the United States. I [am] giving nothing away except to save starving people and even then I hope we can only help them to help themselves.'[2]

In the event he probably disliked it less than he expected. He found Berlin 'an awful city' and never wanted to see it again – but who would not in the circumstances – and he was impatient to get back after a month away. However, he felt that he acquitted himself well. As the only Head of State he presided over the conference. The surprise – and the misjudgment – was that he liked Stalin. He reminded him of Pendergast! To his wife he recorded it without ambiguity: 'I like Stalin' (July 29th).[3] To his diary he was no more circumspect, 'I can deal with Stalin. He is honest – but smart as hell.' (July 17th)★[4]

He was rather less forthcoming about the British, whom he approached with a slightly ungracious suspicion. Before he sailed for Europe he told Bess: 'George VI R.I. sent *me* a personal letter today by Halifax. Not much impressed.' However, he added 'Save it for Margie's scrapbook.'[5] This was an invitation to stay at Buckingham Palace, which visit, to save time, he managed to change to a luncheon in a British battleship. This he approached with little more enthusiasm: 'I've got to lunch with the limey King when I get to Plymouth.' However, to his diary, after the event, he was rather more forthcoming. He found the King 'a very pleasant and surprising person' and the lunch 'nice and appetising'.[6] Perhaps he was primarily concerned to assure Mrs Truman that he was not acquiring Roosevelt's taste for European royalty.

His first judgment of Churchill was more surprising, but also a little cool: 'He is a most charming and a very clever person – meaning clever in the English not the Kentucky sense. He gave me a lot of hooey about how great my country is and how he loved Roosevelt and how he intended to love me, etc. etc. Well,

★ Twelve years later he wrote of himself as 'an innocent idealist' in 1945, but did not deny that he 'liked the little son of a bitch'. (*Private Papers*, pp. 348–9.)

I gave him as cordial a reception as I could – being naturally (I hope) a polite and agreeable person. I am sure we can get along if he doesn't try to give me too much soft soap.'[7]

The change of British Government on July 27th he took with less dismay than, he believed, did Stalin. But here again his comments certainly betrayed no anglomania: 'The British returned last night. They came and called on me at nine-thirty. Attlee is an Oxford man and talks like the much overrated Mr Eden and Bevin is a John L. Lewis. Can you imagine John L. being my Secretary of State – but we shall see what we shall see.'[8]

During his journey back across the Atlantic the Hiroshima bomb was dropped. The final decision to do so had been taken by him at Potsdam a day or so after the full results of the Alamogordo test in the New Mexican desert had been received. This is now regarded as the most controversial, some would say immoral, and therefore difficult, decision of the Truman presidency. At the time it was not so seen. The testimony of Churchill puts the contemporary view with complete authority: 'The historic fact remains, and must be judged in the after-time, that the decision whether or not to use the atomic bomb to compel the surrender of Japan was never even an issue. There was unanimous, automatic, unquestioned agreement around our table; nor did I ever hear the slightest suggestion that we should do otherwise.'[9]

Did this point to short-sighted callousness on the part of Truman and all those around him, including the British? The charge of short-sightedness may have more validity than that of callousness. To evelute either, however, it is necessary to think oneself back into the circumstance of the time. Brutal though the world of the 1980s may be in some ways, and appalling beyond belief though the contingent nuclear threat may have become, the carnage actually experienced in the mid-1940s was qualitatively quite different from that to which countries at peace, or even engaged in sporadic guerrilla fighting, are habituated. Now an accident involving a hundred deaths rings around the world. Then an estimated 45,000 people had recently been killed in three days of 'conventional' bombing of Dresden. The comparable, and still more recent figure for the fire raids on Tokyo was 78,000. Dresden was unnecessary, but nobody thought that the war against Japan could be waged without such raids, and only one close advisor, Arnold, the Commander of the Army Air Force, believed that it could be won by them alone. The rest believed that victory would involve an invasion of the Japanese mainland. In the aftermath of the bloody battle for Okinawa General Marshall estimated that this would cost half a million American casualties. In any direction therefore there stretched a path of carnage.

The news that the Alamogordo test had been a success, and that the bomb was available for use, which reached Truman on the fourth day of Potsdam, came to him as a relief and not as a burden. It justified a huge secret investment of money and resources which had been made on executive responsibility alone. It assured a much quicker victory at a cost of many fewer American casualties, and probably of fewer Japanese ones too. It eliminated the (fairly faint) possibility of the Russians getting the bomb first. And, Truman felt, it strengthened his position in trying to handle Stalin during the remaining two weeks of the conference and beyond.

This did not mean that he intended to threaten the Russians with the use of the bomb against them. Indeed he waited another week before almost casually informing Stalin of its existence, and then did so in terms so vague that had Stalin not been already well-informed through his spy network it might have meant little to him. What it did mean was that the Americans ceased to have an interest in getting the Russians to enter the war against Japan, and were therefore no longer hobbled by this consideration in arguing with them about Poland and the other puppet régimes which they were imposing in Eastern Europe.* Henceforward it was the Russians who wanted to get in before the peace, and the Americans who had become indifferent. This new freedom however only released the flow of American argument and not the peoples of Hungary, Bulgaria and Roumania, where the Russians remained firmly in occupation and control.

Truman half, but only half, realized the qualitative difference between the new bomb and the previous use of massive quantities of high explosive. He recorded in his diary for July 25th: 'It is certainly a good thing for the world that Hitler's crowd or Stalin's

---

* The régimes of these countries, together with the treatment of Italy and the Russian desire for the extraction of excessive reparations from Germany were the main issues of dispute at Potsdam. Even without the need for Russian support against Japan, however, Truman had little prospect of resisting Russian domination of Eastern Europe. The pressure to 'bring the boys home' was so strong, as was the *in situ* position of the Red Army.

did not discover the atomic bomb. It seems to me the most terrible thing ever discovered, but it can be made the most useful.'[10] This immediately followed a passage in which he said that he had instructed Stimson to use it only against military objectives so that 'soldiers and sailors are the target and not women and children'.[11] (Quite how this was reconcilable with what happened at Hiroshima, and still less with Hiroshima plus Nagasaki, is difficult to see. In reality with a weapon of such force, the distinction was unsustainable.)

What had been deliberately decided by Truman and his advisers was that it should not be used against Tokyo or Kyoto. But this saved face and buildings of note, not lives. The second or Nagasaki bomb seems to have been dropped, five days after the Hiroshima one, under a single authorization and without intermediate civilian re-appraisal. (It was a bomb of a somewhat different type but its release could hardly have been justified on the need for further experiment.*) The issue here is tied up with whether more explicit warnings should have been given to the Japanese, both before Hiroshima and between then and Nagasaki, and whether indeed a demonstration in the waters of Tokyo Bay might have been equally effective.

These issues were in turn entangled with a dispute within the US Administration as to whether the unfortunate commitment to unconditional surrender could be interpreted sufficiently elastically to allow the Emperor of Japan to remain upon the throne. An undecisive approach to this, partly in deference to 'progressive' opinion, made it more difficult to send clear messages which might have achieved peace without carnage.† The Americans were also subject to the inhibition that they started with a total of only four bombs. Nagasaki used up the last but one. They did not therefore feel that they had much margin to spare for error, explosions which did not occur, or demonstrations which failed to convince.

* Alamogordo and Nagasaki were plutonium. Hiroshima was uranium, and the only one of its sort then in existence.

† This was an ironical dispute, as the Emperor was eventually decisive in telling his more bellicose war commanders and ministers that they had to surrender without further destruction and might, had he been fully in charge, have done so before Hiroshima. In any event the fact that the formal and almost unprecedented intervention of the Emperor was necessary to overcome military resistance to surrender destroys the argument that the Japanese would have given up without the use of the A-bomb.

Furthermore they were impatient to end the war before the Russians could become effectively involved, and start making in Asia the territorial and political demands which were disfiguring Eastern Europe.

Truman therefore allowed the two bombs to be dropped and the world to enter a new era; and he did so with a good conscience. At the time the decision did not lie heavy upon his mind, and he did not subsequently regret it. The case in his favour is considerable. He believed he was saving rather than sacrificing lives by acting as he did, and he may well have been right. Certainly no alternative figure with whom the ultimate decision could conceivably have rested – Roosevelt, Churchill, Attlee – would have acted otherwise. Equally certainly he did not offend Stalin or provide the Soviet determination to catch up by *dropping* the bomb. Stalin, when told by Truman at Potsdam what he broadly already knew, answered that he hoped the Americans would make good use of the weapon against Japan. What spurred the Russian nuclear programme was the knowledge that the Americans had the bomb, not their decision to use it. Possession Truman could not conceivably have concealed.

The case against him, Nagasaki apart, which in retrospect at least looks unnecessary and therefore inexcusable, is almost more one of style than of substance. He took the decisions and received the results of their being executed with an inappropriate lack of sombreness and sensitivity. He could be excused for not wholly foreseeing the qualitative nature of the change over which he was presiding. Very few people did. But he knew the immediate destructiveness, even if not the longer-term damage of the weapon he had unleashed. His reaction on board USS *Augusta*, when news of the successful attack on Hiroshima came through, which was that of rushing round the ship and proclaiming the news with glee, does not sound right. Nor does his laconic diary comment on the White House staff conference on the morning after Nagasaki 'Nothing unusual to discuss.'* No doubt a wringing of hands would have served no purpose other than that of self-indulgence.

---

* It is perhaps worth comparing the diary entry of Mountbatten, in later life an anti-nuclear prophet, for August 6th, the day of Hiroshima. He was dining at Windsor Castle. 'Everybody was in good form as the atomic bomb had just fallen,' he wrote (*Mountbatten*, Philip Ziegler, Collins, 1985, p. 300). The weapon then meant victory and the end of carnage rather than a threat to the future of mankind.

But he was too brutal about those with less strong stomachs. When Robert Oppenheimer, a key figure in the development of the bomb, expressed remorse a few months after its use, Truman told Acheson that he had no patience with such a 'cry-baby'.[12]

All this must be seen against the background of the death, starvation and disease on an unprecedented scale, not in America, but over much of Europe and Asia, which was Truman's inheritance as President, and which he had just observed in Germany. Truman's state of mind was not perhaps of central practical importance. The bomb was dropped. The war was won. Truman was back in Washington after five weeks. He had survived his first – and last – international conference. His popularity was still high. But his honeymoon was over. The hard slog of routine presidential life was beginning.

6

TRUMAN BATTERED

September 1945 to November 1946 was the nadir of Truman's presidency. Most things went wrong. His Gallup poll rating achieved a spectacular decline from 87% to 32%, and this sustained plunge in the popularity of himself and his administration culminated in a crushing Democratic defeat in the mid-term Congressional elections. The Republicans gained control of both chambers for the first time since 1928. They were 246 to 188 in the House and they edged ahead by 51 to 45 in the Senate.

All this was bad enough, although popularity, except crucially in November 1948, was rarely the hall-mark of the Truman achievement. What made it worse, however, was that during this early period a large proportion of the misfortunes were his own fault. It was rarely a case of statesmanlike decisions, deliberately taken and courageously sustained, being too long-sighted for the short-term whims of a war-weary electorate. Much more was it a question of an administration ill at ease with itself, both at Cabinet and at White House staff level, allowing an uncertain president to stagger from one ill-prepared decision to another.

The Cabinet was inexperienced after the changes of the summer of 1945. It became more so with the retirement of Stimson that September, the resignation of Ickes in February 1946, the promotion of Vinson in April, and the sacking of Wallace in September. Thereafter, of Roosevelt's Cabinet officers, only Forrestal remained, and he knew little of domestic politics. Byrnes was not inexperienced, but his relationship with Truman never recovered from his failure to keep the President informed of the developments at the long Moscow meeting of foreign ministers in December 1945. Thereafter he was always operating on borrowed time, with Truman anxious to replace him with Marshall as soon as was propitious after the completion of the General's China mission. Byrnes privately submitted his resignation, ostensibly on medical grounds, on April 16th, 1946, and on May 9th Marshall in Shanghai agreed, through the agency of Eisenhower, to become Secretary of State when the President wished. Although Byrnes had set a date of July 1st, the changeover was allowed to drag on, as was Marshall's mission, until early 1947.

It would have been much better for the change to have been made much more quickly after Truman lost confidence in Byrnes. In a curious way the damage was exacerbated by the fact that there was no consistent policy difference between President and Secretary of State. They were both in mid-stream without a paddle. They had left the bank of belief in the unity of the wartime alliance, but neither had reached the other bank of wishing to create a new Western alliance, with Britain, basically enfeebled by the war but undevastated and with a continuity of political régime even if not of government, inevitably the initial second partner. Truman had taken Churchill to Fulton, Missouri, in March and had presided benevolently over the 'iron curtain' speech with its remedy of an Anglo-American partnership. A few days later, however, he had distanced himself from it, and in September he swallowed without difficulty the passage in Henry Wallace's Madison Square Garden speech which said: 'I am neither anti-British nor pro-British – neither anti-Russian nor pro-Russian.' Nonetheless he had initially thought Byrnes too soft with the Russians, and then perhaps too hard. Throughout the summer of 1946 the President was playing with the idea of giving them a substantial loan. The fact of the matter was that Truman and Byrnes had become too suspicious of each other ever to be in exactly the same ideological place at the same time.* The mutual distrust compounded what would in any event have been a uniquely difficult period of adjustment for American foreign policy.

The handling of nuclear policy was almost equally uncertain. During the war Roosevelt had made a conscious decision not to

---

* They were infrequently in the same geographical place either. Byrnes spent a remarkable amount of time away from Washington.

share atomic secrets with the Russians. Truman's early post-war position was in favour of such sharing in exchange for a mutual agreement to stop further development and undertake that none of the three main powers (this was in order to include Britain) would use the bomb without the agreement of the other two. Stimson's final act as Secretary of War was to bring a memorandum advocating such a course before a cabinet meeting on September 21st. This led to an animated two-hour discussion and a fairly even split. Stimson was supported by Acheson (in Byrnes's absence), Wallace, Schwellenbach and Hannegan. Most of the new Truman nominees – Vinson, Clark and Anderson – argued the other way. So, with particular virulence, did Forrestal. What was more to the point was that Truman regarded himself as firmly committed to the Stimson side. 'Anyway I'll have to make a decision', he wrote to his wife after describing the line-up, 'and the Ayes will have it even if I'm the only Aye. It is probably the most momentous one I will make.'[1]

His actions did not live up to the promise of his words. He had begun somewhat badly at Potsdam when his laconic announcement to Stalin of the American possession of the bomb omitted any suggestion of shared knowledge or international control. Then under pressure of a hostile Congressional and press reaction to the Stimson proposal, probably inspired by Forrestal, which he skilfully presented as an initiative of the 'soft' Wallace rather than of the 'hard' Stimson, Truman resiled, or at least postponed.

His hesitation, paradoxically in view of subsequent national attitudes, was reinforced by a tripartite meeting with Attlee and Mackenzie King of Canada which took place in Washington in mid-November. Attlee had urged a meeting earlier than Truman would have wished because he was under parliamentary pressure to seek international control. But his interest was in safeguarding British access to American knowledge rather than in extending it to the Soviet Union. 'In my view', he wrote in a preparatory memorandum, 'an offer to do this now would not be likely to effect a change of attitude to world problems by the USSR. It would be regarded as a confession of weakness. The establishment of better relations should precede the exchange of technical information.'[2]

As this was also Byrnes's position it effectively precluded any likelihood of agreement to go further along the lines of the Stimson memorandum. Whether Truman might have wished to do so at this stage is uncertain. What is the case is that in the view of Vannevar Bush, the chief technical advisor on the US side, the conference was remarkably ill-prepared by the Americans. 'I have never participated in anything so completely unorganized or irregular', he wrote to Stimson.[3]

Whether or not he was aware of this, Truman consoled himself with an odd thought in relation to himself and his principal guest: 'Mr Attlee came yesterday and we had a brilliant – most brilliant I'd say – State dinner for him and Mackenzie King of Canada.' Their great quality was that they were anglophone. 'On the visit[s] of the President of Chile and de Gaulle it was a case of one sentence at a time to an interpreter,' he added, 'and by the time I'd arrive at the thought I'd wanted to express I'd forgot what was to be said and gone off on a tangent maybe.'[4]

Truman's next nuclear initiative was to appoint Churchill's friend, Bernard Baruch, as US representative to the United Nations Atomic Energy Commission, and to allow him to present the Baruch Plan to the UN in June 1946. This was an exercise in cynicism on Truman's part, and of statesmanship on nobody's part. Truman had no real respect for Baruch. 'That stuffed shirt will have something more to do than sit on a park bench and pass out impossible advice' he wrote to his wife about Baruch's appointment, adding a little surprisingly: 'There never was a greater egotist unless it was Franklin D.'[5] The appointment was strongly opposed by Acheson and by Lilienthal. And Baruch's proposals never had the slightest chance of being accepted by the Soviet Union. They were good propaganda within the United States. They were not serious diplomacy. They were based on the totally illusory view that Russia would accept, without a veto, the discipline of the then largely American-influenced UN majority. With their failure the road was open to the Soviet achievement of the A-bomb in 1949, the H-bomb in 1953 and the escalating equality of the 1960s and 70s.

A similar uncertainty of touch marked Truman's approach to domestic problems. He knew very little economics. But that was not crucial. Sensible economic policies have been followed by technically ill-equipped political leaders almost as frequently as foolish ones by those who believed they were masters of the dismal

science. Nor was there anything discreditable in the fact that as he
sailed back across the Atlantic from Potsdam he had little idea
whether the major domestic menace confronting the United States
in the post-war world was inflation or deflation. It was perfectly
reasonable to be prepared either for a threat of mass unemployment
as the forces were demobilized and five million defence jobs
disappeared, or for shortages and a wage explosion leading to a
runaway pressure on prices. He did not foresee that it was possible
to achieve both together, but had he done so he would have been
30 years ahead of his time.

At first he was more inclined to fear slump. It was the need to
counteract this threat which primarily informed his long message
to Congress (the longest since Theodore Roosevelt) on September
6th. Three months later he had swung round and when asked at a
press conference whether he regarded deflation as anywhere near
as dangerous as inflation replied unambiguously 'No, I do not.'[6]
Here again a flexibility as events developed could perfectly well be
justified. What was more dangerous was that Truman lacked both
any instinctive philosophical approach to economic problems and
any structured group of advisers who themselves shared the same
basic outlook.

Was Truman a New Dealer, or was he not? He had of course
voted for all its most controversial aspects in the 1930s, but that
may have owed more to party loyalty than ideological conviction.
He was in favour of extensions of welfare provisions, and proposed
several important ones that fall. But he was alleged to be unsound
from a New Deal point of view on deficit financing (but so, it
could be argued were Roosevelt and his Secretary of the Treasury:
they preached virtue and practised sin) and he was not instinctively
at home with the liberals who had been Roosevelt's most enthusiastic supporters before 'Dr New Deal' was replaced by 'Dr Win
the War'. 'Same bunch of Prima Donnas who helped drive the
Boss to his grave are still riding his ghost,' he wrote on his
appointment sheet after a meeting with the Roosevelt National
Memorial Committee on September 5th.[7] And many of those
who were close to him in these early days were pretty vehemently
conservative. Snyder, even before his elevation to the Treasury,
was probably the closest of the lot, both personally and as an
economic adviser. His instincts were those of a business man and
banker and they were not made any more liberal by the fact that

his outlook was that of small town business and banking rather than of the Wall Street establishment.

Snyder, with the cumbersome title of Director of the Office of War Mobilization and Reconversion, was constantly in dispute with Chester Bowles, the head of the Keynesian-oriented Office of Price Administration (Bowles for controls, Snyder for setting the businessman free). He was also the inspirer of a right-of-centre group within Truman's own staff, composed principally of Matthew Connelly, who had served the Truman Committee during the war, and Jake Vardaman, another St Louis banker, whose main service to Truman was to bring Clark Clifford, a vastly abler man than himself, into the White House.* The liberal view was upheld by Samuel Rosenman (former special counsel to Roosevelt, who continued with Truman until early 1946) and Charles Ross, his old Independence classmate and current press secretary. The intellectual weight on this line-up came from Rosenman, the weight of rank and friendship from Snyder. The result was that here again Truman was buffeted about in mid-stream.

In particular he got the worst of both worlds in dealing with the food shortage which beset even the United States more in 1945–6 than during the war itself. It was a sign of America's relatively favoured position that the issue there was the non-availability of adequate sized steaks, whereas in Britain it was about adding bread to a whole list of rationed foodstuffs, and on the mainland of Europe it was about getting enough calories to keep alive. Nevertheless beefsteaks were a major issue up to and over the 1946 elections. Had Truman listened to Bowles alone he might have produced a limited quantity of cheap rationed meat for everybody. Had he listened to Snyder alone he might have achieved butchers' shops well-stocked with expensive meat. As he veered between the two he produced neither and paid a heavy price in votes. There were then few metabolic experts to convince the American people of their good fortune in not being able to dig their graves with steak knives. Many voted with their stomachs. 'You've deserted your president for a mess of pottage, a piece of beef, a side of

---

* Truman eventually over-rewarded Vardaman by appointing him in the Federal Reserve Board, where according to Margaret Truman, 'he repaid (Dad) by voting against every Truman policy for the next seven years. He went round Washington spreading the nasty story that he was kicked out of the White House because he did not drink or play cards.' (M. Truman, op. cit. p. 290)

bacon,' Truman wrote on October 14th, 1946, in one of the several
self-pitying undelivered speeches which he had become addicted
to preparing in the period, 'You've gone over to the powers of
selfishness and greed.'[8]

The mood had been largely fostered by the unprecedented wave
of industrial trouble which he had lived through in the preceding
twelve months. The labour union leaders had of course been crucial
to putting him where he was. Without their pressure at Chicago
in 1944 he would not have agreed to run. Without their support
he would not have been nominated. This however had the curious
and in many ways rather healthy effect that he regarded them as
being more obliged to him than *vice versa*. If they put him in
the White House, they ought to behave responsibly during his
presidency. In his view they did not.

John L. Lewis was of course a case apart. He had separated
himself from the Democratic Party, and acted, in Truman's view,
with total disregard for the national interest before, during, and
after the war. Truman wrote of him with a hard, almost vicious
contempt: 'He is, as all bullies are, as yellow as a dog hound pup.
He cannot face the music when the tune is not to his liking. On
the front under shell fire he'd crack up. But he can direct the
murder, assault and battery goon squads as long as he doesn't have
to face them . . . I had a fully loyal team and that team whipped
a damned traitor.'[9]

The others he regarded differently, but without particular
warmth. 'Big money has too much power and so have big
unions', he wrote to his mother and sister on January 23rd, 1946:
'both are riding to a fall because I like neither.'[10] As the first
half of that unfortunate year went by his feelings became
more embittered, with the leaders of the two largest railroad
brotherhoods, Alvanley Johnston and A. F. Whitney, who had
been his supporters not merely in 1944 but in his nadir year of
1940 as well, moving into the centre of his zone of disapproval.
On top of the long-running steel and General Motors strikes of
the winter, Lewis brought the coal miners out on April 1st,
and a rail strike was called for May 18th and actually started on
May 23rd.

Truman's reaction to most of these and to a few other similar
disputes was a fairly wild programme of temporary seizure of
the industries by the Federal Government. 'In one year,' Robert

Donovan wrote, 'he had seized the coal mines twice; he had seized the railroads; he had seized 134 meat-packing plants; he had seized ninety-one tugboats; he had seized the facilities of twenty-six oil producing and refining companies; he had seized the Great Lakes Towing Company. And all he had on his hands now was disaster.'[11] He was certainly in danger of reaching too automatically for the weapon of seizure and thus of devaluing any symbolic significance that it might carry.

It was not always clear what practical purpose seizure served, except that of dramatization. It could be held to make the strikes *ex post* into political strikes against the Government, but as they had manifestly started as industrial strikes for higher wages or better fringe benefits against the companies this neither got the strikers back to work nor provided a particularly effective propaganda weapon against the leaders. It made it legally possible to use the army, but this was only seriously contemplated in the case of the rail strike, and there was clearly a limit to how quickly, effectively and in what numbers soldiers could turn themselves into railroad operatives. The more extreme step of drafting the striking railroadmen themselves (there was a half precedent from the action of the Briand government in France in 1910, but there the majority of the men were reservists) was actually proposed to Congress by the President on the day the strike was settled. Whether this threat, about the constitutionality of which the Attorney-General was hesitant, contributed to the settlement is doubtful.

The reason that Truman reacted with especial violence against the rail strike was not only that it came on top of the other disputes and led to mounting criticism that he was becoming the President of industrial chaos. It was also that, in what was still (just) the age of the train in the United States, such a strike had much the most immediate public impact. There were always some stocks of coal, steel and automobiles (although none of them were very substantial at that time) but there cannot be any stock of commuter or transcontinental journeys. There may also have been at work a sense of betrayal by his special friends in the railroad unions. In any event it provoked him into composing an appalling draft speech, which mixed resentful hysteria, reactionary populism, and virulent vulgarity of language in about equal proportions. It was all put in terms of American Legion-style patriotism:

'John Lewis called two strikes in War Time to satisfy his ego. Two strikes which were worse than bullets in the back of our soldiers. The rail workers did exactly the same thing. They all were receiving four to forty times what the man who was facing the enemy fire on the front was receiving. The effete union leaders receive from five to ten times the net salary of your President.

'Now these same union leaders on V.J. Day told your president that they would co-operate 100% with him to reconvert to peace time production. They all lied to him.

'First came the threatened Automobile strike. Your President asked for legislation to cool off and consider the situation. A weak-kneed Congress didn't have the intestinal fortitude to pass the bill.

'Mr Murray and his Communist friends had a conniption fit and Congress had labor jitters. Nothing happened.

'Then came the electrical workers strike, the steel strike, the coal strike and now the rail tie up. Every single one of the strikers and their demagog [sic] leaders have been living in luxury, working when they pleased . . .

'I am tired of government's [sic] being flouted, vilified and now I want you men who are my comrades-in-arms, you men who fought the battles to save the nation just as I did twenty-five years ago, to come along with me and eliminate the Lewises, the Whitneys, the Johnstons, the Communist Bridges and the Russian Senators and Representatives and really make this a Government of by and for the people. I think no more of the Wall Street crowd than I do of Lewis and Whitney.

'Let's give the country back to the people. Let's put transportation and production back to work, hang a few traitors, make our country safe for democracy, tell Russia where to get off and make the United Nations work. Come on boys let's do the job.'[12]

What is one to make of this extraordinary document, which caused a good deal of perturbation when it first saw the light of day in 1966? First, it was never of course seriously intended to be delivered. It was Truman blowing a safety valve, not preparing a speech. No sooner had he knocked it off than he agreed that

Rosenman should be summoned from New York (where he had retreated to private legal practice) in order to prepare with Charlie Ross and Clark Clifford a serious text for the broadcast that evening. They did their work, and while what emerged was a tough speech it was also a rational, even cautious speech.

Even so, safety valve or not, Truman's draft ('this frontier diatribe', as Robert Donovan charitably calls it) cannot be totally shrugged off. It is probable that he wrote it early in the morning rather than late at night. Bourbon was therefore unlikely to have made a contribution to its composition. That makes it the more frightening. It was of course wildly inaccurate. There was no question of miners or railroadmen receiving up to forty times the pay of servicemen. Nor did union leaders get 'from five to ten times the net salary of your President'. They were very well paid by British standards. But in the mid-1940s (or for that matter the mid-1980s) they were not on $350–700,000 a year, even leaving aside the benefits in kind of the White House, Camp David and the presidential yacht. Nor, moving on to slightly less factual ground, was 'effete' a very appropriate adjective to apply to Lewis or to Truman's erstwhile friends; his task might have been easier had they been more so. Nor is 'intestinal fortitude' a very nice concept. And, while Bridges may well have been a Communist, who were 'the Russian Senators or Representatives'? This was all language of which McCarthy might have been proud, but might have been too strong for the delicate stomach of the young Nixon (soon to be elected to Congress). It was all very unfortunate. Perhaps Truman can best be considered as being as close as possible to the opposite of Rochester's view of Charles II,

> 'Who never said a foolish thing
> Nor ever did a wise one.'

If Truman rarely (in private) wrote a wise word, he was much less inclined in public to do a foolish thing. And that was much better than emulating King Charles.

On the next day, against the background of Truman demanding draft powers from Congress, the railroad strike was settled. It left considerable short-term bitterness. Whitney announced that he would spend all the resources of the Brotherhood of Railroad Trainment in fighting Truman's re-election in 1948. The CIO denounced him as 'the No 1 strike-breaker'. Sidney Hillman and

Harold Ickes added more moderate but at least equally damaging attacks. Mrs Roosevelt wrote privately and wisely: '. . . I hope you realize that there must not be any slip, because of the difficulties of our peace-time situation, into a military way of thinking . . . I have seen my husband receive much advice from his military advisers and succumb to it every now and then, but the people as a whole do not like it . . . I hope that now that your anxiety is somewhat lessened you will not insist upon a peacetime draft into the army of strikers. That seems to me a dangerous precedent.'[13]

Truman received these attacks, warnings and advice with some surface irritation, but in fact he had substantially calmed down on the issue and indeed saw the need to rebuild some bridges. This became easier because May 1946 marked the peak of post-war labour unrest. John L. Lewis was to have another major joust with the government six months later, but his position had become increasingly isolated. The union leaders as a whole were pushed both into a more defensive position and into a greater need for an alliance with the Democratic Party by the return of a Republican Congress in November. And when it came to 1948, Whitney, so far from throwing all his funds against Truman, strongly supported his re-election.

Truman had made an early contribution to the change of atmosphere by a rapid and bewildering switch of direction almost immediately after the industrial crisis weekend of May 23rd–25th. The draconian draft powers for which he had asked the Congress in his dramatic personal appearance on May 24th were granted by a bemused House of Representatives by a 20 to 1 majority after a token debate. The Senate moved more cautiously. An unlikely combination of Robert Taft and a handful of liberal Democrats blocked precipitate decision. It was a sufficiently ill-considered bill that it could only go through at a rush. Delay was fatal to it. Little more was heard of Truman's draft powers. The Senate compensated, however, not with the administration but with anti-union public opinion, by passing the so-called Case Bill, which Representative Francis H. Case of South Dakota had got through the House in February. This measure was not merely anti-strike (it provided for a 60-day cooling-off period), but also hostile to the long-term growth of union responsibilities; it prohibited for instance the administration by the unions of health and welfare funds paid for by employers' contributions.

A major controversy broke out, publicly between the unions and the employers' organization, more privately within the administration, as to whether Truman should veto it. On June 11th he did so. His message of reasons struck an entirely different note from that of May 25th. He had lurched back into a position of balance, but his performance on the tight-rope was more breathtaking than elegant.

He was not much enjoying it himself. Throughout the fifteen months between his return from Potsdam and the mid-term elections such buoyancy as he retained was largely confined to his famous elasticity of step. There was little in his mind. In November 1945, Ickes recorded after a bilateral meeting: 'Once again he repeated that he had not wanted to be President. He says this to me practically every time that I see him and I wish that he wouldn't. The state of mind of which that is evidence is not good for him or for the country.'[14] Three weeks later Truman told the Gridiron Dinner: 'Sherman was wrong. I'm telling you I find peace is hell . . .'* As a joke this was a little too near to the bone to be wise. As an expression of the President's mind it was joyful compared with his December 28th letter to his wife after a brief and apparently not very successful Christmas visit to Independence: 'Well I'm here in the White House, the great white sepulchre of ambitions and reputations. I feel like a last year's bird nest which is on its second year. Not very often I admit I am not in shape. I think maybe that exasperates you too, as a lot of other things I do and pretend to do exasperate you.'[15]

In February Harold Smith, the Director of the Budget, wrote of Truman's expression of 'various notes of despair about the avalanche of things that were piling up on him. 'While I did not express despair . . . I came away . . . with my own despair, accentuated because of the President's inability to use staff as yet.'[16] This was not a wholly accurate diagnosis. Truman's problem was at least as much that of choosing good staff as of using them properly. Ickes, on his removal from the Department of the Interior in that same month, delivered a damaging blow when he

---

* The Gridiron Dinner was a traditional Washington press and politicians' pre-Christmas occasion, at which Roosevelt had established a firm pattern of self-confident presidential wit. General Sherman's aphorism was not delivered at an earlier Gridiron dinner. He was proving that war was indeed hell by his march through Georgia on the equivalent date eighty years before.

announced 'I am against government by crony.'* This problem
began to cure itself during 1946. Some of the cronies departed.
Others found their level. And Clark Clifford, moving into a more
senior position and well seconded by George Elsey, began to
establish some sort of cohesion in the small White House staff.

Inevitably this took some time to pay dividends, and 1946
continued, as it had begun, as a miserable year for Truman.
Roosevelt had always aroused plenty of bitter opposition, but it
had been balanced by enthusiastic support, and there had never
been any serious suggestion that his personality and style were not
up to the job. Truman, at this period, had the opposition without
the enthusiastic support, and it was precisely his style and character
which were most strongly and woundingly criticized. 'To err is
Truman' was a favourite Republican joke of the time.† But it was
not only Republicans who laughed. The old New Dealers were
disenchanted, and the general sophisticated view (and sophisticated
opinion is always more important, as a counter to country club
and Chamber of Commerce opinion, for Democrats than for
Republicans) was that the White House was occupied by a jejune
little man who had very little idea what he was doing. There were
few who thought that he had the slightest chance of being there
after 1948.

Before there was any alleviation he had to suffer at least two
further humiliations. In September there was the severance from
Wallace. Truman sacked him. This was one of the few popular
things he had done for some time. For Wallace, who had so nearly
been President of the United States, it was the end of effective
power. In 1948 he ran as the Progressive Party candidate for the
presidency and started impressively, but in the outcome Truman
was able to brush him aside like a fly. Thereafter he had seventeen

* With typical curmudgeonly honesty, however, he then modified the blow
by answering a question as to whether he would work against Truman politically
with the response: 'I might work for him in 1948. I can think of worse contin-
gencies.' (Donovan, *op. cit.* p. 183)

† There was a considerable similarity between the treatment of Truman in
America and the treatment of Attlee (whose nadir however came about a year
later) in Britain. Both are now put high in the leagues of presidents and prime
ministers, but both suffered contemporary derision. 'An empty taxi drew up
outside 10, Downing Street and the Prime Minister got out', 'Mr Attlee is a
modest man, with a great deal to be modest about.' These *mutatis mutandis*, are
very much the sort of jokes which might have been made about Truman at the
time.

years of decline, during which he even became disenchanted with
most of his own left-wing views. For Wallace it was therefore
downhill all the way after 1946. For Truman there were to be
a lot of roses. Yet the rupture which set two of Roosevelt's
vice-presidents upon these divergent paths was at the time incom-
parably worse for Truman than for Wallace.

Truman simply made an ass of himself. Wallace, probably
wrong on the issue of how to deal with the Soviet Union, left
with dignity and looking as though he had carried a considerable
part of Truman's constituency with him. He was engaged to make
a foreign policy speech in Madison Square Garden, New York,
the arena in which he had upstaged Truman in 1944, on September
12th. A day or two before he came in and read most of it to the
President. Truman either did not listen, or thought that he agreed
with it. In any event he approved it. When the text was released
during the day of the speech it created a furore. It was manifestly
at odds with the foreign policy that Byrnes was pursuing and
Truman was supporting. The President was cross-questioned
about it at a routine press conference that he was holding that
afternoon. He endorsed the speech, and expounded the manifestly
absurd proposition that it was in line with Byrnes's policy.

A day or two later he tried to pretend that he had merely
endorsed Wallace's right to make the speech. This line clearly could
not be held. So he tried to retreat to one of mildly rebuking Wallace
and getting him to promise that he would make no more foreign
policy speeches until Byrnes returned from the foreign ministers'
conference which was currently taking place in Paris. Then Wallace
leaked highly prejudicial accounts of the long meeting with Truman which had led to this limited truce. Next, under pressure not
only from Byrnes but from Senators Vandenberg and Connally,
Truman's patience cracked, and he dismissed Wallace with an
intemperate letter. Then he withdrew the letter and requested the
resignation more temperately by telephone. Then he half-hesitated.
'[Henry] was so nice about it I almost backed out,' he wrote. But
the deed was done, although in about the worst possible way. It
was certain that he was much to blame. It looked as though he
had only acted under the crack of the whip of his Secretary of
State, for whom he no longer had any respect. And, although in
his private writings he subsequently indulged in rather routine
denunciations of Wallace, there is from the same sources the steady

impression that he liked Wallace more than most of his colleagues, and indeed admired several aspects of his rather elusive character.

The whole farce lasted for eight or nine days. Truman was in no private doubt about his own responsibility. 'Never was there such a mess and it is partly my making,' he wrote to his mother and sister on September 18th, 'But when I make a mistake it is a good one'.[17] 'I don't think I ever spent a more miserable week since Chicago,'* he added to his wife on the following day.

The second humiliation was that he was allowed to take no part in the Congressional elections. He accepted the strong advice of Robert Hannegan that the less the electors saw or heard of him the better would be the chances of the Democratic candidates. The candidates themselves were almost all of the same view. Some played recordings of Roosevelt's voice. None requested similar support from the incumbent president. Once he had reluctantly accepted Hannegan's advice, they would not have got it even had they asked. He journeyed silently across half the continent to vote in Independence. He went by special train but he made no whistle-stop speeches from the rear-platform. Even in his own state, where the train stopped three times, he confined himself to a little hand-shaking with local politicians.[18] He held no rally in Independence, he made no election-eve broadcast.

He spent election night in the same train on the way back to Washington. When he awoke to hear the disastrous results he decided that the Democratic Party needed a new National Chairman (Hannegan had foolishly accompanied his crushing advice with a complacent prediction of the outcome if it were taken), and a new streak of steel in his own soul. Henceforward he was going to be more his own man as President.

At Union Station in Washington there was no one to meet him except Dean Acheson, then under-secretary at the State Department. His lonely, distinguished presence on that railroad platform was in a curious way symbolic of the transition from the first phase of the Truman presidency. Acheson was certainly not a crony. He was a Connecticut gentleman (the son of a bishop) of acerbic intelligence and patrician presence. He had no great wealth, but his education was that of the core of the Eastern establishment: Groton, Yale, Harvard Law School. He never sought elective

---

* The 1944 Democratic Convention.

office. He probably could not have achieved it, for not merely did he not suffer fools gladly: he extended the definition of fool to cover a fairly high proportion of the human race. In his later years he came to embrace, at any rate for the purpose of argument, some fairly eccentric and even reactionary views, but in his middle years he served Truman, America and the whole western world first as under-secretary and then as Secretary of State with a wisdom and flair which made the calumnies to which he was subjected by some Republican members of Congress a squalid disgrace.

The symbolism of his presence at the station on November 6th was two-fold. First, the fact that he was alone showed that Truman's fortunes were at a low ebb. Second, the fact that it was he, and that the President was delighted to see him and insisted on taking him back to the White House for a drink, indicated that Truman was coming to feel at home with a wider and different group from the Missouri cronies and very political politicians with whom, hitherto, he had felt he could alone relax; two and a half years before he would have been amazed to have been told that he would rather have seen Acheson than Byrnes. Third, it showed that his fortitude, decisiveness and high public spirit was attracting the loyalty and admiration of men who could help him fashion the next remarkable phase of American foreign policy. General Marshall would soon be back from China. There were some bright spots on the horizon. Maybe the US cavalry would arrive in time to save his presidency.

In the meantime, however, the morale around the stockade was fairly bad. On the following day such an intelligent Democratic senator as William Fulbright made the extraordinary suggestion that the President should appoint Vandenberg Secretary of State, and then resign, which in the absence of a vice-president and with the constitution as it was then was, would make Vandenberg president. A Republican chief executive could speak to a Republican legislature. Mrs Roosevelt, who perhaps had her own reasons for always being remarkably friendly and encouraging towards Truman, if occasionally a little chiding, wrote more perceptively that Truman might do better with a Republican than with a disloyal Democratic Congress.

Truman thought the same. In any event he was determind to behave like a liberated man. I do not believe that at that stage he had any more faith in his chance of re-election than did most of his fellow citizens. But he was resolved to make the best he could of his remaining time. 'From now on I'm going to do as I please and let 'em all go to hell,' he wrote to his mother and sister on November 18th. 'At least for two years they can do nothing to me and after that it doesn't matter.'[19]

He started with a good holiday in the surprising location of the submarine base at Key West, Florida. He handled John L. Lewis's renewed coal strike with much more sureness of touch than he had shown in the spring, and achieved his capitulation on December 7th. He rose in the polls and got his best press for a long time past. His Christmas holiday in Independence was even briefer than in the previous year, but his spirits were higher, and he approached 1947 with the desperate self-confidence of a man who felt that things had been so bad that they could not easily be worse.

7

TRUMAN RESURGENT

Truman began the hinge year of 1947 on the presidential yacht *Williamsburg*, steaming up the Potomac. He had been for a short New Year's Eve cruise with his staff. He got back to the White House at 8.45 a.m., and soon afterwards telephoned his wife and daughter in Independence. He then recorded: 'Never was so lonesome in my life. So I decided to call the Cabinet* and ex-Cabinet officers.' The 'lonesomeness', a not infrequent complaint, raises the question of why such an uxorious couple as the Trumans chose to spend so much time apart. The President did not *have* to spend short – and sometimes less short – holidays on masculine boat trips. Mrs Truman did not *have* to spend several months a year in Independence.†

The telephoning however appears to have been a great success, so much so that Truman went on from present and former Secretaries to embrace by electric wire General Eisenhower, Senator Vandenberg, Republican majority leader in the Senate, and even Congressman Martin, the new Republican Speaker of the House of Representatives. At that stage he was not confronting or denouncing the Eightieth Congress.

Truman's most important companion for 1947, and the one whom he would probably most like to have greeted on that New Year's Day, was not available. General of the Army George

* Individually, by telephone, not to emergency collective session, which would have been an imperious way of assuaging his New Year's Day loneliness.
† Although, according to the family doctor, General Graham, who left the Army in 1953, returned to Kansas City and looked after them both to the end, she had some health reasons for doing so. 'When she was in Washington, she was always tense,' he recorded, 'and her blood pressure was always high.' As she lived to the age of 97, the condition cannot have been very acute.

C. Marshall had recently moved with the Chinese Nationalist government 1500 miles down the Yangtse from the gorges of Chungking to the plains of Nanking. The change had made him somewhat more accessible, but not sufficiently so for the Bell Telephone Company, brilliant though its performance appeared to Europeans in the 1940s and 50s, to be able to reach him. His mission to this doomed government, almost the only failure of his life, but a failure which was neither his fault nor a significant tarnish of his reputation, came to an end five days later. Fifteen days after that he was sworn in as Secretary of State. He held the senior cabinet office for almost exactly two years. Then ill-health forced him to resign and be replaced by Acheson. Twenty months later, recovered, reluctant but as always loyal in accepting assignments, he came back as Secretary of Defense for one year. He and Acheson between them were crucial to the international success of Truman's presidency. Yet it would be quite wrong to see them as crutches supporting a lame man. Acheson more articulately, but both in their differing ways, regarded their commitment and achievement as stemming essentially from their regard for Truman's leadership and character. As the one was as different from the other as each was from Truman it was a remarkable triangle of disparate respect. It did a great deal to make the Western world of the past four decades. And no period was more crucial to this artefact than the two years of Marshall's tenure of the State Department.

This said, Marshall's quality is not easy fully to comprehend for those who did not know him. He had a high sense of duty, exceptional natural authority, steadiness of judgment, and power of decision. This formidable combination of attributes was enough to make him a great man. But what is more surprising is that the reserve, self-sufficiency and air of impeccability which went with them allowed him also to be likeable. He was always controlled. He never misbehaved. He always spoke in a low, quiet tone to which everyone listened. He always arrived and left every gathering at precisely the time that he intended to. He accepted the few disappointments of his life, most notably Roosevelt's decision to keep him as Chief-of-Staff rather than to allow him instead of Eisenhower to command 'Overlord', without remonstrance. He also accepted calmly the upset of private plans which were involved in his several (apparently reluctantly accepted) recalls to public duty. He never appears to have lost his temper. 'I have no feelings,' he told Dean Acheson, 'except those I reserve for Mrs Marshall.'

It is almost too good to be true, particularly as it was accompanied by what would in a lesser mortal have been considered a certain pomposity of parlance. He always announced himself on the telephone as 'General Marshall speaking'. It was almost as though he had been christened 'General'. As a result nobody – not even Roosevelt, certainly not Truman – except for Mrs Marshall and an obscure major-general who had presumably been at the Virginia Military Institute with him, called him anything else, not even 'Mr Secretary', let alone 'George'.

Yet, on a wide range of testimony, no one found him pompous or priggish. Margaret Truman, meeting him for the first time when she was barely twenty and before her father was vice-president, wrote, 'I fell in love instantly with this remarkable man . . . He was marvellous at making you forget his importance, while simultaneously making you feel that you and what you were saying were important to him.'[1] Dean Acheson, who served under him for his first six months as Secretary of State, succeeded him, and then served alongside him when he returned as Secretary of Defense during the Korean War, wrote of him as 'this noble and generous man,'[2] and recorded the pleasure which he derived both from having him to very small dinners in Washington, when he arrived as precisely at seven as he left at nine, and from visiting him on Sundays at his house at Leesburg, Virginia.

Truman himself wrote of Marshall: 'The more I see and talk to him the more certain I am he's the great one of the age.' This was within a month of his becoming Secretary of State, but the President never subsequently changed his opinion. He also enjoyed a day at Leesburg, although it did not correspond with his normal choice of a pattern of entertainment.

Marshall, although he was certainly not encompassed by military rigidity (Acheson was struck by the fact that even in wartime he thought about military problems, let alone political ones, in a broad political framework) had certain limitations of imagination. He did not create ideas. He needed them to be put to him. He was good at choosing between them. And although he played a major role in calling the old world back into being, not exactly to redress the balance of the new but to stand more or less upright alongside it, I know of no evidence that he ever had a friend amongst the leaders of Europe. Acheson was on close terms with at least three, maybe even five, of them; but not Marshall. Language was no doubt a barrier with some, but hardly much with the British. Yet, although Ernest Bevin's reputation depends substantially upon his partnership with Marshall, and Marshall's depends at least equally upon Bevin's swift response to the Harvard Commencement Speech of June 1947, without which response the Marshall Plan might never have assumed reality, there was no hint of intimacy between them. Mainly through a misunderstanding Marshall thought that Bevin let him down at the London Conference of Foreign Ministers at the end of 1947, and subsequently held this against him. But even before that there had been no warmth. Acheson in 1949, for all his Groton and Yale style, immediately got on close terms with Bevin. He relished Bevin's earthy jokes. Marshall, who did not make many jokes himself – for such a remarkable man there are few anecdotes about him, and those there are somewhat pale – did not have the same appreciation of Bevin's humour. Despite what might have been thought his more promising provenance of Uniontown, Pennsylvania, Marshall always, I suspect, thought Bevin a rather coarse fellow. This showed a certain lack of imagination and narrowness of taste. But even at the superificial level of attraction of personality as opposed to the more important one of solidity of achievement, this is balanced by the near universality of affection as well as respect which Marshall commanded from a wide range of Americans (some of them of very critical temperament) who knew him well.

Marshall was very American. Not only was he unintimate with foreigners,★ he also had little taste for European life or travel. The paradox was that while he saw his duty as being to uphold the interests of his own country, he conceived of them in sufficiently broad terms that, with the possible exception of Acheson, he was objectively the most internationalist of all the 59 (then 49) Secretaries of State in the history of the Republic.

His return to Washington did four things. First, it gave a greater tautness to decision making in the State Department, even though Acheson as under-secretary (in which post he remained for six

★ Sir Oliver (now Lord) Franks, British Ambassador to Washington from 1948 to 1952, was a rare exception. He has something of Marshall's own qualities of calm, authoritative incisiveness. Field Marshal Dill may have been another exception. But he was dead two years before Marshall became Secretary of State.

months with Marshall before leaving government for eighteen months of private law practice) had done his best while Byrnes perambulated the world. Second, on all issues except Palestine, he re-united the policies of the State Department and the White House. Third, he added the weight of his non-partisan authority to Truman's partisan incisiveness in promulgating several major advances in the foreign commitments of the United States. Fourth, and not least important, his presence substantially increased the self-confidence of the President.

This accretion of strength came at a crucial time. In 1947 the defeated countries of Europe remained impoverished and demoralized. France and Italy in particular looked on the brink of revolution. Of the two victorious countries Britain, snowbound and fuelless, was forced to begin the long process of withdrawing from its world power illusions and responsibilities. Russia, moved by a mixture of truculence and fear, had become sullenly uncooperative, iron-handed in Eastern Europe and menacing beyond. There was no approach to a stable balance in the continent.

The third week of February was a climacteric in Britain's adjustment to post-war reality. On February 20th Attlee announced in the House of Commons that power would be handed over in India no later than June 1948. On the 21st Bevin caused notes to be delivered to Marshall informing the United States Government that British aid to Greece and Turkey could not continue after the end of March 1947. For Britain the former was the more momentous decision. But it posed no problem for Washington. It did not immediately affect the East-West balance and gentle support for Indian nationalism had long been settled American policy. Such support had been one of the main sources of friction between Roosevelt and Churchill during the war. No action from Washington was called for.

The eastern Mediterranean decision was quite different. It was to be implemented with brutal speed and it was bound, in the view of London and Washington alike, to result in an important shift of power to the Soviet Union unless America would step in where Britain was forced to withdraw. Bevin indeed would probably not have assented to the decision had he not judged that the US Government was just about ready to accept the new commitment. Major issues were therefore at stake. Had America refused the new burden, not only would a dangerous flank have been opened to

Russian influence, but Anglo-American relations would have been
gravely impaired, and the United States, having once resisted a
'bounce', would have been the more difficult to move in the future.
If the Greek-Turkish gamble had gone wrong the Marshall Plan
would have been unlikely to take shape.

In fact, however, although playing for high stakes, Bevin was
not doing so against long odds. It was overwhelmingly likely that
Truman, advised by Marshall and Acheson, would want to pick up
the check. The more open question was whether the new Republican
Congress would allow him to do so. The key meeting for this was at
the White House on February 27th. Truman, Marshall and Acheson
met the leaders of both parties in both houses. Acheson's account of
what occurred, while somewhat vainglorious, is the most vivid and
well-supported from other sources.

'My distingushed chief [Marshall], most unusually
and unhappily, flabbed [*sic*] his opening statement. In
desperation I whispered to him a request to speak. This
was my crisis. For a week I had nurtured it. These
congressmen had no conception of what challenged them;
it was my task to bring it home. Both my superiors, equally
perturbed, gave me the floor. Never have I spoken under
such a pressing sense that the issue was up to me alone.
No time was left for measured appraisal. In the past
eighteen months, I said, Soviet pressure on the Straits, on
Iran, and on Northern Greece had brought the Balkans to
the point where a highly possible Soviet breakthrough
might open three continents to Soviet penetration. Like
apples in a barrel infected by one rotten one, the
corruption of Greece would infect Iran and all to the east.
It would also carry infection to Africa through Asia
Minor and Egypt, and to Europe through Italy and France,
already threatened by the strongest Communist parties in
Western Europe. The Soviet Union was playing one of the
greatest gambles in history at minimal cost. It did not
need to win all the possibilities. Even one or two offered
immense gains. We and we alone were in a position to break
up the play. These were the stakes that British withdrawal
from the eastern Mediterranean offered to an eager and
ruthless opponent.

A long silence followed. Then Arthur Vandenberg said solemnly, 'Mr President, if you will say that to the Congress and the country, I will support you and I believe that most of its members will do the same.' Without much further talk the meeting broke up . . .'[4]

The Truman Doctrine was effectively launched. The only trouble was that Acheson, determined rightly to get it into the water, had pushed it down the slipway with too much champagne. Well before Dulles the domino theory was promulgated, and the susceptibility of the majority of Congress to the rhetoric of the Cold War was established.

When, therefore, Truman laid before a joint session of Congress on March 12th his proposals to make available an immediate $250 million for Greece and $150 million for Turkey he was proposing something much more far-reaching than the spending of $400 million (although that sum was then a great deal more substantial than it is today) and he was deliberately doing so in ideologically provocative terms. In particular, he set no limit to the geographical framework within which support was to be given: 'I believe that it must be the policy of the United States to support free peoples who are resisting attempts of subjugation by armed minorities or by outside pressure.' This somewhat flat sentence, when supported, as it was, by the Congress, can be regarded as one of the four or five most decisive in American history, even though Truman did not act uniformly upon it throughout the world. Viewed favourably, it proclaimed several decades of the *Pax Americana*. Viewed unfavourably, it set the country on the course to the *débâcle* of Vietnam. Viewed neutrally, it achieved its purpose. Both houses of the Republican Congress voted for the Truman Doctrine by approximately three to one.

Did Truman employ overkill? A surprisingly large proportion of those intimately involved thought that he did. George Kennan, the most important State Department adviser on policy towards the Soviet Union, did. Acheson did not: it sprang directly from his powerful and spontaneous presentation of two weeks previously. In the White House, George Elsey did, but Clark Clifford did not. More importantly, Marshall, who had left Washington for the Moscow meeting of foreign ministers several days beforehand, was somewhat unhappy. Acheson thought that he had got him to clear the draft on his way through Paris, but the Russian expert, Charles E. Bohlen who was with him, recorded that they both found 'the rhetoric too flamboyantly anti-Communist'. So too did Bevin who had just reached Moscow after an endless train journey across the snowbound plains of northern Europe. He and Marshall may both have been somewhat influenced by their knowledge that they were to be shut up in the drabness of an end of winter Moscow for over six weeks,* and a feeling that the President's speech, wholly desirable in substance, nevertheless condemned them to the certainty of an unproductive sojourn. Lord Bullock recorded that Bevin said in his final report on the Conference that 'Truman's announcement removed any chance of agreement on the general principles of a German settlement and changed the whole scene.' Bullock added however that without access to Russian sources Bevin could not really know.[5]

Truman himself was as usual unrepentant about his language. But he had found the decision peculiarly taxing, more so apparently than that to drop the Hiroshima and Nagasaki bombs, nineteen months previously. With the speech out of the way he went again to the familiar submarine base at Key West, Florida for a short holiday. From there on March 13th he wrote a typical and revealing letter to his daughter:

'We had a pleasant flight from Washington.
Your old Dad slept for 750 or 800 miles – three hours, and we were travelling from 250 to 300 miles an hour.
No one, not even me (your mother would say) knew how very tired and worn to a frazzle the Chief Executive had become. This terrible decision I had to make had been over my head for about six weeks. Although I knew at Potsdam that there is no difference in totalitarian or police states, call them what you will, Nazi, Fascist, Communist or Argentine Republics. You know there was but one

* This fourth meeting of the Council of Foreign Ministers was spread over 43 formal sessions lasting from March 10th to April 25th. The pace of late 1940s diplomacy was much more that of the Congresses of Vienna or Berlin than of today's meetings of ministers. Bevin was away from London for more than eight weeks, having spent six weeks in New York in November-December 1946. The condition of his heart meant that he mostly had to set off eastward by train and westward by ship.

Pendergast's last beam. Truman next to T.J. Pendergast, Postmaster-General James A. Farley, the tallest, at the Democratic Convention in Philadelphia, 1936.
(Harry S. Truman Library)

More a skeleton than a feast: Roosevelt and Truman at the White House, August 1944.
(Popperfoto)

The Big Three at Yalta. *(Franklin D. Roosevelt Library)*

The Big Three at Potsdam. *(U.S. Navy, courtesy Harry S. Truman Library)*

idealistic example of Communism. That is described in
the Acts of the Apostles.

The attempt of Lenin, Trotsky, Stalin, *et.al.* to fool the
world and the American Crackpots Association, represented by Jos. Davies,* Henry Wallace, Claude Pepper†
and the actors and artists in immoral Greenwich Village,
is just like Hitler's and Mussolini's so-called socialist states.

Your Pop had to tell the world just that in polite
language.'[6]

Between the proclamation of the Truman Doctrine and
Marshall's Harvard Commencement speech, which is generally
regarded as the launching date of the Marshall Plan, there was an
interval of only 85 days. It was a period of major policy making
at a formidable rate. In fact, the ideas of the Marshall Plan were
ready well before June 5th. There was indeed some thought that
it might have been launched in tandem with the Truman Doctrine,
and proposals for economic aid to Western Europe submitted at
the same time as those for military sustenance to the Eastern
Mediterranean.

It was decided however that this might be too heavy and rushed
a meal for the Congress to digest. More preparation was required.
Furthermore Truman wisely and modestly thought it undesirable
that his name should be memorialized by attachment to a major
programme for spending American taxpayers' money on economic
aid which in principle was to be offered to any state in Europe,
non-Communist or Communist. The Truman Doctrine was one
thing. It was military aid presented in a specifically anti-Communist context. It would be accepted by a Republican Congress
even under Truman's name. For the European Recovery Programme, as it subsequently became, a less partisan label was
required. Marshall provided it. Truman shrewdly saw the tactical
advantage of this. He also thought that the General deserved the
accolade and had no jealousy about letting him have it.

Nonetheless the broad policy behind the Plan was essentially
Truman's policy and the detailed ideas were essentially worked

---

* Joseph E. Davies, 1876–1958, had been US Ambassador to Moscow 1936–8
and was used by Roosevelt, and indeed Truman in his early days, for special
missions.

† Claude Pepper, b. 1900, was Senator for Florida from 1936 until his defeat
in 1950. He returned to Capitol Hill as a congressman in 1962.

out by Acheson, supported by a trenchant series of memoranda
written by Will Clayton, then State Department assistant under-
Secretary in charge of economic affairs. Acheson also commissioned and skilfully used a report from a body known as
the State/War/Navy Co-ordinating Committee. This committee
reported on April 21st and, strangely for a body composed of
three middle-rank military gentlemen (even the State Department
representative was a colonel) deployed with limpid logic the far-
sighted economic self-interest case for generosity. It pointed out
that in 1947 the United States was likely to export $7.5 billion
more goods and services than it imported. But resources to pay
for this export surplus were running down. 'The conclusion is
inescapable that under present programmes and policies the world
will not be able to continue to buy United States exports at the
1946–7 rate beyond another 12–18 months . . . A substantial decline in the United States export surplus would have a depressing
effect on business activity and employment . . . if the export
decline happened to coincide with weakness in the domestic
economy, [the effect on] employment might be most serious.'[7]

Acheson not only organized the back-room work. He also put
on a dress rehearsal of the Harvard speech itself. Truman had
earlier promised local friends that he would address the annual
meeting of the Delta Council, half picnic, half serious-minded
local reunion at the Teachers' College in Cleveland, Mississippi.
It was fixed for May 8th. By early April he had decided that a
combination of his mother's health (she nearly died at the age of
95 in June that year and finally did so in July) and that of Senator
Bilbo (whose equally imminent death was causing a bitter faction
fight in Mississippi politics) made such a presidential visit inappropriate. On April 7th he asked Acheson to go in his place. They
both decided that if Delta could not have a President it ought to
have an important speech. The next month was spent in detailed
and rigorous drafting, with the White House much involved, and
State consulting other relevant departments.

Most of it was done before Marshall got back from Moscow on
April 28th. On May 1st Acheson put on a pre-rehearsal of the
dress rehearsal. He took the speech together with a few of his staff
to an off-the-record luncheon of the officers of the League of
Women Voters, and proceeded to give it what he described as 'a
preliminary canter'. It seemed to go well. With a little further

polishing and some advance briefing of the British press, he set off for Mississippi.

This long-prepared oration was well-received by the audience, reasonably reported by a few papers in the South, but ignored by the rest of the American press. It was however extensively reported in Europe, particularly but not exclusively in London. This interest fed back in a few weeks to America. By then however the next stage of the operation was well in train. Marshall, during May, performed a key rôle. He brought Kennan back to the State Department from the National War College, where he was lecturing and put him in charge of a policy planning staff which directed itself in more detail to the shape of the Plan and produced a report on May 23rd.

His instructions to Kennan were both vague and splendid. 'Avoid trivia,' he said. Kennan did. From the report there stemmed a strand of settled United States foreign policy which persisted at least until the 1970s. This was American belief in the desirability of fostering a union, most desirably federation, in Western Europe. It led over decades to the United States being prepared, on occasion, to subordinate trading difficulties with the European Community to this wider political consideration. It led to Jean Monnet finding some of his best allies in Washington. And it led to continuing mild friction between off-shore Britain and pro-federalist America. At this initial stage however it merely took the form of a resolve to use the aid to promote regional unity in Europe.

Marshall also took three key decisions himself. The first was that speed was essential. Otherwise Europe might disintegrate in front of benevolent but too leisurely American eyes. 'The patient is sinking while the doctors deliberate,' he said.* The second was that Europe get together and produce a plan for its own recovery. The United States would then do its best to produce what was needed to sustain the plan. But it must not produce both the supplies and the plan; or at least not be seen to do so. Third, and most controversially, he decided that the offer must be made to Europe as a whole and not only to the non-Communist part of it. If Europe was to be more deeply divided he wanted it to be done by Moscow and not by Washington. He may have hoped, or

* Broadcast on April 28th.

calculated, or both, that the Russians would neither accept nor allow their satellites to do so. But he was determined (and so persuaded Truman) to take the risk. It was of course a risk, for had they done so it is difficult to see how the objective of using the Plan to promote regional unity could possibly have been achieved. A federation extending from Paris to Moscow was not remotely feasible.

Marshall also made his own decision to use the Harvard speech as the occasion for the next (and as it happened the crucial) major pronouncement. Acheson was against. Like many of the highly educated, he distrusted educational occasions. 'Commencement speeches', he wrote, 'were a ritual to be endured without hearing.'*

Marshall in Harvard Yard gave the impression of not greatly caring whether anyone was hearing him or not. He read a short speech with his head down. His audience revered him but hardly recognized the full importance of what he was saying. Perhaps that has always been so with the great orations in the history of the world, from the Sermon on the Mount to the Gettysburg Address. Marshall did not take precautions to ensure that reverberation was greater than instant appreciation. I do not know how Harvard compared with the Mount and Gettysburg in this respect, but it was certainly less widely trailed than Cleveland, Mississippi. The State Department did not even have a full text when the Secretary of State left Washington for Boston. Once again, the domestic coverage was thin. But Leonard Miall, the BBC correspondent in Washington, acted as an essential disseminator. Ernest Bevin heard it on his wireless early the following morning, and lumbered into the Foreign Office determined to let no time go by before Marshall's most pregnant sentence – 'The initiative, I think, must come from Europe' – was responded to.

The subsequent story of how Bevin both upstaged Bidault and carried him along with him, how they jointly invited 22 nations

---

* Acheson, *Present at the Creation* p. 232. The author, having delivered the Harvard Commencement Address of 1972, a quarter of a century after Marshall, is inclined to concur. I regard my Harvard degree as one of the three or four greatest honours I have ever received. I thought the occasion to speak on the twenty-fifth anniversary of Marshall as one of the greater opportunities of my life. I was mistaken. I enjoyed the rest of the twenty-four hours very much. But the open-air speech to a slightly somnolent post-prandial gathering of 3000 alumni, where 10 or 12,000 had been present in the morning for the degree giving, was something of an anti-climax.

including the Soviet Union to a meeting in Paris at the end of June, how they all came, how Molotov made it clear that Russia would be delighted to get American money, but only on a bilateral cash basis and without any commitment to a common plan, how when this demand for eleemosynary treatment did not work he took seven other nations away with him (although the Czechs only with difficulty and the Finns against their natural instincts) and how the remaining fourteen quickly prepared at least an approach to a unified Western European initiative, is enshrined in innumerable memoirs, biographies and other accounts of events of the following few months.

Three hypothetical questions remain about the Marshall Plan. First, to what extent did its assumption of reality depend upon Ernest Bevin's determined and enthusiastic response? Might it all have got lost if Bevin had followed the recommendation of his permanent under-secretary (William Strang) and asked the Embassy in Washington to inquire what precisely Marshall had in mind? Bevin himself regarded his more positive and urgent reaction as important. It was certainly so in the sense that Marshall had stressed at Harvard that 'the initiative . . . must come from Europe'. There was also considerable vagueness in Washington during the following few weeks as to exactly what was planned in the Plan.* A request for precision might therefore have been counter-productive. But this is a long way from the extreme thesis that Marshall was just musing in Cambridge, and that the dinner for which Bevin so firmly and immediately accepted the semi-proffered invitation was only half intended to take place. The thrust of the Truman Administration had been firmly behind Marshall's words, at least since April.

Second, what would have happened if the Russians, instead of flouncing out with their satellites from Paris, had remained in, half cooperative, half sullen? Most probably the venture would have led only to some limited transfer of funds from the United States to Europe and then run into the ground. Clearly it could not have proved the forerunner to Western European unity, and most probably the Republican Congress would never have voted an

* As late as July 28th, one middle rank State Department official wrote to another: 'The "Marshall Plan" has been compared to a flying saucer – nobody knows what it looks like, how big it is, in what direction it is moving, or whether it really exists.' (Bullock, *Ernest Bevin, Foreign Secretary*, p. 403)

appropriation of $17 billion. Marshall's decision that the Russians and not the Truman Administration should be left to split Europe was a well-calculated risk.

Third, how much difference did the Marshall Plan in fact make to the pace of European recovery? Historians who wish to show that no event is decisive and all landscapes more or less flat are now intent upon proclaiming that Marshall Aid, like the Battle of Waterloo, the repeal of the Corn Laws and Roosevelt's pump-priming, made practically no difference. It would all have happened anyway. As always with this eventless and enervating theory of history there are some facts on its side. There had been massive but relatively unpublicized outpourings of US aid in 1945 and 1946. There was a trough in 1947, which coincided with, although it did not cause, the economic and political foundering of that year in Europe. And in 1948 the economies of Western Europe began significantly to pick up well before they received the flow of Marshall funds. But that was assisted by the fact that governments knew the funds were coming. Previously Europe had lived from hand-to-mouth. Such recovery as had taken place had been based on re-stocking. The Marshall Plan enabled Europe to get its second wind and to embark upon an essential recovery of fixed investment. If it did not start the recovery it crucially underpinned it.

A postscript needs to be added. The British response to the Marshall proposal was at once splendid and ludicrous. London led Europe, as has been seen. Yet, having led it, the British Government tried equally hard to detach itself from it. At a series of late June meetings in London a determined attempt was made to argue that Britain should not be lumped in with the other European countries, but (although at the same time a beneficiary) should also be a co-distributor, with the United States, of the aid to the other countries. The ludicrousness of the claim was symbolized by the fact that Attlee, Bevin, Cripps and Dalton all assembled in 10 Downing Street to argue the point against Clayton, who was no more than equal third in the US State Department. He held firm. They did not, for they had no firm ground on which to stand, and to their credit, once resisted, co-operated enthusiastically on a basis they would not have chosen. Yet the incident was a remarkable and depressing precursor of Britain's relationship with the continent of Europe throughout the 1950s.

Such reflections about Britain's medium-term relations with the mainland hardly dominated Truman's mind in the summer of 1947. He was totally committed to the Marshall Plan, upon which a substantial part of his reputation rests. In the autumn he was to demand and get from a tight-fisted Congress the maximum practical appropriation for its implementation. But after a strenuous spring of foreign policy initiatives he switched back for much of the rest of the year to more domestic concerns.

On June 20th he vetoed the Taft-Hartley Bill. How much this sprang from conviction as opposed to political calculation is open to a little doubt. He was not instinctively against some curbs on union power. 'We have got to have a certain restriction on the union element,' his own records show him as having told a group of broadcasters in January, 'because if we don't, we go haywire. You take the underdog and put him on top, and he is just as bad on top, and sometimes a little worse.'[8] He was straining the old Roosevelt coalition in several directions. The South was already unhappy about the appointment of his Civil Rights Commission and its report, due in October, was almost certain to produce further strains. And his robust attitude towards the 1946 strikes, while good for his general popularity, had subtantially disaffected the labour unions. In 1946 however he was dealing with short-term situations on his own presidential initiative. In 1947 the question was whether he was to endorse long-term curbs imposed by a Republican Congress. If he had, he could have said goodbye to any substantial union support in the 1948 election.

Curiously his Cabinet were almost all in favour of his accepting the bill. The only two against were Schwellenbach, the egregious Secretary of Labour, who naturally had his clients to consider, and Hannegan, the Postmaster-General, whose primary business was not mails but the fostering of the Democratic Party machine. Snyder, Truman's closest Cabinet friend, was particularly strong in favour of his signing the bill. At the least equally curiously, the White House mail on the subject was both huge and overwhelmingly in favour of a veto. Over 750,000 communications were received. It was of course largely an organized campaign, but it was not the sort of organization at which the unions were usually very good.

There was no certainty until the last moment about what Truman was going to do. Then on June 20th he came out against the bill with a message of exceptional length – over 5,000 words. There was no reflection of hesitancy in the tone of this message. The bill was 'a shocking piece of legislation . . . bad for labor, bad for management and bad for the country'. There was an element of bathos about this 'veto', which so far from stopping the bill in its tracks, merely held it up for three or four days while the House overrode the President's view by a majority of 4 to 1 and the Senate by nearly 3 to 1.*

Nevertheless his disapproval of it earned him considerable credit with the unions. A year earlier the President of the Brotherhood of Railways Trainmen had threatened that the Brotherhood would 'open its treasury' to defeat Truman in 1948. Now Alexander Whitney caused his spokesman to state: 'It is indicated that our Brotherhood will throw all its resources behind President Truman and his Administration in an effort to elect a Congress which will back the President's liberal programme', thus demonstrating both the union's flexibility and its faithfulness to good trade union jargon.

At least equally importantly, Truman's 'veto' of Taft-Hartley, following the Marshall speech, clutched back the liberal wing of the Rooseveltians from the enticements of Wallace. In early 1947 Americans for Democratic Action had been founded, with Mrs Roosevelt as its figurehead, a number of old New Dealers as its Praetorian Guard, those patriarchal New York immigrant clothing worker union leaders, Dubinsky and Potofsky, as its godfathers, Walter Reuther of the United Automobile Workers as a whipper-in, and the then relatively junior John Kenneth Galbraith and Arthur M. Schlesinger, Jr. as its young Turks. This body at first had no commitment to Truman. Indeed as late as February 1948 ADA refrained from endorsing him. But the Taft-Hartley veto made them neutral. Wallace's withdrawal from support of the Marshall Plan when the Russians walked out in Paris disenchanted them with him. And the sponsors of his candidature (announced in Chicago in December 1947) made them profoundly suspicious, for they were always firmly hostile to Communist front organizations. Thereafter ADA flirted around a little, even with

* Two-thirds majorities were required in each case. In the House more Democrats voted against the President than with him. The young Lyndon B. Johnson, as Donovan points out, voted against Truman. The still younger John F. Kennedy was one of the 71 who voted for him.

Eisenhower, but never with any seriously possible Democratic candidate for 1948, before coming solidly to Truman's support in the campaign itself.

During most of 1947, however, Truman was far from being pre-occupied with thought of the 1948 election. In the first place he was doubtful whether he wanted to run. Although there is no direct documentary evidence there is strong oral support for the view that at some time (possiby on several occasions) during the year he renewed his 1945 suggestion to Eisenhower and offered to step aside and support him for the *Democratic* nomination. This is testified to by Rosenman who wrote many of Truman's speeches, Steelman of his White House staff, and from the other side of the fence by Milton Eisenhower, the General's brother. The reasons why it was not subsequently confirmed in the writings or words of either of the principals are fairly obvious. Eisenhower did not wish to confirm that he had let Truman think he was a Democrat. And Truman, partly as a result of Eisenhower not rallying to Marshall's defence against the calumnies of McCarthy, moved into a position of such abiding dislike of his successor that he preferred not to recall that he had ever thought of promoting him as President of the United States. But there seems little doubt that, at any rate during the first half of 1947, Truman was still attracted by the idea, and spoke accordingly to Eisenhower, who said that he had no intention of going into politics (such dissimulation was another subsequent count against him in Truman's eyes), but not that he was not a Democrat.

On November 12th 1947, Truman told Forrestal that 'he would be delighted not to run again if it were not for a sense of duty which compelled him to do so.'[9] In other words he had crossed his Rubicon. Duty would make him run. But his reluctance was sincere. He talked of the intolerably constrictive effect which the presidency had upon the life of his daughter and of the limited satisfaction which he derived from it.

As that winter turned into the spring of 1948 Truman's political mood evolved further. By March or April he was determined to fight and if possible to win. It was 1940 writ large. In part this was reaction against Eisenhower, and well before McCarthyism. It was one thing for him to think of handing over the baton to Eisenhower. It was another for others to promote Eisenhower when Truman had already decided that the General had no stomach

for a political fight. Yet this is precisely what happened. The whole
Roosevelt clan (with the crucial exception of Eleanor who was
tempted, but continued to treat Truman as well as ever) and many
of their associates too, were seized with a 'draft Eisenhower' craze
in the early months of 1948. Truman was furious. He was not
going to be dumped for an allegedly non-political general who
had rejected his own overtures. Subsequently he dragged up
Eisenhower's relationship with his wartime English driver, Mrs
Summersby, and his 1945 letter to General Marshall, saying that
he wanted to be relieved of his duty, divorce his wife and marry
Mrs Summersby, as a reason why he could not support Eisenhower
for president.[10] This was very much *ex post*. As Truman knew of
the Eisenhower-Marshall correspondence later there seems little
reason why he should not have known before 1947. Indeed it
would have been more appropriate to disclose it to him as
Commander-in-Chief, while both the generals were serving
officers, than when they subsequently became political figures
of differing affiliation.* While he was not vain, Truman could
occasionally take deep and unforgiving offence if he thought that
someone combined excessive self-regard with an attempt to put
themselves on a higher moral plane than himself. A curious selec-
tion of people fell into this category. Robert Oppenheimer
and Adlai Stevenson†, as well as Eisenhower are amongst their
number.

Nevertheless it remains the case that throughout 1947 Truman
was, for a president, unusually unconcerned with electoral considerations. This did not mean that he was indifferent to politics.
Even when he thought that he might voluntarily go out in 1949,
he wanted to do so with 3¾ years of effective presidency behind
him. He therefore welcomed the big improvement in the polls
which took place in the spring (of 1947), when his approval rate
rose to a very respectable 60% from a low of 32% in September
1946. He wished to preserve a base in the Democratic Party, even

* This comes from Mr Merle Miller's conversations with Truman in 1961
(*An Oral Biography*). If Mr Miller was accurate in recording Truman, and Truman
was accurate on Marshall's reply that, 'if Eisenhower ever came close to doing
such a thing he'd not only bust him out of the Army, he'd see to it that never
for the rest of his life would he be able to draw a peaceful breath' this may go
some way towards explaining Eisenhower's less than heroic defence of Marshall
in 1952. But the existence of this letter is not well-authenticated.

† See pp. 182–202, *infra* for an account of Truman's attitude to Stevenson.

if the South had to some extent to be let go, and he even cultivated with moderate assiduity his relationship with what he was later to denounce as the 'do-nothing, good-for-nothing, worst (ever) Eightieth Congress'. On July 23rd when he was lunching at the Senate he took the unprecedented step of strolling on to the floor after the meal and sitting in his old seat. Vandenberg, who was in the chair and who of course had been carefully tipped off, 'recognized' the ex-Senator from Missouri for five minutes. Truman used the time to make a nostalgic little speech which was well received on both sides.

1947 was notable in the annals of the Truman administration on a number of other counts. It was the year of the National Security Act, which set up the Department of Defense and unified the armed forces, although not in nearly as complete a form as Truman would have liked. The Act also, and almost incidentally, established the CIA. It was the year when Truman, a little afraid but having the courage to go on when frightened, landed himself with a civil rights programme, which was the forerunner of much subsequent legislation in the field, as well as the cause of the Dixiecrat revolt of 1948 and thus the beginning of a substantial geographical re-orientation in American politics. It was also a year, particularly in the latter part, when the Palestine issue obtruded heavily on to both the domestic and the foreign politics of the United States. But that had to some extent been so in 1946, and was to be still more so in 1948, to which year the core and crunch of the story belongs.

Altogether Truman ended the year in much better shape than he had begun it. He had started with the courage of desperation. To most people it looked inconceivable that he could run again, let alone be elected. It looked likely that his own words of 1944 about vice-presidents who succeeded to the presidency ('usually they were ridiculed in office, had their hearts broken, lost any vestige of respect they had had before') were making themselves even more applicable to himself than to most of the others. By the end of the year he had a certain solidity of achievement, particularly in the foreign policy field. His presidency could not be regarded as negligible, whatever was to happen in the future. He had overcome his own reluctance to run again. Given his temperament he probably already thought that he could win. It was still the case, however, that few others did, although they would no longer have dismissed his ability to be nominated.

When Henry Wallace announced his independent candidature on December 19th it did little to spoil Truman's Christmas. Indeed the President organized the holiday rather better than usual, with a large family party in the White House in place of the usual rather bad-tempered dash for thirty hours to Independence. The reason for the family party was that it was the first Christmas without 'Mamma Truman'. Paradoxically but rather typically, however, the large White House party was made up overwhelmingly of relations of Bess rather than of Harry Truman. The President's brother, Vivian, could not come because he had too many of his own family to entertain at home in Missouri. 'I am sure they had a grand dinner', Truman wrote ruminatively, 'a much happier one than a formal, butler served one, although ours was nice enough. But a family dinner, cooked by the family mother, daughters, grand-daughters and served by them, is not equalled by the White House, Delmonico's, Antoine's or any other formal one.'[10] Truman had launched himslf on a modest quest for racial equality but he was a long way from embracing the idea of women's liberation. An ideal to which however his dedication could never be doubted, whether in good times or in bad, was that of a simpler, earlier, more honest America. But it was always something which, whether he was in Washington or Independence or Grandview was just beyond the receding horizon. It was the nostalgia of an incurable romantic, mostly slightly dissatisfied but rarely self-pitying. And unlike some of his successors he did not try to inflict his nostalgia as political stock-in-trade upon the nation.

8

VICTORY OUT OF THE
JAWS OF DEFEAT

1948, in contrast with its revolutionary predecessor a century before and in contradiction of Yeats, was a year when the centre held. The word of Marshall was made flesh in the form of the European Recovery Programme. The foundations of NATO were laid. And Truman confounded Dewey, the *Chicago Tribune* and Dr Gallup by being re-elected President of the United States.

During the first part of the year, however, leading up to the proclamation of the state of Israel on May 14th and its immediate recognition by the United States, the divisive issue of Palestine was repeatedly hovering over the international landscape. It was divisive between the White House and the State Department. It was divisive within Truman's own mind. In an intermittent way it had been all of these things since the first months of his presidency. It was the greatest irritant of the period to Anglo-American relations. It probably was the factor which most inhibited the growth of real respect, let alone affection, between Truman and his most powerful European auxiliary, Ernest Bevin. And it certainly strained the President's relationship with his much admired Secretary of State more than every other issue put together.

Truman appeared, in the eyes of the British Government and to some extent of the State Department, to be determinedly, even carelessly, pro-Zionist. In fact he was much more objectively than subjectively so. He had a general predisposition in favour of a Jewish national home, and indeed a Jewish state, but no great emotional commitment to the cause. He was however subject to a number of influences, personal and political. There were two determined Zionists in the White House staff. The first was David K. Niles, whom he had inherited from Roosevelt, and greatly liked. The second and more central was Clark Clifford, who from 1946 had constant access to the President and never hesitated to take on the State Department. Then there was his old haberdashery partner, Eddie Jacobson, who had re-established himself more successfully in similar business in Kansas City and re-entered Truman's life as an unofficial but extremely effective ambassador of the Jewish Agency in the summer of 1946. On several crucial occasions he applied pressure upon Truman in a way that the President would have accepted from few other people. In addition, Weizmann himself, operating less intrusively but with a grander sweep than Jacobson, never failed on the three or four occasions when they met to exercise almost as magnetic an effect upon Truman as he had upon Balfour thirty years before.

The political pressures came from the Democratic machine, both nationally through Hannegan and his successor McGrath, and from State leaders, primarily but not exclusively in New York. It was funds, still more than votes, that they were concerned about. Their pressure was re-inforced by the fact that the Republicans, Dewey and even Taft, were prepared to outbid the President whenever he veered towards accepting State Department caution towards the rapid creation of a Jewish state.

To Attlee and Bevin, who at least until 1947 when they tried to hand over the problem to the United Nations, had direct responsibility, Truman emerged from all this as a rampant partisan, careless alike of Arab opinion and the prospects of peace in the area and concerned only with the exigencies of American domestic politics. Attlee responded with some tart private messages which Bevin supplemented with occasional exasperated and ill-judged public speeches. In June 1946, he enlivened the Labour Party Conference by saying 'Regarding the agitation in the United States . . . for 100,000 Jews to be put into Palestine, I hope it will not be misunderstood in America if I say, with the purest of motives, that that was because they did not want too many of them in New York.' The hope with which he prefaced his delicate irony, it need hardly be said, was misplaced. Nine months later, he had another go: 'I really must point out that in international affairs I cannot settle things,' he told the House of Commons in typically egotistical terms, 'if my problem is made the subject of local elections. I hope I am not saying anything to cause bad feeling in the United States, but I feel so intense about this . . .'

These statements did Bevin a lot of harm with American public opinion, in New York at least. On one occasion dockers there refused to unload his luggage from the *Queen Mary*★ and on another he was booed at a baseball game in Yankee Stadium. More importantly they infuriated Truman, and acted as a countervailing influence to the irritation with which he reacted to excessive Jewish lobbying. In June 1946 he at first refused to see a delegation of all the New York Congressmen, and finally received them only with obvious impatience. He was no better when the two Senators from the state, Wagner and Mead, brought a former member of the Anglo-American Committee of Enquiry (into Palestine) to see him. 'I am not a New Yorker,' Truman is alleged to have told them. 'All these people are pleading for a special interest. I am an American'[1]† '. . . The Jews themselves are making it almost impossible to do anything for them', he wrote to Edwin Pauley in October.[2] And in August 1947, he used to Mrs Roosevelt the analogy he had applied to the labour unions over a year before: 'I fear very much that the Jews are like all underdogs. When they get on top they are just as intolerant and as cruel as the people were to them when they were underneath. I regret this very much because my sympathy has always been on their side.'[2] A couple of months after this he pretended to Senator Pepper of Florida (to irritate not propitiate him) that he had personally burnt 35,000 pieces of unread pro-Zionist mail.

Then in February 1948 he refused to see Weizmann. This led to Jacobson being sent in to secure a reversal of the decision. He succeeded, but not without touching some of Truman's rawest nerves. He arrived unannounced at the White House and as was habitual got an interview without difficulty, although he was urged not to talk to the President about Palestine. Needless to say,

---

★ There was a peculiar irony in Bevin being the victim of a dockers' boycott. In 1920 he had both made his national reputation and earned the title of 'the dockers' K C' with his presentation of their case before a public court of inquiry; and in the same years he had organized the refusal of the London stevedores to load the *Jolly George* with arms for Churchill's support of the White Russians.

† Attlee listened to R. H. S. Crossman, a member of the same Committee expatiate on the subject for three quarters of an hour and then concluded the interview less provocatively but still more discouragingly by merely saying 'How's your mother, Dick' (Kenneth Harris, *Attlee*, p. 411). Had he and Truman known of each other's interview they might have had more mutual sympathy on the issue.

Jacobson did not for long stick to this advice. 'He [Truman] immediately became tense in appearance, abrupt in speech, and very bitter in the words he was throwing my way,' Jacobson recorded. 'In all the years of our friendship he never talked to me in this manner or anything approaching it . . . I suddenly found myself thinking that my dear friend the President of the United States was at that moment as close to being an anti-Semite as a man could possibly be, and I was shocked that some of our Jewish leaders should be responsible for Mr. Truman's attitude.'[3]

Nonetheless Jacobson used his special powers of persuasion to get Weizmann his interview, which took place secretly on March 18th, 1948. It led to one of the worst foreign policy confusions of Truman's presidency. On November 29th, 1947, the UN General Assembly, with the problem dumped in their laps by the British, had voted by 33 to 13, with 10 abstentions, in favour of partition. As a two-thirds majority was required to give the resolution validity the margin was adequate but not handsome. The United States lobbied hard in its favour. Truman issued instructions that the delegation in New York was not to use 'threats or improper pressure' on other delegations. That instruction, however, even if fully carried out, and there is evidence that it was not, would have left some room for persuasion and 'proper' pressure. What is certain is that without not merely the vote, but the influence of the United States, then far greater in the General Assembly than today, there would have been no chance of the requisite numbers.

The resolution was greeted with Jewish jubilation and Arab violence. When the British announced that they would end the mandate on May 15th and would play no part in enforcing partition it became obvious that, unless Palestine was to be invited by the world peace-keeping organization to fight out its own destiny in a communal war, the policy inspired by the United States required the deployment of a large contingent of United States troops. This Truman was never prepared to contemplate. Without a special draft for Palestine he simply did not have the men available. Nor was this by any means his only consideration. The logical gap permitted a strong counter-attack from the State Department, which was in any event deeply concerned about the effect of the UN resolution upon United States-Arab relations.

Subsequent writers close to Truman, notably his daughter and Clark Clifford, have portrayed this counter-attack as stemming

Whose laughter had least mirth? Byrnes, right, hands over to Marshall as Secretary of State, January 1947, with Attorney-General Tom Clark in the background. *(National Park Services – Abbie Rowe, courtesy Harry S. Truman Library)*

A 1948 whistle-stop. *(AP/Wide World Photos)*

Dewey concedes: bland to the end. *(AP/Wide World Photos)*

from the professional middle ranks of the Department where little
loyalty was felt to Truman. Truman himself provided the base for
this thesis when he wrote in his diary for March 19th, 1948, about
the contretemps which followed his meeting with Weizmann:
'There are people on the third and fourth levels of the State
Department, who have always wanted to cut my throat. They've
succeeded in doing so. Marshall's in California and Lovett's in
Florida.'[4] The false implication of the accurate statement about the
locations of the Secretary and under-secretary stemmed from his
unwillingness to blame those whom he admired. But the thesis is
unsustainable. The views of the official State Department were
shaped by those whom Truman himself had entrusted with the
main responsibility for the formulation and execution of United
States foreign and defence policy, not only by Marshall and Lovett,
but by Forrestal, the Secretary of Defense; and all the indications
from his previous attitude to the desirable scale of Jewish immigration are that they would have been shared by Acheson had he
still been in office. These were not men who were disloyal to
Truman, or whom Truman would ever have accused of so being.

The working out by the State Department during January and
February of an alternative to partition was therefore an enterprise
which carried the authority of the Department at all levels. Moreover it was one of which they kept the President informed and for
which they secured his general approval. A message sent him on
February 21st, when he was cruising in the *Williamsburg*, stated
that if in the face of Arab intransigence the Security Council failed
to work out a satisfactory solution, the issue should be referred
back for re-consideration by a special session of the General Assembly. 'The Department of State,' the message continued, 'considers that it would then be clear that Palestine is not yet ready for
self-government and that some form of United Nations trusteeship
for an additional period of time will be necessary.'[5] The next day
Truman cabled to Marshall: 'I approve in principle this basic
position.' But, confusingly, he added the illogical stipulation that
this should not be interpreted as a shift from the position the
United States had previously taken in the General Assembly. To
compound the confusion the State Department, when sending the
President the text of a speech which Warren Austin, the head of
the US delegation to the UN, was to make in the Security Council
of February 24th, gave him that assurance in relation to the speech.

The assurance was just compatible with the speech itself, but not with the policy for which the speech was intended to pave the way.

Then on March 8th, following the failure in the Security Council on March 5th of a US move to endorse the General Assembly partition resolution, Truman had a meeting with Marshall and Lovett and agreed that trusteeship should be the fall-back position. Then there took place the 'secret' meeting on March 18th between Truman and Weizmann, of which the State Department at least was not informed. The following day Austin made another and more important speech to the Security Council of the imminence of which Truman had not been informed. On March 18th Truman told Weizmann that his policy was still partition. On March 19th Austin told the Security Council that the policy of the United States was to suspend partition, to impose a temporary trusteeship and to summon a special session of the General Assembly. The contradiction was blatant. Almost every articulate Jew in the United States, except for Weizmann, who wisely held his counsel, accused the President of gross betrayal. Truman himself wrote in his diary: 'This morning I find that the State Department has reversed my Palestine policy. The first I know about it is what I see in the papers! Isn't that hell! I am now in the position of a liar and a double-crosser.'[6]

It was of course substantially but not wholly Truman's own fault. Clifford however was instructed to remonstrate with the absent Marshall and Lovett. He got fairly robust answers. Lovett responded with a memorandum setting out the whole issue of the State Department's transactions with the President on the issue. Marshall held a press conference in Los Angeles and spoke with a calm firmness. 'The course of action . . . which was proposed . . . by Ambassador Austin', he said, 'appeared to me after the most careful consideration, to be the wisest course to follow. I recommended it to the President and he approved my recommendation.'[7]

Truman was left with little more to do than to try to explain to a press conference of his own that trusteeship did not exclude partition but merely postponed it, to persuade Mrs Roosevelt not to resign as a member of the UN delegation, and to complain that he was 'feeling blue'.

This inglorious episode in American dipomatic history left

Truman battered and disgruntled and Marshall in charge but unhappy. The point at issue was in fact rather academic. The special General Assembly met in April, but completely failed to agree on trusteeship. Meanwhile the Jews in Palestine achieved partition for themselves and made it clear that they intended formally to proclaim the State of Israel the moment the British mandate ended. On May 8th Marshall warned the putative Israeli Foreign Minister (Moshe Shertok, later Sharett) that if the new state got into trouble he must not expect military help from the Americans. There was no dispute with the White House about this. Truman was no more willing to commit troops than was the State Department or the Pentagon.

What was at issue was the recognition by the United States of the unilaterally proclaimed state, and particularly the timing of such an act. This was considered at a White House meeting on May 12th. Marshall, Lovett and a regional expert represented the State Department. Truman was buttressed by his Zionist advisors, Clifford and Niles. This composition plus the fact that Clifford was invited to open with a fifteen minute exposition of the case for immediate recognition riled Marshall. He was not softened by the explicitly political form in which Clifford put the case. It would enable the President to recover some of the support lost in March. Marshall accordingly responded in the most magisterial terms (or, as Clifford claimed, 'he said it all in a righteous God-damned Baptist tone'[8]):

> 'I remarked to the President that, speaking objectively,
> I could not help but think that the suggestions made by
> Mr Clifford were wrong. I thought that to adopt these
> suggestions would have precisely the opposite effect
> from that intended by Mr Clifford. The transparent dodge
> to win a few votes would not in fact achieve this purpose.
> The great dignity of the office of the President would be
> seriously diminished. The counsel offered by Mr Clifford
> was based on domestic political considerations, while the
> problem that confronted us was international.'

Then he added a most extraordinary bombshell: 'I said bluntly that if the President were to follow Mr Clifford's advice and if in the elections I were to vote, I would vote against the President.'[9]

How the meeting was concluded is in some dispute. Jonathan

Daniels, writing close to the event with good oral sources, says that Truman concluded that there was no alternative but to follow Marshall's advice. Donovan, writing nearly thirty years later with much better written sources, mentions no such conclusion and implies that Truman, miserably shattered, nonetheless withstood the blast. What is certain however, is that whatever Truman said at the meeting, Marshall's advice was not in fact followed. Daniels spans the contradiction by implying that the Secretary of State and his assistant thought they had pushed Truman too hard and recording that Lovett took the initiative to arrange a bridge-building luncheon with Clifford at which a compromise could be agreed. Marshall would accept recognition in return for a few days in which to prepare the diplomatic ground.

The lunch took place at the F Street Club, on Saturday, May 14th, but no compromise resulted. At 6.00 p.m. Washington time (midnight British time) that evening the mandate ended and the new state was proclaimed. At 6.11 p.m. the White House announced *de facto* recognition. And so far from the ground having been prepared the news surfaced in the worst possible way at the worst possible time. The UN General Assembly was in session and the United States was trying to rally support for a vote, just about to take place, on trusteeship for Jerusalem. The White House announcement was received with incredulity turning into consternation by the uninformed US delegation, and with bitter anger by many of the others. The delegate of Cuba, then more or less a client state of Washington, tried to get to the rostrum to announce (presumably without authority) the withdrawal of his country from an organization which had been disfigured by the duplicity of its leading member. The delegate of the Soviet Union, beaten by 24 hours in the race to recognize (which had been one of Clifford's objectives) was able to compensate with a large meal of unctuous propaganda. Marshall sent Dean Rusk, then assistant secretary for international organizations, to New York in case the US delegation resigned *en masse*. They did not, but Eleanor Roosevelt wrote to say that the United States was destroying its capacity to lead by changing its position so frequently and without consultation.

The *déringolade* was greater than that of March, but this time it was Truman who had got his way. He had had his tit-for-tat with Warren Austin, although this was hardly an appropriate pastime for the President of the United States. He had also more than balanced the account with Marshall. This in itself did not give him pleasure, although by so doing he had vindicated the authority if not 'the great dignity of the office of the President' (Marshall's words of May 12th), and was probably influenced by the events of March in acting as he did. The Secretary of State fully accepted this vindication. He did not contemplate resignation. He believed in the sanctity of chains of command. The issues and the series of contretemps strained their relationship but did not come close to breaking it. Marshall almost certainly voted for Truman in November: he twice saw him off from Union Station on electioneering swings with a display of commitment which, if false, would have been disgracefully alien to his public character. Fortunately the world was not confined to Palestine. And in 1948 there were a lot of other things happening in it on which Truman and Marshall saw much more eye to eye than on the tangled story of the emergence of the State of Israel.

The London meeting of the Council of Foreign Ministers over the New Year of 1948, was the end of any serious attempt to govern Germany and fashion a peace treaty upon a four-power basis. No progress was made at this week-long conference on any of the outstanding points. The Western representatives severally rather than jointly decided that if they wanted to move Europe out of the morass they had to move without Russia. Bevin opened up with Marshall the prospect of 'some western democratic system' which could be a barrier against 'further Communist inroads'. Marshall was forthcoming but in a rather general way. In mid-January Bevin followed up this conversation with a much more precise memorandum, submitted through the British Embassy in Washington. He proposed to go ahead with the creation of Western Union, a treaty of mutual defence linking in the first instance Britain, France and the Benelux countries. Around this core a wider European grouping was envisaged, but it could have little military validity unless the United States was prepared to join. Marshall, who had already been advised that a regional defence pact under Article 51 of the UN Charter was a practical and internationally respectable way to proceed, was encouraging. 'The initiative which he (Bevin) is taking will be warmly applauded in the United States,' he wrote to Lord Inverchapel, the British Ambassador.

Thereafter events proceeded with an extraordinary momentum. Bevin got his Western Union treaty signed by March 17th. Six days earlier he had used the occasion of Soviet pressure on Norway to lay before the American Government an *aide-memoire* going considerably beyond the note of January 13th. 'Mr Bevin considers,' it ran, 'that the most effective course would be to take very early steps, before Norway goes under, to conclude under Article 51 of the Charter of the United Nations* a regional Atlantic Approaches Pact of Mutual Assistance, in which all the countries directly threatened by a Russian move to the Atlantic could participate . . .' Within 24 hours on March 12th Marshall responded with another of the handful of momentous statements in American diplomatic history: 'Please inform Mr Bevin that . . . we are prepared to proceed at once in the joint discussions on the establishment of an Atlantic security system.'

The rapid authority of this response would not have been possible without the coincidence of three factors. First there was the Secretary of State's confidence in the President's capacity for robust decision making. Second there was solid bipartisan support in the Senate for a forward position in Europe. When the 'Vandenberg Resolution', which gave general endorsement to the idea of an Article 51 military engagement, was put to the vote in April it was carried by 64 votes to 4. Third, and this made speed necessary as well as possible, there was a background of mounting menace in Europe. On February 25th there had been the Communist take-over of the Czech Government. On March 10th Jan Masaryk had been found dead on the flagstones of the Prague Foreign Ministry. During the same weeks, as plans developed for the setting-up of a West German government, there came the first sporadic signs of Soviet interference with Western military rail traffic to Berlin.

These events helped to concentrate many minds in Washington. Even so, the speed and firmness of decision making was prodigious by any standards. That spring the Marshall Aid appropriations were obtained from Congress. Truman came out with a demand for compulsory selective service accompanied by universal military training on a part-time basis. A clear decision was made within

---

* He had been well briefed about the direction of official thinking in Washington.

the administration that even though the Nationalist régime in China was declining into defeat, a strict limit should be set to the amount of bolstering support which it would receive from the United States. '. . . the costs of an all-out effort to see Communist forces resisted and destroyed in China would . . . be impossible to estimate,' Marshall stated. 'But the magnitude of the task and the probable costs thereof would clearly be out of all proportion to the results to be achieved.'[10] Europe was to have priority, even though this was to involve a lot of trouble for Truman with the China lobby. The 'bipartisanship' which lubricated US foreign policy in Europe did not extend to the Far East.

This priority expressed itself in the momentum with which the creation of NATO was carried forward; and the need for it was demonstrated when the sporadic harassment of the spring turned into the full Berlin blockade of the summer. On June 20th the new currency that was to be at once a cause and symbol of the *wirtschaftswünder* was bestowed by the allies upon West Germany. At first the deutschmark was not intended for Berlin. But when the Russians retaliated by introducing a new currency of their own into all sectors of the city, the allies re-retaliated by extending the D-mark to the three Western sectors. The next day, June 24th, a full blockade was imposed by the Russians.

Truman responded with a mixture of firmness and restraint. There were three possible courses. One was to give in, to allow Berlin to be strangled into the Soviet zone. The second was to send an armoured train up the railway track, or perhaps more plausibly, a fighting column up the *autobahn*, with orders that if necessary it should try to shoot its way through. The wisdom of this course depended upon a calculation that the Russians would climb down when confronted with the challenge of war. In the days when the Americans still, just, had a nuclear monopoly, it was not an obviously foolish course. It was advocated by General Clay, the American military commandant in Berlin, and some Air Force opinion (although not by the Joint Chiefs of Staff), as well as by Aneurin Bevan from within the British Cabinet. It clearly had its risks but it also offered the chance of a quick victory, attractive at any time but particularly so in an election year.

It was not however the course which Truman chose. He

preferred the third option of the airlift. That carried the risk that it might not work and the near certainty that it would involve months of hard slog. But it offered less of a flash-point of danger, it was in accordance with the weight of advice which he received, and it was best calculated to hold the allies together. The fact that Truman chose it is another example of his happy capacity to act more wisely than he often spoke or wrote.

All of these issues had to be faced with lonely courage rather than the gregarious self-confidence which comes with a back-drop of popular esteem. Personally and politically Truman suffered a wounding spring and summer. His rising ratings of 1947 proved to be a false dawn. A sharp plunge began that autumn. By April 1948, his Gallup approval rating was down to 36%, almost as low as in 1946. On February 17th the Democrats had suffered a sensational loss in a by-election in the Bronx, one of their safest seats; the victor was not a Republican but a supporter of Henry Wallace. This accompanied by serious sulking in the South made it look as though the Democratic Party under Truman's pilotage was losing both its left and its right wings. There were some who did not hesitate to point this out to him. Ickes wrote with a special venom: 'You have the choice of retiring voluntarily and with dignity, or of being driven out of office by a disillusioned and indignant citizenry. Have you ever seen the ice on a pond break in every conceivable direction under the rays of the warming spring sun? That is what has happened to the Democratic Party under you, except that your party has not responded to bright sunshine.'[11]

Meanwhile his own personal contribution was to get involved in two unfortunate controversies. A few people close to him (Edwin Pauley in a big way and General Wallace Graham, his doctor, in a small way) were exposed by the Senate Appropriations Committee as having engaged in commodity speculation, acting allegedly on inside knowledge. This might not have mattered too much had not Truman denounced such speculators in October as particularly heinous contributors to inflation. Still more controversially he decided to build a stone balcony between the second and third floors (in American parlance) on the south front of the White House. It was against the advice of the Commission of Fine Arts. It was regarded as presumptuous interference with a national monument by a peculiarly temporary and unaesthetic tenant. Apart from anything else it would involve the re-designing of twenty dollar bills. However Truman persisted in creating this 'monument to a Missouri mule' as it was sometimes called. The passage of time has tended to justify him in this, as in bigger things. It certainly improved the amenity of the White House, and probably the appearance too, for it got rid of the canvas awnings, which were always previously used in summer, and would look more cluttering today than they did in 1948. At the time, however, it seemed a singularly ill-judged enterprise for Truman to undertake in what was so widely assumed to be the last year of his presidency.

This was the background against which he formally announced his candidature on March 8th. At this stage at least it looked as though there was no direction in which he could go except up. That however proved an illusion. His declaration, so far from being steadying, coincided with the beginning of a widely-based but ill-considered 'draft Eisenhower' (and 'dump Truman') campaign which continued from then until the threshold of the Democratic Convention in mid-July.

It began, paradoxically, on the left of the party. During March and the first week of April two of the Roosevelt sons, several important labour leaders, both the (liberal) senators from Alabama (one of whom, Sparkman, was to be Adlai Stevenson's running mate in 1952) as well as the equally liberal Senator Pepper of Florida all issued anti-Truman and broadly pro-Eisenhower statements. Colonel Arvey, the effective boss of Chicago, joined in the chorus from a slightly different angle. The common keynote of the statements made them particularly wounding. It was not just that they preferred Eisenhower. They were all predicated on the view that Truman was incompetent, unappealing and unelectable. It was his duty to the party to withdraw. 'I hope (he) will not be a spite candidate like Henry Wallace' one of the labour leaders said. On April 12th, Americans for Democratic Action formally repudiated his candidature and urged one of Roosevelt's former dark horses, Justice William O. Douglas, as an alternative if Eisenhower would not run.

There is not the slightest indication that Truman was ever tempted towards withdrawal by these disavowals and appeals. Once he had got over his hesitations of 1946–7 it was the mule-like rather than the modest side of his character that was to the fore.

He privately denounced the liberals.* In public he mostly ignored them. He had come to a more realistic view of Eisenhower's intentions than they had: 'General Eisenhower, I am sure, is not a candidate for President', he wrote unusually temperately in a political letter at the end of April, 'and I don't think he would be a candidate on the Democratic ticket anyway – his whole family are Republicans and I know them all.'[12]

Eisenhower's behaviour in 1948, let alone 1952, fully bore out the truth of this statement. But still the extraordinary wave of liberal support for him rolled on. It was joined by two major tributaries: some of the most important machine politicians in the northern cities and the leaders of the disaffected South. As the General persistently said he had no intention of being a candidate he had no need to declare his position on any issue from civil rights to Taft-Hartley to farm support. All who wanted to get away from Truman could cluster under his branches.

As late as the first week of July, with the Convention opening on July 12th, a group, including in addition to those already mentioned, Hubert Humphrey, then Mayor of Minneapolis, Strom Thurmond, Governor of South Carolina and soon to be 'Dixiecrat' candidate against the ticket, two other southern governors, Chester Bowles, former head of Roosevelt and Truman's Wages and Prices Administration and successful aspirant to the governorship of Connecticut, Mayor O'Dwyer of New York City, and 'Boss' Hague of New Jersey, came together in a last minute appeal for the Convention to offer, and Eisenhower to accept, a draft. It was a remarkable coalition by any standards. Walter Reuther of the Automobile Workers, David Dubinsky of the International Ladies' Garment Workers, and Philip Murray of the CIO, had also been involved at earlier stages in moves for the promotion of the General and the demotion of the President.

On July 9th, in reply to a final ploy of Pepper's which was that he should be drafted by the Convention, not as a Democrat but as a 'national' candidate, Eisenhower issued a refusal sufficiently

---

* During the Convention itself, when he was unsuccessfully urging Douglas to accept the vice-presidential nomination, he wrote exasperately: 'I call him, tell him I'm doing what FDR did to me. He owes it to the country to accept. He belongs to that crowd of Tommy Corcoran, Harold Ickes, Claude Pepper crackpots whose word is worth less than Jimmy Roosevelt's . . . No professional liberal is intellectually honest . . . Most Roosevelts aren't either.' (*Private Papers*, p. 8)

comprehensive and categoric to bring everyone at last to their senses so far as he was concerned. Arvey and O'Dwyer, as 'pros', responded by immediately endorsing Truman. Pepper responded by announcing his own candidature, which lasted for little more than 24 hours. The chairman of ADA responded by trying to launch Douglas. Douglas killed that on the Sunday (July 11th). On the Monday he killed Truman's attempt to get him to accept the vice-presidential nomination. 'I can't be a No. 2 man to a No. 2 man,' he was reported to have said.[13] On the Tuesday there was a brief 'Barkley for President' boomlet; he had made a notable keynote speech on the previous night, and it still did not take much to set some people flapping towards anyone but Truman. On the Wednesday Truman himself, having disposed of Barkley by getting him to accept the vice-presidential nomination, for which it was alleged that he had been angling at every Convention since 1928, made the short train journey to Philadelphia and arrived at 30th Street Station 'in the rain at 9.15,' as he recorded. Margaret Truman put it more graphically: 'Philadelphia on that night of July 14th seemed to be wrapped in a huge suffocating blanket of heat and humidity.'[14]

It was nearly five hours before he could make his acceptance speech. This was because of the general incompetence with which this despondent Convention was run rather than because of any particular difficulty at this stage over his nomination or that of Barkley. His dangerous rivals had eliminated themselves. Irwin Ross, the authoritative chronicler of the 1948 campaign,* thinks that even had Eisenhower entered the contest, the sundering of his totally disparate coalition, which must have followed from a declaration of his position on civil rights, would probably just have given Truman the edge. But it would at best have been a very close run thing. As it was Truman cantered to a formal victory, with 947½ votes to 263† for Senator Russell of Georgia, who, as an anti-civil rights candidate had a strictly limited constituency, the more so as Mississippi and Alabama had already walked out of the Convention.

Truman's nomination was not then made unanimous as was customary. Rayburn, in the chair, although pro-Truman, could

* *The Loneliest Campaign*, published in 1968.
† An ex-governor of Indiana got a half vote.

not risk it. The South was too adamant, and had been made more so by the main excitement of the Convention, which had occurred earlier that day. The liberals, deprived of Eisenhower, compensated with an amendment for a stronger civil rights commitment, moved by Hubert Humphrey, and carried against the platform by 651½ votes to 582½. The Truman forces–McGrath, Clifford, Niles, the Missouri delegation – had all been against the amendment, so it was perhaps a little hard of the South to deny him the unanimity which they had always given to Roosevelt and which they gave to Barkley on this occasion. His daughter suggests that he had already said enough and that they (Thurmond at least) paid him the compliment of believing that, unlike Roosevelt, he meant what he said on the issue.

The absence of unanimity was however the last of the series of insults which the Democratic Party had been delivering to Truman. His speech, to a packed audience in a foetid convention hall in the middle of the night, was a remarkable success. He used his new technique, which he had been developing under advice since early May, of speaking not from a text, of which his reading was always deadening, but from a series of headings. These left room for improvisation and animation, and the fact that they gave a certain staccato quality to his speaking suited his style:

'Senator Barkley and I will win this election and make the Republicans like it – don't you forget it. We will do that because they are wrong and we are right.'[15]

The lash was almost as harsh on the shoulders of the somnolent, warring, defeatist delegates as on the despised Republican Party 'of special privilege'. It was not a visionary general offering his legions new frontiers or a freedom from fear. It was a sergeant-major telling his squad to get off their backsides. It worked rather well. They sat up. They listened. They cheered. For a moment they almost thought they might win.

Truman had one skilful ploy in his speech. The Republicans meeting in the same hall three weeks before, had adopted a liberal candidate and a notably liberal platform, substantially at odds with the record of the 80th Congress. If Truman was going to make a success of his strategy of portraying them as a party of reactionary ogres he had to expose the contradiction and keep that Congress to the fore. So he announced that he was using his presidential powers to summon it back for a special fifteen day session on July 26th. During these fifteen days he invited the Congress to do a good four years' work: to deal with rising prices, the housing problem, education, civil rights, and to provide for an increased minimum wage, a national health programme and extended social security benefits. He topped off this extravagant ice-cream sundae of satirical propaganda by offering a ready-made disparaging nickname for the special session. July 26th, he said, was called 'Turnip Day' in Missouri. A local jingle advised people to 'sow your turnips wet or dry' about then, but most of the few who knew it thought it referred to the 25th rather than the 26th.

However both the name and the idea served their purposes. It was a fairly outrageous use of executive powers which produced predictably exaggerated howls of execration from the other side. 'Never in the history of American politics has a Chief Executive stooped so low,' pontificated Senator Brooks of Illinois. The ploy was good, rather undignified, partisan propaganda. However, Truman was not running on non-partisan dignity. He left that to Governor Dewey, the young statesman, still well under fifty, again as in 1944 the Republican candidate.

Dewey had to fight harder for the nomination in 1948 than in 1944. It was regarded as a much more worthwhile prize, an almost certain key to the White House. He had two serious rivals. Robert A. Taft of Ohio, son of a president, effective party leader in the Senate, disdainful of the tricks of political packaging but widely respected and even revered, the core and conscience of the Republican Party; and Harold Stassen of Minnesota who had made himself something of a boy wonder as a successful governor in his early thirties, who was as liberal and internationalist as Dewey, over whom he physically towered, and a great deal more genial.

However, Dewey, whatever he lacked in warmth and stature, had a beautifully oiled machine and once he had decisively beaten Stassen in the Oregon primary, both in debate and votes, looked the favourite, although not irresistibly so. He was ahead on the first two ballots and won on a landslide on the third. Earl Warren, Governor of California and future Chief Justice, was unanimously chosen as vice-presidential candidate. The Convention was one of the best organized in American history. There was enough uncertainty to create interest, but not enough bitterness to leave dangerous wounds. Few doubted that it was a prelude to victory. The ticket, with New York and California, was excellently balanced geographically, much better than the Democratic one with Missouri and Kentucky. But it was not balanced ideologically. Warren was as liberal as Dewey. He was also as bland.* However there was nowhere else for right-wing Republicans to go. The strain on their loyalties did not begin to approach that needed for a break. The ideological splits and the prospects of the erosion of votes were all within the Democratic Party.

Dewey behaved throughout the campaign with dignity and decency. He also behaved with complacency. He was totally dedicated to being President, but at least equally dedicated to being a good one. He was uninterested in collecting cheap plaudits or scoring demagogic points on the way. This was the good side of his somewhat cold personality. If it was true, as a New York Republican lady was reputed to have said, that it was difficult to decide which was the chillier experience, having Tom Dewey ignore you or shake you by the hand, it was also true that he was intellectually honest and rarely stooped to conquer.† His most brazen demagogic point during the 1948 campaign was to claim that the Republicans would not have to spend a lot of time and money rooting Communists out of the government because they would not have them in in the first place. This elipsis apart, his pronouncements on how to deal with internal Communism were impeccable ('You can't shoot ideas with a gun' 'We will not jail anybody for what he thinks or believes'), and a model which his successors would have done well to follow. The principal lesson which he drew from his 1944 joust with Roosevelt was that he did better when he behaved as a statesman and worse when,

---

* This blandness (which did not repeat itself in his firm and courageous Supreme Court judgments nearly twenty years later) perhaps reached its epitome in his speech at Charleston, West Virginia, on October 5th, with its engaging image of a beneficent traffic policeman directing the economy: 'The little jeeps of small business should have a chance to keep moving, just as well as the ten-ton trucks of big business.' Watch needed, however, to be kept on 'the economic road hog'. (Ross, op. cit. p. 210)

† Mrs Longworth (Alice Roosevelt, the daughter of the 26th President) who was credited with the remark that he was like the bridegroom on the wedding cake, would no doubt have thought that he could not stoop without disappearing from sight.

exceptionally, he took the low road, notably in a vituperative Oklahoma City speech.*

With this experience behind him, with his confidence bolstered by every poll and every editorial writer, the choice between stooping and conquering never seriously presented itself to him. All he needed to do was to avoid gaffes and remain securely ahead. He made few gaffes. He appeared to remain securely ahead. He behaved like an incumbent president and never mentioned Truman's name. In the words of one reporter he rarely left 'a high road of rich baritone homilies'.† Truman naturally and happily fell into the inverted role of the challenger. But he was not running against Dewey any more than Dewey was running against him. He was running against a mixture of the 80th Congress and the reactionary aspects, real and imaginary, of the Republican tradition. As a result the two main candidates of the 1948 campaign were, for different reasons, like darkened ships which passed in the night without recognition or engagement.

Dewey's confidence was not based exclusively upon the polls. These were not in fact as annihilating of Truman as is commonly assumed in retrospect. The Roper Poll, which had achieved an impressive record for accuracy in the later Roosevelt elections, gave Dewey 46.3% against 31.5% for Truman in early August. Gallup at approximately the same date gave Dewey a lead of 48% to 37%. On September 9th Roper (on material collected in August) showed Dewey still leading by 44.2% to 31.4% and foolishly announced that he was giving up polling as the issue was so far beyond doubt. But on September 24th Gallup only gave Dewey 46.5% against 39% for Truman. On the eve of the election Gallup had narrowed the gap to 49.5% over 44.5%, and the Crossley Poll confirmed this with 49.9% against 44.8%. While Dewey was never out of the lead, these later figures, particularly when seen against the big movement since August, do not now look like a solid basis for certainty.

They were however buttressed by other considerations. It looked as though Truman would be still weaker in the Electoral

---

* 'Shall we expose our country to a return of the seven years of New Deal depression because my opponent is indispensable to the ill-assorted power-hungry conglomeration of city bosses, Communists and career bureaucrats who now compose the New Deal,' he had there said of Roosevelt. (I. Ross, *op. cit.* p. 47)

† Edwin A. Lahey of the *Chicago Daily News*, quoted in Ross, *op. cit.* p. 216.

College than in the popular vote. While they might not do a great
deal for themselves, Thurmond and Wallace would surely at least
have this effect. Thurmond would rob him of a part of the hitherto
solid South, and Wallace would make it impossible for him to
carry some of the populous northern states, most notably New
York, which had been safely in the Roosevelt column. In fact both
these things happened: Thurmond won in Mississippi, Alabama,
Louisiana and South Carolina and the Wallace vote demonstrably
robbed Truman of New York, Michigan and Maryland. But
Truman, even though he also lost Pennsylvania and New Jersey,
which had been for Roosevelt in all his four elections, was able to
ride these defeats.

In addition there was the low repute of the President, the low
morale of the Democratic Party (most of them thought they were
fighting to hold governorships and Congressional seats, with no
hope of the White House), and the crippling shortage of funds
which went with this. Truman was sometimes cut off the air
before he had finished a broadcast speech because there was no
money with which to pay for a little extra time. In Oklahoma
City, at the end of September, Margaret Truman says that they
did not have enough money 'to get the train out of the station'
without an on the spot fund-raising effort.[16]

Against all the evidence Truman pretended from the beginning
that he would win. Whether he believed this in August and
September is impossible to say. His letters and private writings are
silent upon the point. The pretence had to be complete. What can
be authenticated, however, is that for the last three weeks of the
campaign he was operating on a basis of genuine and (as it turned
out) accurately based confidence. On October 13th, as the campaign train steamed south through eastern Minnesota, he sat with
George Elsey at the dining table and wrote out a state-by-state
prediction. It was about 85% accurate, with most of the errors on
the side of optimism. He gave himself 340 electoral votes; he got
303. He gave Dewey 108; Dewey got 189.

Truman campaigned harder than Dewey. He did it almost all
by train, and depended essentially on direct contact with the
electorate and short speeches from the rear platform. Television
was still of negligible importance, the number of his radio broad-
casts was limited by money (his voice was not very good for that
medium in any event) and although he occasionally addressed large

rallies – 23,000 in Chicago, 12,000 in Philadelphia – these set-piece occasions, unlike the Roosevelt practice, were not the core of the campaign.

He did no journey by aeroplane. The train was quite an elaborate affair of sixteen coaches. Truman travelled in the rear car, which had been specially built for Roosevelt and contained bedrooms, bathrooms, kitchen, dining-room and sitting-room. Next was a dining car converted into a suite of offices for his staff. Then came a newsroom, then a signal corps car, followed by sleeping and living accommodation for all the assorted personnel, including about sixty journalists and photographers.

After a short Labor Day foray into Michigan the first main trip began on September 18th and ended fifteen days later. He covered eighteen states, out to San Francisco by Chicago, Iowa and the mountain states, down to Los Angeles, through the sunbelt and back by St Louis. He worked himself very hard, starting at 5.45 a.m. on his first full day and making his last appearance at 8.10 p.m. On some days he made as many as sixteen speeches. 'Truman was at his best,' Irwin Ross wrote, 'in his whistle-stop appearances.' Mr Ross also gives us a succinct account of the shape of his speeches on such occasions:

> 'Truman's impromptu talks held to no set sequence, but they usually contained the same ingredients: a plug for the Democratic candidate for Congress or the Senate, a passing reference to the local college or baseball team (sometimes only the local weather was worthy of note), a brief exposition of some problem of local or national concern (housing, farm price supports, public power) which the Republicans had managed to muck up, and a plea for his audience to register and vote. The final turn in his routine was to introduce his wife and daughter. "And now I would like you to meet Mrs Truman," he would say, at which point the blue velvet curtain behind him would part and the First Lady would appear to smile at the crowd. "And now my daughter Margaret," or in southern states "Miss Margaret" . . . Crowds were large, curious, good-natured, but not especially enthusiastic.'[17]

Reporters who made the trip found it very difficult to estimate whether Truman was gaining votes. The crowds were certainly friendly, but were they convinced? What did they make of the contrast between the hyperbole of his language in denouncing the Republicans and the flat folksiness of his delivery? Did they find his appeals to them to keep him in the White House so that he might not suffer 'from a housing shortage on January 20th, 1949' as embarrassing as did most of the members of his staff? Did they find him lacking in dignity for a president or agreeably close to their interests and style? Would they rather have been listening to one of Dewey's carefully prepared set-piece orations, dealing in sonorous depth with a single major topic? All of these questions remained unanswered when the train got back to Washington on October 2nd. But one thing was already certain. The election was probably lost, but the campaign was not a flop. Three million people had turned out to see him. They appeared to have enjoyed listening to him. He had enjoyed talking to them. There would be no problem of his maintaining his morale until November 2nd.

Truman next set out on his travels on October 6th. He then did a three-day tour of Delaware, Pennsylvania, New Jersey and up-state New York. The crowds had become very big, and the President was reported as being in crackling form throughout. The limited importance of either of these considerations is however underlined by the fact that Truman succeeded in losing all four of the 'Roosevelt' states covered by this expedition.

On the last day of this trip the news of the aborted 'Vinson mission' to Moscow had broken. This was, to say the least, amateurishly handled. At the end of his transcontinental journey Truman was persuaded by two of his speech-writers that it would be good politics, and maybe good diplomacy too, to send the Chief Justice on a special peace mission to Stalin. It was a gesture rather than a negotiation which was planned, for it was never clear what Vinson was intended to say when he got to Moscow, and he had little foreign policy experience and no personal *entrée* to the Russians. However it could be argued that with tension high over Berlin and all the traditional channels of negotiation clogged, such a public display of America's desire for a peaceful solution might remove some part of Russian suspicion.

Clearly however it required careful consideration with the Secretary of State. Marshall was in Paris where he had just agreed with the British and French foreign ministers that there was no point in further seeking direct negotiation with the Russians on

Berlin, and that the three Western powers should rather jointly submit the issue to the Security Council. Marshall was therefore bound to be against the Vinson proposal. Truman however did not bother to discover this before he had, first, persuaded a reluctant Vinson that it was his duty to perform the mission, and, second, had told Charles Ross to negotiate with the broadcasting networks for a half hour of 'non-political' time for the evening of Tuesday, October 5th. Not unnaturally, in the middle of an election, they asked what the presidential speech was to be about. Ross told them 'in confidence'.

It was only at this stage that Truman telephoned Marshall in Paris. Marshall spoke faithfully. At the end of the conversation Truman went back and told his disconcerted staff that, election or no election, the enterprise was off. This has sometimes been presented as the supreme example of Truman's attachment to responsibility rather than votes in matters of foreign policy. Certainly it makes an interesting contrast with his dealings with Marshall over the recognition of Israel five months previously. But it could also be presented as an example of his ill-considered rashness when he was operating more or less on his own and before he was brought up against the likely consequences of his actions.

Inevitably, of course, the 'confidential' discussions with the broadcasting companies leaked, and Truman came near to getting the worst of both worlds. He had no vote-winning peace mission, but he was portrayed as having sought to play politics with major issues of national security. There was general dismay around him, but he himself treated the matter with some equanimity. He thought that there might be advantages in appearing as a man of peace who had nonetheless subordinated his instincts (and his need for votes) to the imperatives of General Marshall's orderly foreign policy. This was not a position compatible with high presidential authority, and could not conceivably have been held to be helpful had he been running as an unruffled incumbent. But as he and Dewey had spontaneously reversed roles, leaving the President to be the cheeky challenger, he was possibly right in hoping that the incident had done him little harm. And he was almost certainly right in thinking that Dewey's principal campaign gaffe, made a week later, was more damaging with the public, because it was much less sympathetic. In rural Illinois, where the Governor of

New York was making one of his relatively rare back platform appearances, the train suddenly moved a few feet into the crowd during the speech. Dewey snarled with ill-humour: 'That's the first lunatic I've had for an engineer. He probably ought to be shot.' The words do not sound too serious, but they were enough to move a lot of public sympathy from the imperious little candidate to the engine driver, and Truman subsequently kept the incident skilfully on the boil.

For the last three weeks of the campaign Truman concentrated on the eastern half of the continent. Some of it proved to be stony ground for him, and the foundations of his success came from the West (beyond the Mississippi Dewey carried only Nebraska and Oregon), but the broad tactic was nonetheless right for it enabled him to make a major impact on two of the three most marginal states which were crucial to victory: Ohio and Illinois. His October 10th to 16th trip was particularly productive. Not only did he cover these two states but also three others – Wisconsin, Minnesota and West Virginia – which he won fairly comfortably. Then he went to Miami for the convention of the American Legion, where he gave a good explanation of his Vinson initiative. Then he had a day in Pennsylvania, which he failed to sway, even though he made one of his most successful anti-Dewey speeches in Pittsburgh.

On Sunday evening, October 24th, he left Washington for what most of those around him still thought was the last time before another president was elected. He went to Chicago (another visit to Illinois), Cleveland (another visit to Ohio), Boston (the centre of one of the only two north-eastern states that he carried), New York (a predictable waste of effort in view of the strength there of Dewey and Wallace, but obligatory), and then home to St Louis and Independence. In Harlem, on the Friday before the poll he made his only civil rights speech of the campaign. In Madison Square Garden the previous evening he had made his strongest commitment to Israel and claimed full credit for the United States victory in the race to recognize. Everywhere he continued to berate the Republicans without much respect for restraint or even truth. In Chicago he appeared to compare Dewey to Hitler as a tool of reactionary big business interests. In Boston he boxed the compass and denounced him as being the one the Communists wanted to win. It was however all done with considerable good humour.

Even his prepared big city rally speeches were by this stage interlaced with successful passages of mocking raillery.

Truman's last meeting was in St Louis on the Saturday evening. Then he went to Independence and eschewed campaigning for the last two days. He had travelled 21,928 miles and delivered 275 speeches.[18] On the Tuesday he voted in the Independence Memorial Hall, before attending a luncheon for about thirty old friends given by the Mayor at the Rockwood Country Club. He reminisced about Missouri politics in a relaxed and expansive mood. Then he left, unaccompanied by anyone other than three Secret Service agents, and drove secretly to a hotel in Excelsior Springs, a small resort thirty miles north-east of Kansas City. There he had a Turkish bath, a sandwich and a glass of milk and went to bed and to sleep early in the evening.

At midnight he awoke and listened to the radio for a few minutes. He was a little ahead in the popular vote, but was still predicted to lose. At 4.00 a.m. he was awake again, to be greeted by the news that Ohio, Illinois and California had been left holding the balance and that he had already won Illinois. He decided that that was it, had a harder drink than milk, and motored to the Muehlebach Hotel in Kansas City, where his staff were installed and where he arrived in dapper condition at 6.00 a.m. He had to wait another four hours for Dewey's concession. This was not due to any ill-grace on Dewey's part (indeed his concessionary press conference was one of the most gracious of his career) but to the fact that he had gone to bed very late, with the issue still unresolved, but with his hopes draining away as fast as his disappointed supporters were leaving the ballroom of the Roosevelt Hotel in New York City, and had not awakened until 10.30 a.m.

That evening Truman attended an informal impromptu celebration of 40,000 people in Independence, and on the following day took the train back to Washington. At St Louis, where there was a huge crowd at the station, he held up the famous Wednesday morning edition of the *Chicago Tribune*, with the headline 'Dewey defeats Truman'. In Washington there was more than a solitary Dean Acheson to greet him on the railroad platform. 'Barkley and I must have shaken hands with at least five or six hundred – some of them johnnie come lately boys,' he did not fail to note. (He felt the same way about $750,000 in back-dated cheques which Louis Johnson received for campaign funds after the result.) However it was all highly satisfactory after the troughs which Truman had been through, and the crowds which greeted him between Union Station and the White House were immense and enthusiastic. There were only two immediate snags. The first was that Bess Truman had a bad sore throat, and that the President had to be up at 3.00 a.m. administering medicine to her on the night after his return. The second was that the White House was falling down. It was already propped up inside like a mine working, and immediate arrangements had to be made for a move across the street to Blair House, which was expected to be for ten months but in fact extended to forty. First, however, he was able to get away to his beloved submarine base at Key West for two weeks.

How did this spectacular and unexpected victory occur? To take a downbeat aspect first, it was achieved on a very low poll. Only 51% of the electorate voted. That probably favoured the Democratic Party, which was somewhat better organized at local level, although certainly not better funded at national level. On the popular vote Truman was significantly although not magnificently ahead. He had a lead over Dewey of 4½%, which would be equivalent in a British constituency election to a majority of about 2,500. He just failed – by 0.4% – to get over half of the votes cast, but he compensated for this by keeping Dewey to a slightly lower percentage of the total than he had achieved against Roosevelt in 1944. Truman had to contend with Wallace and Thurmond, which Roosevelt never had to do.★ Thurmond polled nearly 1,200,000, just over 2%, and because he was geographically concentrated got nearly 8% of the votes in the Electoral College. Wallace did a shade worse, more or less up to expectations in New York, from which state he got nearly a half of his national total, but was badly down in California, thought to be his other pillar. Geographically unconcentrated, however, he got no votes in the Electoral College.

Even without his 50%, Truman nonetheless gained a higher percentage than any British Prime Minister since the war, over 7 points more than Mrs Thatcher in 1983; 2 points more than Lord Wilson in 1966, half a point more than Lord Attlee in 1945.

★ Samuel Lubell, a notable political commentator of the period, argued however that on balance both these candidatures helped Truman. Wallace took the Communist curse off him and strengthened his position with right wing Democrats, particularly Catholics. Thurmond helped him with the black vote. Lubell's *The Future of American Politics* was published in 1952.

Nonetheless his result, under the Electoral College system, could have been easily overturned, or at least put into the House of Representatives. It was not dissimilar from the Kennedy result in 1960, although his popular majority was greater. Truman carried Ohio by only 7,000 and California by 17,000. A switch of 12,000 votes in these two states would therefore have left the House to decide. In Illinois the majority was only 33,000. A switch of another 17,000 there would have given Dewey an absolute victory. In a poll of nearly 50 million a well distributed shift of 29,000 votes, just over .05 per cent of the total, could have produced a reversal.

Truman immediately attributed his triumph to union support 'Labor did it', he was reported by the *New York Times* as having said on the morning after. It is certainly true that in spite of the upsets of 1946 the leaders of both the AFL and CIO worked far more committedly in that campaign than they ever had before, and probably carried most of their members with them; only the ever-aberrant John L. Lewis, flanked this time by Alvanley Johnston, were for Dewey. They also provided the necessary money and foci of organization for his campaign. Several of his most successful major rallies were labour-sponsored. Yet, when all that is said, to suggest that a candidate who lost in Michigan, New York and Pennsylvania was carried to victory on the backs of the union leaders is verging on the fanciful. It was much more the farmers who 'did it'. This was certainly Dewey's view, and it was substantially borne out by Truman's remarkable string of successes across the Middle West, the mountain states and the Pacific. For a Missouri Democrat to carry Kansas suggested that something was stirring deep in the farm belt. One cause was a fall in the price of corn from $2.25 a barrel in July 1948 to $1.26 in October. It was not dissimilar to the 1921 decline. Then it bank-rupted Truman. In 1948 it was a major factor in keeping him in the White House. It was a triumph of his campaign that this collapse was blamed not on the incumbent president, but on the outgoing Congress and the candidate who was tarred with their brush.

Truman also did well, but by no means sensationally so, amongst blacks. Most did not vote at all, but of those who did twice as many were for Truman as were for Dewey. In the big cities Truman maintained the traditional Democratic majority, but substantially less strongly than had Roosevelt. The best summing up seems to be that he held together, on a declining asset basis, the traditional Roosevelt coalition, sustained it with a special injection of farm votes, and was fortified by an over-confident Dewey campaign which discouraged marginal Republican supporters from voting.

However achieved, it was a famous victory. As Mrs Truman, through her sore throat, told the White House assistant usher on the morning after their return to Washington: 'It looks like you're going to have to put up with us for another four years.'[19] There was also going to be a great deal with which Truman himself, and vicariously Mrs Truman, would have to put up during that forthcoming four years.

9

THE LIMITATIONS OF
VICTORY

Just as defeat in the mid-term elections of 1946 had liberated
Truman in his own mind from the shadow of Roosevelt's splen-
diferous personality, so his much more important victory in 1948
gave him a new freedom in the minds of most of his countrymen
both from this formidable shadow and from the limitations of his
own occasionally jejune impact. He had joined a small company
of three presidents who had succeeded through death and subsequently been re-elected in their own right. Theodore Roosevelt
was the first predecessor, Calvin Coolidge the second. Truman
could no longer be regarded as a president simply of chance and
gaffes.

This gave him no immunity from criticism. But no president
including Washington and Jefferson has ever approached such
immunity. Lincoln and Franklin Roosevelt, to cite the other two
(with Washington and Jefferson) now most commonly regarded
as in the first league, were peculiarly far away from it.

Roosevelt, by virtue of the beneficent power of the United
States when Hitler menaced the world, approached immunity
internationally, but not internally. Lincoln, on the other hand,
signally failed to achieve it either abroad or at home. The London
Times under one of its most distinguished editors (Delane) accomplished the considerable feat of describing the Gettysburg
Address as 'rendering ludicrous' what might otherwise have been
an impressive ceremony of dedication. Nor, beset by the relentless
ambition to replace him of his Secretary of the Treasury, Salmon
P. Chase, and by his own capacity for selecting incompetent
generals, did he stand high internally until victory for the Union
was manifestly within his grasp. The American democracy has

many qualities, but appreciating great presidents during their terms of office is not amongst them.

It should therefore be no surprise that, while Truman's election was recognized as remarkable, it gave him no guarantee of four years of unchallenged authority. Even before his inauguration on January 20th, 1949, there had been two precursors of the troubles of the second term. In December 1948, Alger Hiss, a State Department official who as a young man of promise had occupied junior but central posts, had been indicted for perjury in denying that he had passed classified documents to a Communist agent. During the same late autumn it became obvious that the Chiang Kai-Shek régime would be driven out of mainland China. Those who wished to oppose the administration said that this was due to supineness in Washington. Those who wished to support the administration thought it was an inevitable result of the corruption and inefficiency of the Kuomintang. It opened a great foreign policy divide in American politics. Towards Europe there was an adequate community of approach. Towards the Far East there was no such thing. Vandenberg's health was declining. (He died in April 1951.) The China Lobby was rising. Truman was to have more foreign policy trouble at home during the second term than during the first.

Acheson replaced Marshall as Secretary of State because of the latter's kidney complaint on January 7th, two weeks before the Inauguration. For all his fine creative qualities of mind, and total ability to defend himself in any forum, Acheson's return probably exacerbated rather than calmed the incipient political conflict. His coruscating confidence was sometimes a liability with the Congress. It in no way prevented his getting on with Truman (of whose presidential prerogatives he was always very respectful) or with his most important foreign colleague, Ernest Bevin (although Bevin and Truman could not get on with each other). But it seemed too much of an arrogantly carried emblem of the liberal Eastern foreign policy establishment to endear him to many members of the Senate or the House.

As the second term wore on and as McCarthyite populism achieved its formidable if short-lived wave of success, Acheson became a red rag to the red-baiters. But his provocation was splendidly done. It began with his examination for confirmation before the Senate Foreign Relations Committee. When asked about

his relationship with Hiss, which in fact was not particularly close
– it was so with Hiss's brother – he replied that his 'friendship was
not easily given nor easily withdrawn'. Nor was he then going 'to
abandon (Hiss) and throw rocks when he was in trouble'. This
created some consternation, but Vandenberg was still there to find
a way round. Acheson agreed to balance it with the publication of
a statement (in fact drafted by Vandenberg) saying that he abhorred
Communism – and no doubt sin too. That for the moment was
enough to get him a unanimous favourable recommendation from
the committee, and confirmation by the whole Senate on a vote
of 83 to 6. But Vandenberg was not going to be there for long,
and the 6 (all Republicans) were a cloud bigger than a man's hand,
particularly as they voted adversely mainly because of China, about
which Acheson was most vulnerable and knew least.

The inauguration was a more spirited affair than the one at which
Truman had previously been sworn in. Roosevelt endured a tired
acceptance of his fourth mandate on a sodden White House lawn
in 1945. Truman was not tired. Indeed he began the day with a
seven o'clock breakfast with 98 surviving members of Battery D
and their wives. Nor was he blasé about the proceedings. 1945
was Roosevelt's fourth inauguration. 1949 was Truman's first, and
he already had a pretty clear idea in his own mind that it would
be his last as well. Furthermore there was quite a lot of money to
spend. The 80th and Republican House of Representatives had felt
little doubt that Dewey would be elected. They had generously
voted an exceptionally large sum for his inauguration. Liberation
from 16 years of Democratic rule would have been worth celebrat-
ing. They had also put up the President's salary from $50,000 to
$100,000 and added $50,000 of tax-free expenses.

Truman was the beneficiary of these premature Republican
eleemosynary acts. The $150,000 of income (equivalent to about
$¾ million today) enabled him to live more easily than ever before.
The $80,000 voted for the inauguration enabled him to mount a
procession alleged to be seven miles long. 'The weather . . . was
perfect,' Margaret Truman recorded, 'very cold, but with bright
winter sunlight pouring down from a clear blue sky.'[1] The White
House was closed and the post oath-taking reception had therefore
to be held in Mellon's National Gallery. To compensate for this
there was no hated rival with whom Truman had to do an un-

comfortable 1½ mile drive along Pennsylvania Avenue. There was only old Alben Barkley. But they both put on their theatrical costumiers top hats and cutaway coats as though they were Harvard Overseers on Commencement Day rather than Missouri and Kentucky politicians.

At the Capitol Truman delivered an address of little oratorical distinction but considerable substance. He laid down the four cardinal points of American foreign policy. The first was support for the United Nations; the second was the use of Marshall Aid to achieve the recovery of Western Europe; the third was the provision of military assistance to sustain 'freedom-loving nations' against the threat of Soviet aggression; and the fourth, the surprise one, announced a new programme for assistance to the underdeveloped world. This was christened Point Four (by the press, not by Truman) and was the beginning of Third World Aid. The inaugural speech was almost entirely devoted to international issues. National ones had been dealt with in the State of the Union message on January 5th.

Then he had provided his own label, having himself written a commitment to a 'Fair Deal' into the draft speech. The domestic programme he outlined put more emphasis on social measures, as opposed to those for economic recovery, than Roosevelt's New Deal had done. The post-war economy was in good shape and could largely be left to look after itself. By dint of heavy military cutbacks behind the shield of the solitary possession of the atomic bomb, Truman's first term had been broadly one of balanced budgets. This financial probity, which was sensible enough when the economy called for no deficit stimulus, he hoped to continue and even intensify in the second term, in spite of proposals for Federal health insurance, increased Federal aid to education and a major public housing programme. There were also proposals with no spending implications. The Taft-Hartley Act was to be replaced and civil rights legislated upon.

Remarkably little of this programme was to be achieved. The budget balance was to be undermined, first by the end of the United States nuclear monopoly, and then, more powerfully in the short-term, by the Korean War. And the 81st Congress was too dependent for its Democratic majority upon conservative Southerners, many of whom held committee chairmanships, for it to show much appetite for liberal legislation. By November

1949, Truman was complaining to his diary: 'Trying to make the 81st Congress perform is and has been worse than cussing the 80th.'[2]

Domestic blockage mattered less to the world, and probably to Truman himself, than foreign policy blockage would have done at the time. Internationally, in spite of the China fissure, McCarthy's antics and MacArthur's insubordination, the President was able to command policy for most of the second term. The first six months were particularly productive. The North Atlantic Treaty was signed in April and the Berlin blockade came to an end in May.

The latter event was a major victory for Western patience and non-provocative firmness. It was the first turning of a tide which, in spite of the presumed power of nuclear supremacy, had flowed relentlessly in favour of the Soviet Union throughout 1947 and 1948. It created a special bond between the United States and the emerging Federal Republic of Germany, popular as well as official, which was to be an unvarying factor in world politics for the next 25 years (but no longer). It also presaged a new, unacknowledged, but real stability in East-West relations on the central front which was to persist until the renewal of Soviet probings, first in Berlin again, and then in Cuba, in the early 1960s. The brinkmanship of the Dulles era was around the periphery, not in the more dangerous centre.

The creation of N A T O was essential to this new stability in Europe. Looked at from any perspective it was one of the most remarkable feats of international political engineering of modern history. It was all put together in little more than a year, and that year was bisected by the election of November 1948, which the incumbent President, as we have seen, was almost unanimously expected to lose. Twelve founder members signed. But the United States was not just one of a dozen. In the late 1940s and for most of the next two decades, but not in the 1970s, its power was not merely pre-eminent: it was qualitatively different and overwhelming. And the United States, from this solar position, had to make by far the greatest contribution in terms both of resources and of sacrifice of tradition.

The fact that a major political act, which is normally slow and messy, was performed with the speed and precision of a surgeon is a tribute to the leadership which the Western world then enjoyed. Bevin was the impresario, but Truman had to provide the commitment, and he did so with an unfussy resolution which practically no other president could have rivalled.

Although twelve countries signed the treaty (another four have since joined), it was effectively made by five: the United States, Britain, Canada, Belgium and the Netherlands. France had not then developed Gaullist detachment, but was more interested in immediate American military supplies than in wider or longer-term aims. The French Government did however perform the considerable service of insisting on having Italy in. There had been considerable doubts about this. The objection was not that she was an ex-enemy but that she was Mediterranean rather than Atlantic. These doubts had been seriously felt by Truman himself. However the French convinced Acheson, and Acheson convinced Truman. Exclusion would have been a disaster for Italy and a major misfortune for the Alliance.

The Treaty was signed in Washington on April 4th, 1949. The celebratory dinner had to be held in the Carlton Hotel. The White House was still closed, and Blair House was not big enough. But the value of the Treaty was not diminished by the substitute nature of the surroundings. It contained the Soviet threat to Western Europe. The position never again looked as menacing as it had done in 1947–8 when Berlin was beleaguered and the Communist parties in France and Italy seemed poised for a takeover. It maintained peace for a generation on the central front, which was the most dangerous for it was there that the armies and influence of the super-powers were in immediate juxtaposition. If Truman had created nothing else in his second term, NATO would have justified his re-election.

It can of course be argued that with Dewey we would have got just as effective a NATO, and a less sour Republican Party, because they were not completing twenty years of exclusion from office, and consequently a greater immunity to McCarthyism. Maybe. Maybe Seward would have waged the Civil War more effectively than Lincoln. Maybe if Roosevelt had not broken convention and gone for a third term and James A. Farley or one of the other aspirants had seized the crown, the war would have been at least as quickly won and the alternative president would have been more skilled and less tired in dealing with Stalin at Yalta. Maybe if Halifax had become Prime Minister instead of Churchill in 1940 (as he so nearly did) Hitler would have been still more resolutely opposed and Britain's resources less exhausted at the end. No hypothesis which was not put to the test can be retrospectively proved to be wrong. They do not however carry great plausibility. Perhaps the Dewey one has a little more than the others. But the fact remains that under Truman's presidency NATO was created with remarkable speed, vision and determination, and that he deserves full credit for it.

The Senate ratified the Treaty by 82 votes to 13 (with Taft at the head of the minority) in July. Together with the ending of the Berlin blockade on May 12th and the creation of the Federal Republic of Germany (the Basic Law was passed on May 8th and the first elections were held in August) and satisfactory progress within O E E C for the implementation of the Marshall Plan, it was a summer of considerable achievement in Europe. On the other side of the world United States troops, apart from a few advisory specialists, were withdrawn in late June and without much attention from the southern part of the little-known Korean peninsula. At Potsdam this protuberance had been rather casually and arbitrarily divided for post-Japanese occupation between the Soviet Union and the United States. Russian troops, surprisingly, had gone earlier.

These assuagements were soon to be balanced by less favourable developments. On August 5th the State Department published a long and unsuccessfully defensive 'China White Paper', setting out over a thousand pages its own perfectly reasonable account of events since 1944. It was badly received by, for example, Senator Vandenberg, John Foster Dulles and the *New York Times*. It failed to create a climate of calm resignation in America for the proclamation of the People's Republic of China on October 1st.

Even the most persuasive document in the world might however have failed to achieve this in view of the superimposition of the proclamation, at an interval of only a week, on the news that the Soviet Union had achieved an atomic bomb. The device had in fact been exploded in late August. It was similar to the bomb which the Americans had exploded at Alamogordo four years and one month previously. The monopoly had been short-lived. The Russian bomb was between three and six years in advance of Washington intelligence expectations. Its early arrival aroused public suspicion that it had been assisted by Soviet spying penetration of United States establishments. The suspicion was to some extent well-founded, though it was in fact the British defector Fuchs who had done most to help the Russians. It created a more fertile soil for the start of McCarthy's campaign five months later.

It also created strong pressure for the stepping up both of America's nuclear armament and of its conventional defence. In the former case the result was an immediate decision to increase the stockpile of atomic bombs, followed by Truman's more reluctant decision, taken in the following January, to begin work on the thermo-nuclear or hydrogen bomb. He had a three to two recommendation against from his Atomic Energy Commissioners. The majority of three believed that the destructive qualities of the new bomb – perhaps a hundred times those of the A-bomb – would be too great to make its possession, let alone its use, acceptable. But a special committee of the National Security Council, composed of the Secretary of State, the Secretary of Defense and Lilienthal, reported by a slightly less clear two to one in favour of going ahead. Truman was finally persuaded to give his approval by the argument that the Russians could and would make their own H-bomb. The Americans had their bomb by 1952. The Russians had theirs in 1955. So the nuclear race was firmly launched.

The end of the American nuclear monopoly also meant the end of four years of a relatively relaxed approach to conventional military strength in the United States. This change came at an unfortunate time for Truman. Major politico-military decisions he made with firmness and even wisdom. But with the internal organization of defence he never had a felicitous touch. 'The disorder in military policy,' Robert Donovan has written harshly but not without justification, 'had its origins in Truman's first term, and reached a climax in the second.'[3] This was mainly because of unfortunate Cabinet dispositions, which accentuated what would in any event have been a bitter Navy rearguard action against what it regarded as the depredations of the Air Force, part of the Army until the National Security Act of 1947, but from that date a fully-fledged service. This was a botched act. It was supposed to unify the services, and did indeed create the office of Secretary of Defense. But it did so in such an attenuated form as to make unity almost meaningless. The Secretaries of the individual services (their number paradoxically swollen from two to three by the establishment of an independent air force) retained their existence and most of their prerogatives, while the new Secretary of Defense was given neither adequate staff nor effective power.

James Forrestal was largely responsible for this. He came late into Roosevelt's Cabinet, but was its only member to survive deep into the Truman administration. A former head of the Wall Street firm of Dillon, Read, he was a tense, able man. From 1944 to 1947 he was Secretary of the Navy. As such he effectively resisted a National Security Bill in a form which would have given real power to the head of the Pentagon. Having made a shell of the office of Secretary of Defense he was then appointed to occupy it. The result, not unnaturally, was that he became more tense and increasingly frustrated. He ostensibly stood back from Truman's 1948 campaign and made it dangerously clear that he believed in a Dewey victory. On March 3rd, 1949, Truman sacked him, partly because General Vaughan, the White House joker who occasionally indulged in more serious pursuits, harped on his disloyalty, and partly because his behaviour was becoming increasingly irrational. Ten weeks later Forrestal committed suicide.

In his place Truman appointed Louis Johnson, who had a claim on his loyalty as the 1948 chairman of the Democratic Finance Committee. He had not raised many dollars before the result, but he had at least tried. He was a lawyer from Clarksburg, West Virginia, who had first made a political impact as national commander of the American Legion in 1932–3. He became Assistant Secretary of War in 1937, but flounced out in 1940 when Roosevelt failed to promote him and brought in the Republican Stimson as Secretary. Johnson was a committed Democrat but a very conservative one. However his greatest commitment was to his own political advancement. He quickly made it clear that his principal intent was to use the Department of Defense as a stepping stone to the Democratic nomination in 1952. As Truman's own intentions for that year were unannounced this was not the best way of underpinning his relations with the President and his staff. He also began a running feud with Dean Acheson, confident that on most aspects of foreign policy he knew more than did the Secretary of State. By dismissing Forrestal and appointing Johnson Truman had replaced a neuropath with a megalomaniac.

Johnson's entry into his demesne of the Pentagon was conducted with more bombast than finesse. He evicted generals from their offices, had a great new room created for himself, commandeered General Pershing's old desk and barked orders across it in a determination to show that he was in charge in a way that Forrestal had never done. Generals were shouted at, but it was the Navy above all that was to be brought to heel. One of the last results of Forrestal's stewardship had been the laying of the keel of a vast new aircraft carrier, the *United States*, at Norfolk, Virginia. This was not just a very big ship. It was a symbol of the Navy's future as an airstrike service. The naval staff had abandoned plans for the construction of thirteen smaller vessels in order to concentrate funds upon this flagship.

In late April Johnson ordered cancellation. The Secretary of the Navy, John Sullivan, whom he had not even bothered to inform beforehand, resigned. Truman was displeased. He supported Johnson on the issue, but thought that his handling was ham-fisted. The President was also beginning to be offended by Johnson's general boastfulness and incontinent ambition. Although he remained as Secretary of Defense for another sixteen months, he never wholly recovered his position with Truman. Nothing was heard of his candidature in 1952. He did however secure from the Congress a considerable strengthening of the executive powers of the Secretary of Defense, well beyond the puny coordinating role which was all that Forrestal had created for himself. The modern administrative shape of the Pentagon stems substantially from this period of office. His one and a half storm-tossed years, for all the braggadocio, were therefore not without some result.

Still less than with Truman did his relations with the Navy recover. They were not helped by the appointment of Francis P. Matthews, a political 'pro' from the not notably nautical state of Nebraska, as Sullivan's replacement as Secretary of the Navy. Sullivan was a Catholic, and Matthews was a still more prominent one. Truman apparently thought that act of balance was enough without any regard to whether Matthews could tell one end of a battleship from the other. It was a mistake which Roosevelt, for all his skilful playing from the episcopalian heights of Hyde Park of Catholic politicians of Brooklyn and the Bronx, would never have made, at least with the Navy. As a result the admirals, and many below them, were by the autumn not only discontented with the Navy's role but disenchanted with both tiers of the political leadership in the Pentagon. The consequence of this was the so-called 'admirals' revolt' of October 1949.

The House Armed Services Committee was holding hearings

on the B-36 bomber programme, which the Navy regarded as pre-empting its role as well as its funds. Sparked off by a disputatiously bold naval captain called Crommelin, who published a statement claiming that the Navy's offensive power was being 'nibbled to death', the majority of admirals of note rushed either to issue statements of support or to testify before the Committee in a sense deeply hostile to the views of their civilian chiefs. Denfeld, Chief of Naval Operations, did so, Radford, C-in-C Pacific, did so, as did the C-in-C Atlantic and a clutch of other senior serving officers. They were supported, from retirement, by several of the great naval names of World War II, Nimitz, King and Halsey. Radford's testimony was the most hostile to Johnson, speaking of the lack of confidence in his office felt by senior officers throughout the Navy. But Denfeld's caused the greater stir. He was the senior serving naval officer. His disloyalty was jugular. It was damaging to the administration, particularly in the month following the news of the Russian A-bomb. Truman, however, was better at dealing with insubordination than at avoiding it. A week or so later he laconically announced that Denfeld had been transferred 'to another post'. He got the C-in-C Mediterranean, one of the few senior officers who had not been involved in the dispute, perhaps because he was far away, to accept the vacant command. Matthews tried to resign, but Truman allowed him to stagger on for nearly another two years, in spite of a major gaffe in August 1950, when he echoed Bertrand Russell in suggesting that a pre-emptive nuclear strike might be necessary and desirable. A State Department refutation was required and forthcoming. Acheson gladly supplied it. Until he got Marshall back, a month after this, without one kidney but still full of authority, Truman was not lucky in his Pentagon appointments.

The Navy, however, settled down much more quickly and calmly than might have been expected. They were floated off the shoals of inter-service dispute by the splurge of expenditure which followed the outbreak of the Korean War. The Air Force got its B-36s and they got the *United States*, a lot of other equipment as well, and ultimately the underpinning of their nuclear strike rôle through the development of the Polaris submarine programme. Once the exigencies of Korea had caused budgetary probity to be abandoned, there was room for everyone, admirals, generals and aviators, at the trough of public expenditure.

Before then, however, still in the autumn of 1949, Truman
was further damaged by the suggestions that his staff, although
certainly not himself, were taking a few teaspoonsful out of that
public trough. It was very minor stuff, centred around General
Vaughan. He had done a few favours for gentlemen of mild dubiety
of character who claimed that they could procure government
contracts on a 5% basis, and had given the General one or two
unsolicited but durable consumer goods. As a result the terms
'Five Percenters' and 'Deep Freezers' acquired the temporary status
of catch-phrases which could be depended upon to send Republican
audiences into paroxysms of derision and mirth. Truman reacted
to this with his usual fierce, incautious loyalty. When Vaughan
offered to resign he said 'Don't ever mention such a thing to me
again. We came in here together and we're going out of here
together. Those so-and-sos are trying to get me, through you. I
understand exactly what's going on.'[4]

The wound to Truman at this stage was only a fairly light flesh
one. But it paved the way to more damaging accusations a couple
of years later. 'Deep Freezers' helped to create an atmosphere in
which by 1952 'the mess in Washington' was accepted as having
an objective reality. The 1949 scandals were about as relevant to
the record of the Truman administration as the equally petty
Belcher scandal was to the achievement of the Attlee Government
in Britain. The main difference was that while both were totally
honest, Attlee was sharply censorious of pecadillos in others while
Truman (if he liked them) was tolerant.

More serious in substance than these attacks was the solid refusal
of the Southern conservative Democrats to vote for the Fair Deal.
By the end of 1949 it was obvious that the President was not going
to get any effective civil rights legislation, that Taft-Hartley was
to remain unrepealed, that the Brennan Plan for agricultural support was not to be enacted, and that social security and education
legislation had run into the sand. Almost the only enactment of a
domestic plank of the 1948 platform was the National Housing
Act. 'I've kissed and petted more consarned [sic] S.O.B. so-called
Democrats and left wing Republicans than all the Presidents put
together. I have very few people fighting my battles in Congress
as I fought FDR's'[5] he wrote in his diary on November 1st.
However he consoled himself with the thought that he had got
enough through on the international front that on balance things

could be regarded as going *'fairly* well'. And his daughter insists that throughout the first eighteen months of the second term, that is up to the outbreak of the Korean War, Truman was fairly content with life. She wrote in relation to this whole period that 'Dad's optimism soared'.* Not even the first effusions of McCarthy in his 'McCarthyite' period, which began quite abruptly in February 1950, dimmed this ebullient mood.

McCarthy was a strange phenomenon. At the beginning of 1950 he was a forty-one-year-old small-town lawyer from Wisconsin who had got himself elected as a circuit judge in 1939, and then, in the Republican primary of 1946, after a period of war service in the Pacific, had defeated Robert M. La Follette, Jr, who had recently been voted in a poll of newspaper correspondents and political scientists 'the best' of the 96 senators. He had done so by a campaign of energy, calumny, indestructible bounce and massive (and mostly lying) direct mail advertising. After three rather tawdry years in the Senate, he was still looking for a satisfactory groin into which to put his knee. He had achieved little beyond that of reversing La Follette's distinction and being voted 'the worst' Senator. Then he alighted, half by accident and half by a pervertedly inspired populist instinct, on the anti-Communist issue.

For its exploitation he had several unusual advantages. He half wanted to be liked, but he was quite indifferent to being respected. Truth or logic meant nothing to him. He could not be effectively caught out, because this is at least half a subjective state, and he was impervious to refutation. He simply moved on to the next unsupported accusation. He was argumentatively indestructible. What cast him down was the failure to attract attention, not the failure to convince. Even when he had no notable issue, he was good at the phrase which stuck, the scene which had to be reported.

* She attributed this mood of optimism principally to the excellent functioning of the White House staff, and gave the chief credit for this to Charles S. Murphy, who had been there since 1947, but who succeeded Clark Clifford in the top job only at the beginning of 1950. This was a little unfair to Clifford, who had flair and had rescued Truman's office from chaos in 1946. Murphy, an intelligent North Carolina lawyer, was more self-effacing and perhaps meshed more easily with Truman's personality.

The staff remained tiny by present-day standards. Truman himself took a 30-minute meeting with ten or twelve of them – which was effectively the lot – each morning at 9.30. (Margaret Truman, *op. cit.* p. 449)

As a result he quickly became a figure of world fame. In his own country his lowering features and rather flat, dispassionate voice became still more familiar than the sights and sounds of Truman, Eisenhower or Stevenson. He was the first demagogue of the television age, a poor speaker but the provider of compulsive viewing. In his five-year span of dreadful influence he weakened two presidents, but he was never himself even a remote prospect for the White House. He sapped other men's leadership rather than promoted his own. His demagogy did not set the nation alight. It was too wheedling and his self-righteousness too shallow. He at least half knew that he was a fraud. His anti-Communism was more of a racket than a crusade. He once shared an elevator with Dean Acheson and greeted him with the off-duty false bonhomie of one travelling salesman in a line of doubtful goods to another in a different but similar line. This was a technique which often produced a friendly, almost grateful response from weak opponents. With Acheson it was less successful. The murderously cold silence and apoplectic forehead of the Secretary of State penetrated even to McCarthy. He was amoral rather than immoral. In the words of Richard Rovere, 'though a demon himself, he was not a man possessed by demons'. As a result, when his spell was broken, he collapsed more quickly and completely than most of his victims. He passed into obscurity in 1954 and died less than three years later, still only 48, and probably as a result of a drinking bout instigated by bad news from his stockbroker. It was a death suited to neither a hero nor a fanatic. It did not even attract much attention.

Nor, as a matter of fact, did his early 1950 effusions, although that was a weakness soon to be rectified. Armed with his new issue he asked the Republic campaign committee to arrange some speaking engagements for him over the Lincoln's birthday weekend in mid-February. They gave him a fairly undistinguished list: a Women's County Republican Club at Wheeling, West Virginia and meetings of similar grade at Salt Lake City and Reno. But if the venues were unnotable the speeches were not. He spoke without texts and there has always been some uncertainty as to what exactly he said. The best authenticated version is that at Wheeling he announced:

'While I cannot take time to name all the men in the State Department who have been named as members of the Communist

Party and members of a spy ring I have here in my hand a list of 205 that were known to the Secretary of State as being members of the Communist Party and who nevertheless are still working and shaping the policy of the State Department.'

The language was neither elegant nor precise, but the broad message was clear. The United States Government was riddled with Communists, and it was the mission of the Junior Senator from Wisconsin, armed with the most detailed evidence, to get them out. Perhaps his cleverest trick was his appreciation that detail always sounds convincing. It did not greatly matter if it was spurious or even non-existent, provided that claim was laid to it. The detail of Wheeling was certainly spurious. What he 'held in his hand' might have been anything from a blank sheet of paper to a laundry list, but it was not a list of 205 State Department Communists. Nor did he have any particular attachment to 205. By the time that he got to Salt Lake City it had become 57 'card-carrying members'. On the floor of the Senate eleven days later it had become 81. Three months later, again in the Senate, it had climbed back to 121. 'I am tired of playing this silly numbers game', he replied when asked to explain the contradictions.

Immediately, the Wheeling speech was not widely reported. The *Chicago Tribune*, appropriately, was the only newspaper outside West Virginia to pick it up on the following day. The others soon caught up. McCarthy was launched on his five year parabola. At first the trajectory was more that of a turbo-prop than a jet. Truman did not take the onslaught too seriously – he was used to almost equally immoderate attacks from more senior Republican figures – although he did pay McCarthy the hidden compliment of writing him one of his famous unsent letters on the day after Wheeling. And six weeks later he told a press conference that 'the greatest asset that the Kremlin has is Senator McCarthy'.[6]

At first the Korean War stole McCarthy's thunder. Then it gave him a still more favourable climate in which to operate. He spent the later summer and early autumn of 1950 working quietly against two Democratic senators – Tydings of Maryland and Lucas of Illinois – who had been particularly vociferous against him on Capitol Hill. By November he had destroyed them both. He began to acquire a certain reputation for electoral omnipotence which made senators treat him with a new wariness. Senators attach a great importance to the standards of the club, but most are at least

equally concerned with their continued membership of it. The
general Republican mood towards him began to change. Towards
the end of twenty years of Democratic power, 'two decades of
treason' as he was later hyperbolically to describe them, the Grand
Old Party was sick for power. Perhaps this vulgar huckster had
found the key. Perhaps he could help to achieve it, where Landon,
Willkie and Dewey, Taft, Vandenberg and Knowland had failed.
They were not squeamish in its quest.

Favoured by this new atmosphere McCarthy soared to even
greater heights of destructive misrepresentation during 1951. He
inflicted major damage on figures of moderate note such as Owen
Lattimore and Philip Jessup. He weakened the morale and self-
confidence of much of the State Department. And he even forced
Acheson on to the defensive to the extent of making him assure a
Senate hearing that Communist China would *never* be recognized,
and such a course was not even *discussed* within the Department.
In June he launched a 60,000 word indictment of General Marshall.
He read part of it on the floor of the Senate, and put the rest unread
into the Congressional Record. Even he stopped short of claiming
that the Secretary of Defense was himself a Communist, but he
did claim that, 'steeped in blood' Marshall was a man 'whose every
important act for years has contributed to the prosperity of the
enemy'. He 'would sell his grandmother for any advantage'. How
could he be believed 'under oath or otherwise'? The effrontery of
the attack was breathtaking. Even some of his normal allies were
a little shocked, but, like all McCarthy's enterprises at that time,
it half worked. Marshall was off his pedestal for a lot of Americans.

Thus with Marshall chipped and Acheson scarred, McCarthy
inflicted substantial damage on the last three years of the Democratic administration. Truman was staunch but he lacked the guile
in dealing with him that Roosevelt would have shown. He was
not good at digging pits for the Senator and mocking him when
he fell into them. Lack of guile, however, was better than lack of
courage, which was the deficiency which Eisenhower displayed,
and which was to make the period of his campaign and the first
eighteen months of his presidency the apogee of McCarthy's
parabola. In Truman's day he sullied America. In Eisenhower's he
ran amok and threatened to undermine the Army as well as the
State Department. Fortunately he over-reached himself and the
quick collapse began.

10

TRUMAN'S THIRD WAR

The dominant event of 1950 was not however the eruption of McCarthy but the outbreak of the war in Korea. It was also the great test of Truman's second term. Did it strike him out of a clear blue sky? The answer is mixed. In his State of the Union message on January 4th he had stated unequivocally: 'The greatest danger has receded . . .' He was referring, with justification, to the improvement of the position in Europe. But the statement was geographically unqualified, and was given practical backing by the fact that he announced a defence budget for the fiscal year July 1st, 1950 to June 30th, 1951 of $13.5 billion against $14.4 billion for the year then in progress. Despite the early Russian achievement of an atomic weapon the United States was planning to continue with its post-1945 policy of a military establishment dictated by economy rather than by any attempt at conventional balance.

Nevertheless, within a month, Truman commissioned a major internal government study of the future risks and needs of US defence policy. This was carried out largely by Paul Nitze, working under the direction of Acheson, although with some Pentagon participation. The result was a secret document known as NSC (National Security Council) 68. It was delivered to the President on April 7th. It was an explosive state paper. It predicted Soviet nuclear equality by 1954 and said that by then the United States, because of a defence budget totally inadequate to the commitments it had assumed, would be in a 'disastrous situation'. The shield of atomic superiority, let alone monopoly, would be gone, and the American people would be placed 'in their deepest peril' by their weakness in conventional forces. This danger could only be counteracted by an entirely different scale of defence effort.

What was needed was a budget not of $13–14 billion, but of $40–50 billion.

What Truman would have done, in the absence of the Korean War, about this deeply disturbing document is almost impossible to conjecture. It was not without its critics within the government. Kennan and Bohlen thought it exaggerated and even hysterical. But its message was such that it could not comfortably be set aside. But its costs were such that they seemed impossible to accommodate within the framework of responsible peace-time finance. The only assuagement was that while the threat was dire it was not immediate in the sense of requiring action within a few weeks. In any event the recommendations clearly could not be implemented without a major programme for the education of public and congressional opinion.

This was a fence that Truman did not rush. In May he made the most extensive speaking tour of his second term. The nominal purpose was to dedicate Grand Coulee Dam in Washington State. He did the journey both ways in the presidential train and was away from Blair House for two weeks, making 57 speeches in twelve states. It was nominally a non-political trip, but this did not unduly inhibit the President's combative style. There were a lot of pre-election swipes at the Republicans. Margaret Truman, who was of the party, wrote of it as the high point of the second term, engendering in her father a feeling which presaged 'smashing Democratic victory in the fall elections'.

'It was a delightful trip,' she added. 'There was none of the tension of 1948.'[1] Perhaps there was not enough tension. It was certainly no Midlothian campaign conducted by a latter-day Gladstone. Truman stuck mostly to domestic issues, although he interlaced them with warnings against the perils of isolationism. But he sounded no call to arms, or even a call to pay vastly more for arms. Nor did he engage head-on with McCarthyism. This was due, not to cowardice but to his mistaken belief that the evil Senator's machinations would quickly snuff themselves out if not fanned with too much attention.

At the time of the Grand Coulee trip Truman had already decided and committed firmly but privately to paper that he would serve no more than another 2¾ years. Only nine days after he had received NSC 68 (but not I think in any way because of it) he chose a peculiarly fine Sunday, with Washington suffused in sunshine and cherry blossom, to commit himself to not staying there any longer than he had to.

'I am not a candidate for nomination by the Democratic Convention', he rather quaintly began.*

'. . . I have been in public service well over thirty years, having been President of the United States almost two complete terms.

'Washington, Jefferson, Monroe, Madison, Andrew Jackson and Woodrow Wilson as well as Calvin Coolidge stood by the precedent of two terms. Only Grant, Theodore Roosevelt and F.D.R. made the attempt to break that precedent. F.D.R. succeeded.

'In my opinion eight years as President is enough and sometimes too much for any man to serve in that capacity.

'There is a lure in power. It can get into a man's blood just as gambling and lust for money have been known to do.

'This is a Republic. The greatest in the history of the world. I want this country to continue as a Republic. Cincinnatus and Washington pointed the way. When Rome forgot Cincinnatus its downfall began. When we forget the examples of such men as Washington, Jefferson and Andrew Jackson, all of whom could have had a continuation in the office, then we will start down the road to dictatorship and ruin. I know I could be elected again and continue to break the old precedent as it was broken by F.D.R. It should not be done. That precedent should continue – not only by a Constitutional amendment but by custom based on the honour of the man in the office.

'Therefore to re-establish that custom, although by a quibble I could say I've only had one term, I am not a candidate and will not accept the nomination for another term.'²

This was a firm and honest statement of his view that he did not want another term, and did not believe that, even if he did, constitutional propriety entitled him to one. It was a little over-embellished by bombast and self-righteousness. It was ridiculous, after the narrow squeak of 1948, to believe in 1950 that he would be unassailable in 1952. Eisenhower would probably have beaten him as effectively, although half for different reasons, as he beat Stevenson. And it was a little far-fetched and nigglingly anti-

---

* It was a quaint beginning because no Democratic Convention could possibly take place within 2¼ years.

Roosevelt to equate a third term with the beginning of the end of republican virtue. It was always Truman's way, when putting his thoughts on paper, to be provocative, mock-modest, and critical of the standards of others. However, there is no doubt that he meant what he wrote and that he had taken the decision for largely unselfish reasons.

Furthermore he had the good sense to keep it to himself. He showed the paper to no one until November 1951. Then, with fourteen months of his presidency still to go, he read it to his immediate staff, whose futures were almost as much affected by the decision as was his own. They kept the secret remarkably well. He made no public announcement until a Jefferson/Jackson Day dinner at the end of March 1952. He wisely delayed turning himself into a lame duck until the last reasonable moment. This was of great benefit, particularly during the year from June 1950, when, with the Korean War at full blast, MacArthur insubordinate, Vandenberg dying and most of bi-partisanship with him, Acheson and even Marshall sufficiently hobbled by McCarthyism to be unable to sustain him at home as they had done in 1947–49, he needed every ounce of presidential authority that he could muster.

Truman flew to Independence at the end of Saturday morning, June 24th. He had to begin the day with a speech for the inauguration of Friendship International Airport in Baltimore. But he had intended the next 48 hours to be a relaxed midsummer weekend of family visiting, both with his wife and daughter, who had already retreated from Washington, and with other less frequently-seen relations.

His plans were blown up. So were the ill-trained and ill-equipped eight divisions of the Republic of Korea which were subject to a full-scale attack from the Communist Democratic People's Republic of the north, launched at dawn on Sunday, June 25th. Differences of time enabled Acheson to receive news of this at his Maryland farm soon after dinner on the Saturday evening. After an hour's digestion of the news he informed the President.

Truman's first instinct was to summon the presidential plane (which was at Kansas City Airport) and make an immediate return to Washington. Acheson dissuaded him. Such a long night flight was, somewhat surprisingly, considered to be dangerous, as well as unnecessarily alarmist. There were still a lot of uncertainties. It was better that he should carry on as though nothing had happened until at least the next day, when the question of return could be reviewed.*

The uncertainties were manifold. They related to the scale of the invasion, to the ability of South Korean troops to repel it, and to the degree of commitment of Russia and China to Kim Il-sung's adventure. Upon this third uncertainty, there turned the likelihood of the invasion leading to a world conflagration, either because this was already planned by the Soviet Union, with moves against Berlin, or Yugoslavia or Iran or all three likely to follow, or because of a more spontaneous escalation if it became necessary for United States troops to be directly involved.

The first two questions were substantially and disagreeably cleared up by lunchtime on the Sunday, when Truman received his second telephone call from Acheson. There was no doubt about the seriousness of the invasion. It was no frontier raid, comparable with those which had quite frequently occurred in the previous months, but a determined military attempt to re-unite the peninsula under Communist control. Nor was the South Korean performance giving any basis for confidence. Syngman Rhee, their seventy-five-year-old president, who had returned from nearly forty years' exile in the United States, was a master of fulmination, almost as much against the pusillanimity of the West as against the aggression of the Communists. But at this stage at least he could not make his army fight. Within the first twenty-four hours, Seoul, the capital, together with the main airport of the country and the second maritime port were all imminently threatened. What was immediately proposed by Acheson was the calling of an emergency session of the United Nations Security Council in the hope that it would not only denounce the aggression but pass a resolution of action. If it did so the main burden of implementation would clearly fall on the United States. If it did not the responsibility on the leading nation for trying to deal with the resultant diplomatic chaos and the exposed military impotence of the UN would be greater still. Truman therefore decided to return immediately and to summon a dinner meeting of his principal advisers, civilian and military, at Blair House for that evening.

Having decided on the return he set off in such a hurry that half

* It was also surprisingly decided that Truman should make no allusion to the invasion when he went about his ordinary business – a visit to his brother's farm – on the Sunday morning. Were not the Agency tapes clattering away?

his staff, the whole of the accompanying White House press corps and (almost) the navigator* were left behind. When confronted with a crisis he was seized with an almost excessive appetite for rapid decision-making. If Goering, when he heard the word culture, reached for his gun, Truman, when he heard the word problem, reached for a decision. The danger was that he would take one before he had heard the relevant evidence; the miracle was that he made so many wise ones. He was therefore impatient to get back. But there was no joyful anticipation. He was not bellicose. The last thing that Truman wanted at this stage was a war in Korea. There was no question of his being like Churchill (before he became older, more battle-scarred, and above all oppressed by the almost infinitely destructive power of nuclear weapons), who, at midnight on August 4th, 1914 was recorded by Margot Asquith as 'with a happy face striding towards the double doors of the Cabinet room.'[3]

Truman flew over Missouri, Illinois, Kentucky, Ohio and West Virginia towards his Blair House rendezvous in a mood of alert determination, but not with a happy face or heart. The war solved one problem for him, that of NSC 68. Within twelve months the United States had a defence budget of over $50 billion a year, and by no means all of the increase went to Korea. But from every other point of view the consequences were heavy. A deep shadow of death and divisiveness was cast upon the last two and a half years of his presidency. The climate of frustration in which the United States, with its still overwhelming nuclear superiority, had to fight desperate and costly conventional battles, in order to limit the dangers of escalation and calm the nerves of its European allies, gave McCarthyism a second and stronger wind. It was also a peculiar misfortune that if there had to be a long but limited war in a distant theatre it should be within the area of responsibility of Truman's most famous and insubordinate commander. General Douglas MacArthur did not allow the remarkable fact that he had not set foot in the United States for thirteen years to prevent his being one of the most 'politi-

---

* In fact the navigator arrived and clambered up a rope ladder as the plane, under Truman's orders to leave immediately, was beginning to taxi. Truman then wasted far more time by landing at St Louis to pick up Secretary Snyder, probably a less useful member of the team than the navigator. But with Truman old friendships died hard, and he liked familiar faces in a crisis, even if he looked more to the advice of those who were less familiar but better informed.

cal' generals ever to hold high command; and neither his politics nor (mostly) his policies were those of Truman.

Truman of course could not foresee all this on June 25th. If told that the war could be limited to the Korean peninsula, he would probably have been amazed to be equally informed that United States casualties would approach a half of those in World War I. Yet his thoughts, during the previous 18 hours and in the plane, were sombre. He believed, according to the clear testimony of his daughter who was present at Independence, that the Korean invasion was probably the 'opening round' in World War III.[4] This was in fact, as he was well advised by his Chiefs of Staff that night in Washington, rather heavily against any balance of rational probability. The Soviet Union was in a substantially weaker position vis-à-vis the United States than it was likely to be in a few years' time. It could not possibly have sustained a successful all-out war. It would therefore have been extremely foolish to launch one.

On the other hand there was no doubt in the minds of Truman's advisers, any more than in his own, that the invasion was Moscow-planned, and that forces far greater than Kim's own, successful though they were so far proving, had to be taken into account. In fact, if Krushchev's memoirs are to be believed,[5] this somewhat exaggerated the degree of central control. The initiative for the attack came from Kim Il-sung. Stalin acquiesced, but only after consulting Mao Tse-tung, and fairly soon began to wish that he had not done so. The strong reaction of the United States, and indeed of the United Nations, was not foreseen.* Khrushchev's account clearly brings out the vast difference compared with today in the Far Eastern strategic balance because of the then apparently impregnable alliance between the Soviet Union and the People's Republic of China. Behind North Korea stood China, and behind China stood Russia.

Truman was therefore deeply apprehensive. He was also convinced that the invasion could not be allowed to succeed, and that the United States must be prepared to take whatever risks were necessary to prevent this. This conviction sprang at least as much from his view that Korea was a crucial test for the effectiveness of the United Nations as from his proper attachment to the prestige

---

* This may have been partly the fault of Acheson who in March had made a speech which appeared to exclude South Korea from the United States perimeter of defence.

of the United States and to the balance of power in the Far East. The UN of those days, with its membership of less than 60 and its substantial 'American' majority (provided by South America, Western Europe and the old British Commonwealth countries) was regarded by its Western protagonists as an organization which could impartially enforce the international rule of law on great and small powers alike, and by the majesty of its authority redeem the weakness of the pre-war League of Nations. Truman was emphatically one such protagonist. He was prepared to fight for Lake Success and take the risks involved, which if anything he exaggerated rather than under-estimated. But he wanted to minimize these risks, both because he knew that this was necessary to get as many other members of the UN as possible to join with him (even if in little more than a token way) in fighting for international order,* and because he had seen enough of World Wars I and II to profoundly unanxious to be the President of World War III. This meant that he would have to fight in Korea, but that he must do so in a limited way, seeking only to restore the *status quo ante*, and suffering operational disadvantages in order to avoid giving even the smallest possible excuse for any widening of the conflict.

These assumptions and this strategy were inchoately in his mind when he got to Washington. He was met by Acheson, by Secretary of Defense Johnson, and the three Secretaries of the individual services. They already had the news that the Security Council had acted satisfactorily, as to both speed and outcome. A resolution condemning the attack, calling for the immediate cessation of hostilities and North Korean withdrawal to the 38th parallel, and also, and most significantly, urging all members to render every assistance to the UN for the execution of the resolution, had been carried by nine votes to nil, with one abstention. The absence of an adverse vote, and indeed of a veto, was due to the fact that the Soviet Union had pursued an 'empty chair' policy since January, in protest against the continued presence of a representative of

---

* The outcome was remarkably successful. Britain and Turkey contributed the most. Canada, Australia, New Zealand, the Philippines, Thailand, Colombia, France, Greece, the Netherlands, Belgium, Luxembourg and Ethiopia all sent land troops, and some sent naval and air support as well. South Africa sent an air unit but no ground forces. Italy, India, Denmark, Norway and Sweden sent non-combat medical units.

Nationalist China. The one abstention came from Yugoslavia.*

The party proceeded to Blair House where they were joined by the Chiefs of Staff, and four of Acheson's senior State Department officials. Snyder was also present. For some extraordinary reason particular importance was attached to the quality, and indeed the formality, of the dinner. It was almost as though the seriousness of the occasion called for some sacerdotal communal feast. The occasion echoes throughout almost every memoir of the evening. Truman wrote to his wife: 'Had them all to dinner at eight, and the dinner was good and well served.'[6] Acheson wrote about 'an excellent dinner . . . gotten up by the staff on a Sunday afternoon at the shortest notice.'[7] Margaret Truman wrote of the meal in a tone of still greater reverence: 'From the air (the President) wired Charles Claunch, the White House usher, to warn him that a Very Important Dinner should be ready at Blair House by 8.30. Mr Acheson would give him the guest list. Claunch called Alonzo Fields, the head butler at the White House who recruited two cooks and made up a menu en route to Blair House in a taxi.'[8] What miracles of gastronomy they concocted during this short journey is nowhere on record, but it was presumably a considerable improvement on the normal standard of American official meals.†

Nor was the quality of the meal allowed to be spoiled by sombre

* There was doubt until the last moment as to whether Malik, the head of the Russian delegation would re-take his seat and block the whole proceedings. He did so neither on this occassion nor, for the second key vote, two days later, although for no obvious reason he suddenly resumed his place on July 20th. The second vote was on a resolution to give teeth to the Sunday one. In effect it called for military sanctions. It got through by seven votes to one, Yugoslavia having moved from abstention to dissent, India and Egypt from assent to abstention. It was still a powerful majority.

† A typical such meal, made unusual only by its solitariness and the grandeur of the service, had been recorded in his diary by Truman on November 1st 1949: 'Had dinner by myself tonight . . . A butler came in very formally and said "Mr President, dinner is served." I walk into the dining room in Blair House. Barnett in tails and white tie pulls out my chair, pushes me up to the table. John in tails and white tie brings me a plate, Barnett brings me a tender loin, John brings me asparagus, Barnett brings me carrots and beets. I have to eat alone and in the silence in candle-lit room. I ring. Barnett takes the plate and butter plates. John comes in with a napkin and silver crumb tray – there are no crumbs but John has to brush them off the table anyway. Barnett brings me a plate with a finger bowl and doiley and John puts a glass saucer and a little bowl on the plate. Barnett brings me some chocolate custard. John brings me a demitasse (at home a little cup of coffee – about two good gulps) and my dinner is over. I take a hand bath in the finger bowl and go back to work. What a life!' (*Off the Record*, pp. 168-9)

or contentious conversation. Discussion of the subject which was the purpose of the gathering was banned by Truman until the table was cleared and the servants had withdrawn. This was partly a put-down of Louis Johnson, who had attempted before dinner to pre-empt the discussion towards a mingling of the Korean and Formosan issues: Truman was determined that Acheson should lead, and also knew that the Chinese Nationalist cause was a lead balloon at the UN. But it was also partly due to a temporary obsession with secrecy over what was essentially a public issue, which had already led to the farce of Truman pretending to his brother that morning that nothing had happened.

These preliminaries over, however, Truman got down to a very crisp discussion. 'My conference was a most successful one,' he wrote to his wife,[9] and that was the general view of the participants. They filled in some of the gaps in his knowledge and confirmed most of his instinctive judgments. He stiffened them with his resolution. North Korea was not to be allowed to get away with the aggression. The United States, with the moral backing, it was hoped, of United Nations authority and the material backing of as many other member states as possible, would resist. The crucial question that remained unanswered was whether this objective could be achieved by a combination of naval movements, air cover, and lavish supplies to Republic of Korea troops. Of the service chiefs present, the admiral and the Air Force general thought 'yes'. Omar Bradley and the Army Chief of Staff, Lawton Collins, thought 'no'. Truman desperately hoped that the former were right. He did not want to be responsible for the deployment of United States infantry, with the casualties and diplomatic risks that this would involve, and at least until mid-week he thought that there was a good chance of avoiding it. When however it became clear, both from the inability of the South Korean troops to form and hold any defensive line and from MacArthur's prognosis that this degree of detachment could not be sustained, he did not hesitate to authorize the shipment from Japan of three American divisions. MacArthur's visit of inspection to Korea took place on Thursday, June 29th. On the following morning at an 8.30 meeting Truman agreed to the request.

Doing so was not made easier by the fact that there was already widespread distrust of MacArthur in Washington, not only for his politics but for his generalship. John Foster Dulles was in

Tokyo at the time of the North Korean attack, and had been deeply shocked that none of the General's aides had the courage to rouse him.★ Dulles had to do it himself, and on his return, most ironically as events were to work out, used his position as the senior Republican attached to the State Department to advise Truman that he ought forthwith to replace MacArthur with a younger and more vigorous general (MacArthur was 70).

Truman acted throughout that last week of June with more than sufficient deliberate speed to justify his daughter's summing up of the march of events: 'Step by step, in six fateful days, searching for alternatives before each move, my father found himself fighting his third war.'[10] The speed was greater than the deliberateness. It was partly responsible for Truman making two, maybe three, of his four mistakes of the week.

First, he authorized United States naval and air action sixteen hours in advance of the second UN resolution which gave him the authority of international legality. The Soviet Union and its apologists were later to make mildly effective play with this. It was however a very minor fault, and one on the right side.

Second, he omitted throughout to get any authority from the Congress for his actions. He held quite a lot of informal consultations on a cross-party basis with the leaders at the White House, but he sent no formal message on the war until July 19th. He just acted under executive prerogative, citing many precedents, but for the commitment of troops rather than the engagement in hostilities. It was not that he was without warning – Taft fired quite a powerful shot across his bows on the Wednesday – or that he doubted his ability to obtain a quick majority: a bill to extend selective service for one year went through the House by 315 to 4 and the Senate by 76 to nil. It was more his determination to get on with things and to defend, indeed enhance, the prerogatives of the presidency. It was probably an error of medium proportions. Robert Donovan in a chapter entitled 'A Costly Mistake' wrote: 'The political rather than the legal aspect of war without congressional approval was to hurt Truman, to make the prosecution of the war more difficult for him, and to cause future public con-

★ This was a perfect illustration of what had provoked Marshall, during a wartime conference, to respond to MacArthur's 'My staff tells me . . .' by saying: 'General, you don't have a staff; you have a court'. (Acheson, *Present at the Creation*, p. 424)

cern about what was to be called the "imperial presidency".'[11] Acheson controverted (in advance) this thesis. The difficulties of the war followed from the difficulties of the war and not from lack of a congressional vote. And while such a vote would in itself have manifestly done no harm, the process of obtaining it might well have done a great deal. His not altogether surprising conclusion was that the President, advised by Acheson, was therefore right. Nevertheless Truman's method of procedure established a precedent which thereafter effectively deprived the Congress of the power to authorize or prevent war, which had explicitly been bestowed upon it by the Constitution.

Third, and stemming to some extent from his desire not 'to go to war'* and his decision not to go to Congress, he publicly underplayed the seriousness of the issues and the size of the stakes. This was one reason for the 'business as usual', semi-secret approach of the Saturday evening, Sunday and Monday. By the Thursday it coalesced with one of his most frequent and unfortunate habits, that of allowing reporters to put words into his mouth, to create a phrase which was to reverberate against him for the next two years and more. At a press conference he denied that the United States was at war. 'Mr President, would it be correct,' he was then asked, '. . . to call this a police action under the United Nations?' 'Yes, that is exactly what it amounts to,' he replied. The trouble was that police actions which cost half a million casualties on the law and order side are liable to be regarded as somewhat bungled.

The fourth mistake never surfaced. Chiang Kai-shek, as anxious as Louis Johnson and MacArthur to get his own defence muddled up with that of South Korea, rushed in to offer 33,000 Nationalist troops which were to be equipped and transported by the United States. Truman clutched at this straw as a possible alternative to the commitment of US ground forces. Acheson and the Chiefs of Staff joined forces to get him away from the idea. This required only one meeting. The scheme would have been somewhat wasteful in resources and gravely damaging to the prospect for military contributions from other members of the United Nations.

These blemishes apart, and none of them was of the first order,

* 'I don't want to go to war,' he declared to those around him like a plaintive but nonetheless dutiful recruit, at the end of the Monday meeting at which naval and air action was determined upon. (Donovan, *op. cit.*, p. 223)

Truman's performance during what was arguably the most crucial week of his presidency was of a very high quality. He paused enough to consider the options but never so long as to lose the initiative. As a result he married the military potential of the United States with the moral authority of the United Nations to sustain his policy of containment. It was a remarkable feat. He astonished the world, and certainly the Soviet Union, by the resoluteness of his response.

At the end of the week he sent Acheson a note of congratulation:

> 'Your initiative in immediately calling the Security Council
> . . . was the key to what followed afterwards. If you had
> not acted promptly in that direction we would have had
> to go into Korea alone. The meeting Sunday night at Blair
> House . . . and the results afterwards show that you are a
> great Secretary of State and a★ diplomat. Your handling of
> the situation since has been superb.'[12]

The tone of this note not only illustrates Truman's instinctive generosity, but points also to a certain buoyancy following the satisfactory turning of a most difficult corner.

All of that buoyancy was going to be needed, for there then began a most dreadful four weeks of military débâcle. For its first year the Korean War simulated the trajectory of a yo-yo. But during its first downward swing no one could tell whether it was going to come up again. The Korean peninsular is on roughly the scale of England and Scotland, with the frontier running near to Leeds rather than north of Carlisle. Seoul, fifty or so miles from the 38th parallel, had already fallen by the time the first Americans arrived, and they made their first contact with the enemy about another fifty miles south of it. They (the 24th Division) were gradually driven back about another eighty miles to Taejon where they fought a desperate but essential five-day delaying action, from July 16th to 21st. This enabled two more divisions to land at Pusan, the port in the far south-east. Around this they were able to hold a foothold about the size of Kent. The remains of the 24th Division – they had lost their commander, General Dean, and a great number of others too – retreated within this perimeter and a stable line was established for the first time by July 27th–28th. Without

★ Surely a redundant indefinite article.

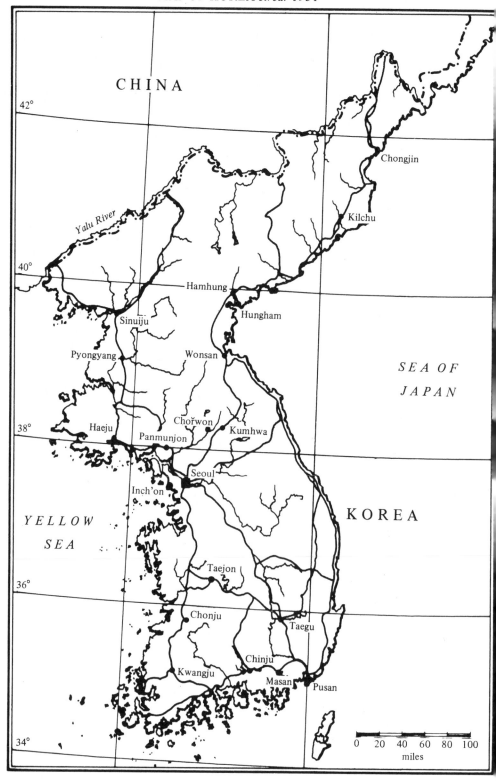

CHINA

42°

Chongjin

Yalu River

Kilchu

40°

Hamhung

Sinuiju

Hungham

Pyongyang

Wonsan

SEA OF
JAPAN

38°

Haeju

Chořwon

Kumhwa

Panmunjon

Seoul

Inch'on

KOREA

YELLOW
SEA

Taejon

36°

Chonju

Taegu

Chinju

Kwangju

Masan

Pusan

34°

0   20   40   60   80   100
miles

the successful delaying action at Taejon the invading troops would almost certainly have cleared the peninsula.

United States air superiority held back the mounting of a major North Korean onslaught on this bridgehead until the last days of August. MacArthur, however, injected some political fireworks into the relative calm a few days before the Communists re-started their military ones. He sent a message to the Chicago convention of the Veterans of Foreign Wars which sharply contradicted the policy of the administration, and still more of the UN, whose servant in a loose way he was supposed to have become. Truman was furious, although he does not appear to have contemplated the recall of MacArthur at this stage. The coffin into which the incident drove a final nail was rather that of Louis Johnson. Truman was insistent that MacArthur should be made to withdraw his statement, even though it had already rung around the world. Johnson made about four attempts to stop the transmission through the Pentagon of this instruction. On September 12th he was out and Marshall was back in the government in his place.

The end of August or the beginning of September would in any event have been a peculiarly difficult time at which to replace MacArthur. There was violent fighting on the perimeter, although the conduct of this defensive battle was more the responsibility of General Walton Walker. MacArthur was engaged in his last military coup. On September 15th he changed the whole balance of the war with a successful amphibious landing mounted at short notice and carried out on a most difficult coast two hundred miles behind the bulk of the North Korean army which was hammering away at the Pusan redoubt. He put the X Corps ashore at Inch'on, the port of Seoul. Eleven days later the capital returned to the possession of the Republic of Korea and an armoured column from the south joined up with the seaborne American invaders. The 38th parallel was crossed in early October. By November 21st the Yalu River, the north-western frontier between North Korea and the Manchurian provinces of the People's Republic of China had been reached. The yo-yo had remounted the string to the limit.

In view of subsequent events MacArthur was criticized for having advanced so far. He claimed that, as he was expressly (and in his view perversely) forbidden air strikes or reconnaissance north of the Manchurian border, it was the only way in which he could find out what was happening in the extreme north of the country,

let alone carry out his instructions from the Joint Chiefs of Staff
to 'destroy the North Korean armed forces'. Certainly he was
explicitly authorized by a message from Truman on September
29th and, more ambiguously, by a resolution of the UN General
Assembly on October 7th, to advance north of the 38th parallel.

A somewhat different criticism was that his generalship was at
fault in allowing two entirely separate commands, responsible only
to himself, the 8th Army in the west and X Corps across the
mountain chain to the east, to operate on too wide a front. Certainly
when on the night of November 25th–26th the Chinese attacked
the 8th Army with a strength of 18 divisions and followed this up
on the 27th with an attack of about 12 divisions on X Corps, the
effect was devastating. The 8th Army reeled back and X Corps
was cut off and had to be evacuated (very skilfully) by sea. By
December 15th X Corps were embarked and the 8th Army had
managed to consolidate on a line just north of Seoul. The yo-yo
was half way down again.

The political repercussions of the Chinese intervention were at
least as great as the military ones. The autumn had been a period
of fluctuating fortune for Truman, as for MacArthur. They had
met once, for a few hours on Wake Island on October 15th.
Typically, Truman travelled 4,700 miles and MacArthur only
1,900. He persuaded the President, who was not particularly eager
to have him in Washington, that he could not separate himself
from his troops for a longer journey. The President found him at
a peak of benignant condescension and complacency. 'We arrived
at dawn', he wrote for his diary. 'General MacArthur was at the
Airport with his shirt unbuttoned, wearing a greasy ham and eggs
cap that evidently had been in use for twenty years. He greeted
the President cordially . . .' He also assured the President that 'the
Chinese Commies would not attack, that we had won the war and
that we could send a Division to Europe in January 1951'.[13]
Truman in return gave MacArthur a fourth cluster to his Distinguished Service Medal, bestowed with a presidential citation
which expressed not merely confidence but adulation. So there
was a good exchange of misinformation.

The mid-term elections were on November 7th. Truman did
little campaigning but accidentally made what might have been
expected to be a substantial contribution to a good result. On
November 1st he escaped a serious assassination attempt outside

Blair House. It was mounted by two young Puerto Rican nationalists. One was shot dead, as was a Blair House guard, with two others wounded. The other would-be assassin was imprisoned until 1979. It was at 2.20 in the afternoon. Despite the month the temperature was 84°F, and Truman perhaps for this reason, but clearly contrary to the perception of his habits, was asleep on his bed at the time. He rather dangerously rushed to his bedroom window, but otherwise took the attack calmly.

It may be that the incident averted worse misfortunes at the polls but there was no direct evidence of its favourable effects. The poison of McCarthy was well into the national blood stream by then, and the results were worse where the Senator had pursued personal vendettas than overall – a sign to all except the most courageous that he was a dangerous man to oppose. As a result it was more the quality than the quantity of the losses from which the Democrats suffered. They retained control of both chambers, although 28 seats changed hands in the House and five in the Senate, reducing the margin there to two. Scott Lucas, the majority leader, was defeated in Illinois, as was Myers, the majority whip, in Pennsylvania. Millard Tydings, into whom McCarthy had plunged his knife most deeply, went down in Maryland, and Richard Nixon, to the particular chagrin of Truman, beat Helen Gahagan Douglas in California.

This was not a glorious outcome for Truman's last electoral battle, but nor was it a disaster on the scale of 1946. More seriously on his mind during that November was the deteriorating situation in Korea. This was a paradox, for the month was mostly one of rapid, even reckless advance. But it was one in which the Pentagon and the State Department lost almost all remnants of confidence in MacArthur. They were pretty sure that Chinese intervention was coming, and thought that his approach to this alternated between provocation and panic. They distrusted his strategy of advancing far and fast with increasingly splayed out forces and a divided command. And they knew that his continuous public complaints about not being allowed to attack the Chinese were not only gross insubordination but also gravely damaging to the unity of the United Nations allies.

Acheson conveyed the atmosphere well, and also gave vent to a rare burst of self-criticism, when he wrote:

'All the President's advisers in this matter, civilian
and military, knew that something was badly wrong,
though what it was, how to find out, and what to do
about it they muffed. That they were deeply disturbed
and felt the need for common counsel is shown by the
unprecedented fact that in the three weeks and three
days from November 10th to December 4th, when
disaster was full upon us, the Secretaries of State and
Defense and their chief assistants met three times with
the Chiefs of Staff in their war room to tussle with the
problem, the two Secretaries met five times with the
President, and I consulted with him on five other
occasions. I have an unhappy conviction that none of
us, myself prominently included, served him as he
was entitled to be served.'[14]

This may somewhat exaggerate the extent to which the advisers
were baffled rather than intimidated. They knew well enough that
the main thing that was wrong was MacArthur, but were inhibited
from recommending his removal by a combination of fear of the
political explosion which would follow and a natural caution about
changing horses in mid-stream. General Ridgway, who was not a
full member of the group and might also have been expected – as
a likely successor – to be the most inhibited, was the only one who
blurted out his impatience that they would not face up to and deal
with the MacArthur problem. But he did not do so until December
3rd, when most of the damage was done.

The subsequent *mea culpa* of the advisers (or at any rate some of
them) has naturally been eagerly used by defenders of the President.
His daughter seized upon Acheson to write: 'During these fateful
weeks my father did not receive the kind of support and advice he
deserved . . .'[15] No doubt he did deserve to be better served, but
there must also be responsibility upon him for not better serving himself. He could not shelter behind the Secretary of State
or the Chiefs of Staff when it came to sacking MacArthur and
there is no reason why he should shelter behind them for not
sacking him earlier. It was not as though he had himself proposed
such a course and been dissuaded from it by the weight of
professional and Cabinet advice. At the Wake Island meeting
he had assumed a certain symbiotic relationship with the General.

He had even been impressed. He talked about 'the ideas of two intellectually honest men when they meet . . .'[16] This mood was only gradually worn away during November. As late as the 30th of that month he wrote for his diary more in sorrow than in anger, but certainly giving no impression that he was being restrained with difficulty from demanding the General's head on a charger:

> 'This has been a hectic month. General Mac as usual has been shooting off his mouth. He made a pre-election statement that cost us votes and he made a post-election statement that has him in hot water in Europe and at home. I must defend him and save his face even if he has on various and numerous occasions tried to cut mine off. I must stand by my subordinates . . .'[17]

On that same day he himself had in fact rivalled MacArthur not in insubordination, for that is a sin which by definition a President and Commander-in-Chief cannot commit, but in creating confusion around the world. He had held a press conference in difficult circumstances. Rattled by MacArthur's alternations between bombast and panic, his military advisers were undecided as to whether it would be possible to hold on in Korea at all or whether it would be necessary to seek a cease-fire and/or contemplate evacuation. He had to bluff his way over this weakness, which he did successfully. In the course of doing so, however, he let fall some ill-considered remarks about the possible use of the atomic bomb. After saying that the United States would take whatever steps were necessary to meet the military situation, he was asked: 'Will that include the atomic bomb?' 'That includes every weapon we have,' he said. Then he was asked: 'Does that mean there is active consideration of the use of the atomic bomb?' 'There has always been consideration of its use,'* he replied. Then, later, he was pressed on whether the weapon might be used against military or civilian targets. He said: 'It's a matter the military people will have to decide. I'm not a military authority that passes on these things.' The next question was whether United Nations authority would be required for the use of the atomic bomb. 'No,' said Truman,

---

* This was his familiar mistake of allowing words to be put into his mouth.

'it doesn't mean that at all. The action against Communist China depends on the action of the United Nations. The military commander in the field will have charge of the use of weapons, as he always has.'[18]

It was a devastatingly foolish series of answers, and the President could hardly complain that it was interpreted around the world as meaning that MacArthur had been given discretion as to when to use a nuclear weapon and would probably do so very soon. Within an hour the White House issued a retraction which rather engagingly began by stating that 'The President wants to make it certain that there is no misinterpretation of his answers to questions at his press conference today . . .' It then pointed out, accurately but eliptically, that what he had said must be nonsense for, by law, only the President could authorize the use of the atomic bomb, and that no such authority had been given. But the alarm bells around the world could not quickly be stopped ringing.

One of them rang in London at a particularly sensitive time. The House of Commons was holding a major foreign affairs debate when news of the President's press conference came through in the late afternoon. The attendance in and around the chamber was augmented by the tense parliamentary situation of that short Parliament of 1950–1, with a government majority of only six. The news from America, however, united rather than divided the House. It did so in rather an ignoble way, with members crowding and clucking around the main tape machine like animals around a meal trough. A mood of near panic set in. I had certainly never seen anything like it. That was not altogether surprising, as I had then been a member for less than three years. What is more surprising is that I have never seen anything like it in the subsequent 35 years.

Attlee was quickly confronted by a letter of dissociation with America signed by half his back benchers. Churchill and Eden expressed slightly more measured dismay. Attlee calmed the House by proposing an immediate visit to Washington. This was a remarkable event, for he was no great traveller. He mostly left such things to Bevin. But Bevin was too ill to go, and in any event had been confined to travelling by ship for several years past, and the schedules of the Cunard Line were hardly adequate for such an emergency.

Attlee proposed to Truman a fairly broad-based three-pronged agenda, but the impression given to the House of Commons and the world was that he was going to read the riot act to the Americans. He was nonetheless able to command a full-scale Washington heads of government conference at very short notice. A significant part of the special relationship persisted, and the British had a hard-fighting brigade in Korea. Accompanied by a strong military team, Attlee flew to the United States on the night of Sunday, December 3rd, and had four full days of talks with the Americans.

This visit was, and remains, one of the most varyingly inter- preted diplomatic events of the post-war decade. The extreme British and pro-Attlee interpretation is that the Prime Minister arrived at the White House like a feared but respected schoolmaster striding into a disorderly class-room and proceeded to tell Truman, with his well-known economy in the use of words, that he had better pull himself together, give up foolish notions of using the A-bomb in or around the Korean theatre, discipline Mac- Arthur, and generally reduce commitment in the Far East in order to get a better balance in Europe. The extreme American and anti-Attlee version suggests that the Prime Minister arrived in Washington as a lugubrious and unwelcome guest at a time when a tense administration needed sustenance not criticism, proceeded to whine a doctrine of total appeasement in the Far East, and was duly chastened by his firmer minded hosts until he departed, none too soon, with his tail between his legs.

It is not easy to determine exactly where, between the two, the truth lies. First, the myth that Attlee's visit stopped Truman starting nuclear warfare in Korea can be quickly disposed of. Truman had no intention of doing any such thing, but he had mainly himself to blame for the fact that such a fear had become widespread. Second, it was probably the case that the news of Attlee's imminent arrival aroused little enthusi- asm in the White House. Margaret Truman, who normally reflects the atmosphere well, refers to the trip as being 'un- necessary' and 'defeatist'. On the other hand, Acheson, who was in most ways the sharpest critic of the visit, actually recorded that on December 3rd he successfully 'opposed efforts to obtain a cease-fire until Mr Attlee had arrived and been consulted'.*[19] And the whole administration, President, State Department and military establishment, put themselves out to a remarkable extent for the exchanges. Apart from the four days of formal talks there was a Potomac cruise and a British Embassy dinner attended by Truman. Perhaps the dismayed administration was glad to have something to do other than listen to the mixture of bad news and bad advice from MacArthur. In any event it was treatment which no allied head of government could now secure in Washington, even at 96 days' notice, let alone 96 hours'.

Truman's own account of the meetings, given respectfully and at considerable length in his *Memoirs* (published in 1956) contains no criticism of Attlee. Unfortunately that amounts to little by way of evidence, for these *Memoirs* were written (certainly not entirely by Truman himself) with all the bland, formal accuracy of British Cabinet minutes. They are a good, flat account of the events of his presidency, purged of any authentic contact with his habits of phrase or thought. In books which better capture his views and personality he is mostly silent upon the visit.

Acheson therefore becomes an important if not wholly conclusive witness. Apart from anything else, he comes near to contradicting himself. He strikes a different note in his own memoirs (published in 1969) and the interview which he gave to Mr Kenneth Harris for his *Attlee* between then and his own death in 1971. *Present at the Creation* is, to say the least, waspish about the Attlee visit. 'December opened by bringing us a Job's comforter in Clement Attlee . . .' he warmly began. 'He was a far abler man than Winston Churchill's description of him as "a sheep in sheep's clothing" would imply, but persistently depressing. He spoke, as John J. Chapman said of President Charles W. Eliot of Harvard, with "all the passion of a woodchuck chewing a carrot". His thought impressed me as a long withdrawing melancholy sigh.'[20]

---

* The fact that a cease-fire, which could only have been obtained on humiliating terms, was under active consideration at the time shows how defeatist (without any help yet from Attlee) had become the atmosphere in both Tokyo and Washington. The centre of infection was MacArthur himself, who had been advising, out of a mixture of panic ('blue funk' in Acheson's words) and special pleading, that Chinese intervention left a choice only between the use of atomic weapons and the evacuation of the peninsula. The false dichotomy of this advice may well have been largely responsible for Truman's indiscretion of November 30th. The President was determined to give no hint of scuttle. In order to give Scylla a wide berth he steered too close to Charybdis.

For the rest he described how he had to rebuke Attlee for believing that the United States could be expected to combine a policy of determined commitment in Europe with scuttle in Asia, and for saying that nothing was more important for the West than retaining the good opinion of Asia: 'I remarked acidly that (there was) the security of the United States.' For the rest he recorded that 'the chief impression left with me was a deep dislike and distrust of the "summit conference" as a diplomatic instrument'.[21]

The bridge between this account and that which he gave to Mr Harris was provided by his description of the difficult general battle he had to fight to prevent Attlee skilfully leading Truman into a cumulative acceptance of his argument, and the specific battle over the excision from the communiqué of an undertaking by each of the two countries not to use the atomic weapon without consultation with the other. This, it was alleged, would be as much against United States law as the President delegating such authority to MacArthur. Talking to Mr Harris, Acheson paid high tribute to Attlee, although rather in the way that Churchill described Baldwin as 'the most formidable politician he ever knew', and several times using rather inappropriate words:

'Churchill never asked or got so much as Attlee did,' Acheson was recorded as saying. 'He was a very remarkable man . . . Attlee was adroit, extremely adroit, his grasp of the situation was masterly. His method was seduction:* he led the President, step by step, to where he wanted to get him. He would make a statement of what the British wanted as though it were a statement of what the Americans wanted, and pause and say, very quickly, "I take it we are already agreed about that," and Mr Truman, who was no slouch himself as a negotiator, would answer "Yes, we are." I was horrified. I began stepping on the President's foot . . . I found that Attlee had been very much underrated. He was a damn good lawyer.† All through the talks he was out to get everything he could out of Truman's hands, and into his. The idea that he came over just to expostulate about MacArthur and the Bomb is most misleading; if we hadn't watched him like a hawk,

---

* An unusual judgment.
† He was not.

he would have gone back to London leaving American policy hamstrung.'[22]

There remains the question of personal relations between Attlee and Truman. Truman was not particularly good at getting on with those from a different background whom he did not much know. Attlee was still worse. In the circumstances they seem to have managed very well. Lord Franks, who was British Ambassador at the time, but whose judgment is much less affected by achievements as a host than is that of many diplomats, has told me that the embassy dinner on the Thursday evening (the third day of the talks) was in his view an occasion of break-through. Truman and Attlee sang World War I songs together. This particular choral manifestation is not mentioned elsewhere, although both Truman and Acheson give the impression that the dinner was a considerable success.

This was the more remarkable as it took place at the end of 24 hours which had been exceptionally wearing for Truman. On top of having to cope with the *débâcle* in the Far East and the Attlee talks, he had just sustained the sudden death of the member of his staff to whom he was closest. Charles Ross, his press officer, with whom he had been at school in Independence, had dropped dead at his desk on the Wednesday evening, within minutes of completing a briefing on the progress of the talks during the day on the presidential yacht. Later that evening, Margaret Truman gave a concert in Washington. The music critic of the *Washington Post* reviewed it in terms which, while not wholly hostile, were fairly critical. Truman read the review at 5.30 the next morning, walked across to his office in the White House, and there poured out to the thirty-four-year-old critic 150 words of bile which was as childish as it was concentrated.★ This was pre-eminently a compo-

---

★ 'Mr Hume: I've just read your lousy review of Margaret's concert. I've come to the conclusion that you are an "eight ulcer man on four ulcer pay".

'It seems to me that you are a frustrated old man who wishes he could have been successful. When you write such poppy-cock as was in the back section of the paper you work for it shows conclusively that you're off the beam and at least four of your ulcers are at work.

'Some day I hope to meet you. When that happens you'll need a new nose, a lot of beefsteak for black eyes, and perhaps a supporter below!

'(Westbrook) Pegler, a guttersnipe, is a gentleman alongside you. I hope you'll accept that statement as a worse insult than a reflection on your ancestry.

Harry S. Truman'

'My whole political career is based on my war service and war associates'. Reunion Parade of the 35th Division, Little Rock, Arkansas, Summer 1949. Defence Secretary Louis Johnson on Truman's right, General Vaughan on his far left.
(Harry S. Truman Library)

A trio of master builders: Dean Acheson, Ernest Bevin and Robert Schuman, London, May 1950. *(Keystone Press Agency)*

A throat-gripping hand-shake? Truman and MacArthur, Wake Island, October 1950. (*Dept. of State, courtesy Harry S. Truman Library*)

The Americans who made the Western Alliance: Marshall, left, and Acheson welcome Truman back from MacArthur, October 1950. (*UPI/Bettmann Newsphotos*)

sition which should have joined Truman's large collection of letters he did not send. His staff would quickly have gathered it in had he put it in his out tray. Instead he stuck a three-cent stamp on it and got a White House usher to go and put it in an ordinary mail-box. Hume published it two days later. The informed reaction was one of shocked surprise that the President of the United States should attack such a small target so intemperately. But the incoming mail was largely on his side and he wrote defiantly in his diary about what he had done. It was not the best preparation for an embassy dinner with visitors with whom he had already spent most of the previous 72 hours.

On the other hand I must record that when I went to see Truman in Kansas City nearly three years later and tried to get him to discuss his relationship with Attlee, I could elicit little warmth. It was Churchill, with whom he worked for the last fifteen as for the first three months of his presidency, for whom he reserved his enthusiasm and whom he wished to see again. He liked to stress his own homespun virtues in favourable contrast to the grandeur of F.D.R., but he confused the issue by showing much more appreciation of the grandeur of Churchill than of the more homespun quality of Attlee.

The essential skill of Attlee on this visit, which Truman probably appreciated more than Acheson, for all the latter's high perception, was that he put under the talks the safety net of fairly frequently telling the Americans that the British would in the last resort support them more or less whatever they did. He did this both in public and in private. He told the National Press Club: 'As long as the Stars and Stripes flies in Korea the British flag will fly beside it.' In this way he kept American impatience at some of his views well under control and gave himself a relatively safe position, up on the tight-rope, from which to tell them that he hoped the courses in which he would support them would not be too foolish. As a result he could return to London feeling that he had got satisfactory moral (although not formal) assurances about consultation before any future use of the bomb, and that he had made the Americans more aware, not merely of MacArthur's bad and rash generalship in the context of Korea (it needed 'no ghost come from the grave to tell [them] that'), but of the dangers of his strategy distorting the whole balance of their world effort.

In Washington the President and his advisers were left to live with the consequences of their crushing repulse in North Korea. The alarmist view that it left only the choices of all-out war or evacuation proved ill-founded, but was refuted only at the price of another six months of bitter and fluctuating warfare with heavy casualties. Compared with the great swoops of the previous six months the advances or retreats became slower, but this stickiness of movement brought more and not less carnage. The line, more or less on the old frontier, which General Walker was able to establish in December, could not be held. Walker himself was killed on December 23rd and replaced by Ridgway, who soon afterwards took over command of all the UN forces in Korea, thereby relegating MacArthur to the role of a semi-spectator in Tokyo.

Ridgway successfully set about restoring the morale of the 8th Army, and of X Corps when it again took the field. His first task was, however, the melancholy one of containing the second Communist invasion of South Korea and again evacuating Seoul. He was back forty or so miles south of the capital by mid-January. On January 25th he launched a counter-offensive and, after a period of setback in mid-February, he regained Seoul by March 15th and was at the 38th parallel by the end of the month. He advanced cautiously north for another three weeks. Then the Chinese launched their expected spring offensive. Once more the UN troops were driven back south of the parallel but managed to hold a line just to the north of Seoul. It was in this withdrawal that the British suffered particularly heavily, with the near massacre, following a most gallant stand, of a battalion of the Gloucestershire Regiment.

By May 20th the Communists were stopped. On May 23rd the UN command began yet another offensive which took them once again north of the parallel and to the occupation by June 12th of the two tactically important towns of Chorwon and Kumwha. There, as the anniversary of its outbreak approached, the war settled down. On June 23rd Malik proposed at the United Nations that cease-fire negotiations should be opened between the participants. They were, but not with a great will to peace. It took another 25 months before an armistice was signed at Panmunjon.

These long drawn-out negotiations were punctuated by occasional outbursts of hard fighting, by substantial American trouble with the intransigence of Syngman Rhee, and by North

Korean accusations, strongly supported by Dr Hewlett Johnson, the 'Red Dean' of Canterbury, that the UN forces were engaging in germ warfare, all against the theme of continuing dispute over the repatriation of prisoners of war. This issue was greatly complicated by the facts that the Communists had engaged in some remarkably successful brain-washing of American and British prisoners and that many of the North Koreans in the hands of the UN were determined not to go back. The war dragged on as a running irritant throughout the last eighteen months of Truman's presidency, and the need to break the log-jam of the stalled negotiations was successfully exploited by Eisenhower in the 1952 campaign. But the crisis went out of the war after June 1951.

During the course of the war Truman had faced three major crunches: first, the decision to resist and then rally the United Nations in June 1950; second, the absorption of the shock of defeat six months later, and the decision to fight back in a still limited war, resisting alike the rival temptations of withdrawal and escalation; and third, the belated dismissal of MacArthur in April 1951.

Although this last was belated, overwhelmingly justified, and essential if the authority of the presidency was to be maintained, it was nonetheless an act of stark courage. I doubt if Franklin Roosevelt would have done it. He would have more successfully massaged MacArthur, while patronizing him a little and certainly not allowing the reverse to happen, as at Wake Island. And he would have shunted him gradually sideways and downwards, so that he ended up somewhere between a grand emissary to the then powerless Emperor of Japan and a keeper of American war graves in the Pacific. But he would probably not have sacked him.

Truman did not decide to do this following the defeat and the Attlee protests of December. In January he was still trying hard, using a mixture of flattery and logical exposition, to find a *modus vivendi* with MacArthur. This was a hopeless task, for MacArthur, particularly after Ridgway took over the joint command in Pusan, was looking for departure with a flourish and not for quiet co-operation. In mid-March, with South Korea again free of invading troops, Truman ordered careful work to be done on preparing a cease-fire proposal to be put to the Chinese. MacArthur was consulted on the key paragraphs. Thereupon he issued his own ultimatum to the Chinese, couched in terms of such insulting rhetoric that there could be no possibility of their accepting it. That made it impossible for Truman to send his message to the Chinese, and, he subsequently claimed, was when he made up his mind to get rid of him:

> 'That is what he got fired for . . . He prevented a cease-fire proposition right there. I was ready to kick him into the North China Sea at that time. I was never so put out in my life. It's the lousiest trick a Commander-in-Chief can have done to him by an underling. MacArthur thought he was proconsul for the government of the United States and could do as he damned pleased.'[23]

General Marshall subsequently put much the same point in more restrained and logical language: 'What is new and what brought about the necessity for General MacArthur's removal is the wholly unprecedented situation of a local theater commander publicly expressing his displeasure at, and disagreement with, the foreign policy of the United States.'[24]

MacArthur did not however go immediately after his epistle to the Chinese. Truman showed some guile over the timing. He needed to get some important congressional votes on appropriations for the Marshall Plan and NATO out of the way before lobbing his bomb into the political arena. He also wanted to be under pressure from his advisers, rather than vice-versa, to agree to the removal of MacArthur. He therefore waited for a further act of provocation, which was a letter from the General to Representative Joseph Martin, the Republican minority leader, which again set out his own foreign policy and which was duly read to the House by Martin on April 4th.

Truman conferred that day and subsequently with a group composed of Marshall, Acheson, Harriman and General Bradley. By April 7th they unanimously recommended to him that MacArthur be relieved of his command. Bradley had conferred with the three service chiefs, and on April 8th brought them to see Truman, when they each gave him their opinion that he should act as proposed. This somewhat deliberate method of proceeding had the great advantage that it led to them all giving extremely firm testimony to a special Senate Committee which subsequently and inconclusively considered the merits of MacArthur's dismissal.

It was the direct opposite of the mood which Louis Johnson had achieved amongst the witnesses before the House Armed Services Committee in 1949.

Its disadvantage was that it defeated the plans for the most courteous possible conveying of the news to MacArthur. This was to be done personally by the Secretary of the Army, Frank Pace, who was in Korea and was to proceed to Tokyo and quietly inform the General. Instead there was a leak, the announcement had to be brought forward, and MacArthur was first informed, not by Pace, but by his incredulous wife, who had just heard it on the radio. This infelicity gave him an exploitable, but hardly decisive, grievance. It is doubtful if he would have taken the news well had it been conveyed to him a week in advance of publication by a joint deputation of every other five-star general in the US Army.

For the moment, however, it was the reaction of the public rather than of the General which made the impact. 'Quite an explosion,' Truman wrote fairly laconically in his diary for April 10th. 'Was expected but I had to act. Telegrams and letters of abuse by the dozen.'[25]

'By the dozen' was something of an understatement. 78,000 pieces of mail on the issue eventually reached the White House, and they broke approximately twenty to one against the President. On the Gallup Poll he did somewhat better, only 69% supporting MacArthur as against 29% for the President. The loyal 29% were not enough to prevent Truman being burnt in effigy in many places across the nation, and there was a great deal of muttering about impeachment, some of it from relatively responsible members of the Congress. The press was substantially better than the public. The *New York Times* and the *Washington Post*, not then the heavenly twins of East Coast liberalism which they subsequently became, both supported the President. So did the *New York Herald Tribune*, the *Boston Globe*, the *Christian Science Monitor*, the *St Louis Post-Dispatch*, the *Chicago Sun-Times*, to cite only a few.

There was however a second spasm of the earthquake still to be faced: the return of MacArthur to the United States. As it was the first time he had been seen in America since 1937, his arrival would in any event have caused considerable interest. In the circumstances it aroused hysteria. He reached San Francisco on April 17th. He was greeted by a crowd of 100,000 and seemed to show himself a dangerous master of sententious demagogy by announcing: 'The only politics I have is contained in the simple phrase known well by all of you: God Bless America.'

He then proceeded to Washington for the joint session of Congress which he had been invited to address. Truman made a good if daring joke by sending General Vaughan to greet him. The Pentagon, even though firm on the issue, was more respectful. Marshall, Bradley and the three Chiefs of Staff were all present on the tarmac at National Airport. The address to Congress was powerful and provocative. The Cabinet, apart from Truman and Acheson, were sunk in gloom. They both believed there was an element of bathos about the much-acclaimed speech. They turned out to be right, but it required some bravado on their part to feel it at the time.

Perhaps MacArthur made a symptomatic mistake by ending in ambiguity. '"Old soldiers," he said, "never die; they just fade away." And like the old soldier of that ballad, I now close my military career and just fade away – an old soldier who tried to do his duty as God gave him the light to see that duty. Goodbye.'

Immediately he faded away to the Waldorf Tower in New York, but from there he made several powerful early forays. However his balloon fairly quickly began to subside. Truman, not the most impartial of witnesses perhaps, thought the beginning of the exhalation was when he was half laughed at at a baseball game in Queen's. Certainly he was never seriously considered as a presidential candidate for 1952. He was of course immensely old, even by more recent sandards, to *start* a political career. He died, almost forgotten, in 1964, at the age of 84.

Truman, when led in that direction by an interlocutor,[26] said that the sacking was the greatest test of his presidency. In a negative sense it was. But it required more nerve than judgment. It was a question of enduring the noise of bombardment, which was fearsome, but which, once he had got the rest of the military establishment on his side, was unlikely to prove fatal. And Truman was very good at that. Other crises of the war called for a rarer combination of qualities, and ones which came less easily to him. These, too, he surmounted well. The Korean War destroyed any hope of a joyous second term, but in all but the small change of short-run partisan advantage, it enhanced his reputation.

II

THE LAST PHASE

There were nineteen months between June 1951, when the Korean War subsided into a bickering stalemate, and the end of Truman's presidency. After the searing years through which he had passed, and as an introit to the subsequent soaring of his reputation, it would be agreeable to record that they were a period of calm fulfilment and grateful recognition.

Unfortunately it would be completely untrue. The best that could be said for this final year and a half was that, by the standards of his presidency, relatively little happened during it. But most of what did occur was disobliging to Truman, and some of it was humiliating. His administration was plagued by the eruption of one petty scandal after another, cumulatively very damaging, although only those permeating the Bureau of Internal Revenue reached objectively serious proportions. Partly as a result his poll rating at the end of 1951 was down to 23%, substantially worse even than in 1946. He had to sack his Attorney-General and replace him with the third second-rater he had appointed to that post since getting rid of Roosevelt's Biddle. He finally lost Marshall, who withdrew from the Department of Defense in September 1951, and he witnessed the sad spectacle of Acheson's authority at home being increasingly undermined because the President lacked the power to protect his Secretary of State from McCarthy's vitupera-tion. Confronted with a steel strike Truman once again shot impulsively and probably illegally from the hip (although this time it was the companies, not the unions, who were his target), and was overturned by the Supreme Court.

As the 1952 elections approached he made almost every possible misjudgment about who the Republican candidate was likely to be, who the Democratic candidate ought to be, and which party was likely to win. He played with the idea of changing his mind and running again himself, but was dissuaded by the near unanimous advice of his family, his friends and his staff: a candidate with an age of 68 and a poll rating of 23% might reasonably be regarded by even his most fervent supporters as having got things nearly the wrong way round. He then had an unhappy campaign relationship both with Stevenson, whom he tried unsuccessfully to make his protégé, and with Eisenhower, with whom he entered into a bitter feud for a mixture of about one to two of good and bad reasons. After threatening darkly (to himself at least) that he would do nothing throughout the election but 'sit on his front porch' – or, as it was the White House,★ the south or back porch – he then conducted a frenetic, ill-judged and unwelcome campaign on behalf of Stevenson.

His last two months of office, apart from a few prickly brushes with Eisenhower, were fairly satisfactory. With a strong sense of the august nature of the presidency (but not of the President) he naturally felt to the full the change in his life which was about to occur. He had a lively awareness of doing things for the last time. But he did not regret this. He felt he had served his time and done his duty. He was ready to go. And when he went he had a grand send-off.

Some of the newer members of his staff sensed a certain lack of grip. Joseph Short, who had replaced Charles Ross as press secretary, thought that Truman was much too inclined to believe that the minor financial scandals could be left to blow themselves out. Roger Tubby, Short's assistant, wrote an extensive and often worried journal. During a holiday visit to Key West a little before the beginning of the final nineteen months, he wrote: 'Poker, poker, I wonder why he played so much . . . a feeling of vacuum otherwise, no struggle, excitement? . . . companionship, banter, escape from the pressing problems of state?' Then, the train of his thought being obvious, he added: 'I read the *New Republic* editorial expressing fear lest Truman end up in as bad repute as Harding – though that hardly seems possible . . . the

★ The Trumans had at last returned to the reconstructed Executive Mansion on March 27th, 1952.

stuff so far [has] been such chicken feed compared to Teapot Dome.'*¹

No doubt the newer staff found it less easy than the longer serving ones to understand the peculiar mixture of his weave of relaxation and decision taking, which had certainly not left the country short of firm government. There was no suggestion of disloyalty developing amongst either group. What was striking, however, was the unanimity with which they all said 'no' when, in early March 1952, he seriously considered running again.

This did not mean that his private memorandum of renunciation, by then nearly two years old, which he had revealed to his staff in the previous November, was just a piece of play-acting. He genuinely thought that it was right and desirable that he should not serve again. He also no doubt had a roseate vision of finding a satisfactory Democratic candidate, whom he could promote, instruct in the ways of presidential politics and government, and then protectively install in the White House.

Truman's approach to the 1952 election cannot be understood without comprehending that he firmly believed a Democratic candidate could and would win. This was based partly on his fierce partisanship, which made him overestimate the continuing appeal of his own and Roosevelt's record. It was also based on the view, which he held steadfastly up to the opening of their Convention in early July, that the Republicans would nominate Taft, whom he regarded as eminently beatable. In Truman's view therefore any presentable Democrat (certainly including himself, in spite of the 23% poll rating) would be President and not merely a sporting runner. This view, except possibly for the inclusion of Truman himself within the electable category, was broadly shared by much informed opinion over the winter of 1951–2.

* Teapot Dome was a naval oil reserve (in Wyoming) which under the Harding administration was transferred to the Department of the Interior (from the Navy Department) and then leased to a private group in return for a direct bribe to the Secretary of the Interior (Fall). It put Fall in gaol and led to the resignation of the Secretary of the Navy. The Attorney-General was also implicated. The result was the *débâcle* of the administration. Harding cocooned himself in a long train trip across the continent which became an almost unending series of increasingly frenzied poker parties. The cocoon could not however prevent the messages of doom from getting through. They annihilated Harding, who was not personally corrupt. He collapsed and died on the West Coast, and, the train brought his body back to Washington through a grief-stricken nation which knew nothing of the emerging scandals.

At the beginning of that winter, on November 19th, Truman for the first time discussed the succession freely with his staff. Adlai Stevenson, who at the age of 51 was three years into a successful term as Governor of Illinois, was the first name to be mentioned in this inner group, as it was already becoming the first name in more public circles. Truman spoke against him, on somewhat inconsequential grounds. According to his daughter he expressed his hope that the Democratic Party 'would be smart enough to select someone who could win. And by that I *don't* mean the Stevenson type of candidate. I don't believe the people of the United States are ready for an Ivy Leaguer.'*

Truman's choice was his own appointment as Chief Justice, Fred Vinson, a former Kentucky congressman who had been briefly Secretary of the Treasury before elevation to the Supreme Court. As Chief Justice, which office he occupied respectably rather than with distinction, Vinson remained surprisingly close to the President's inner circle (he was a poker player). Truman, as in the case of the abortive mission to Stalin in 1948, tended to credit him with both a greater sagacity and a higher public repute than he in fact possessed. What was indisputable was that he was a man with whom Truman felt comfortable. This combination of qualities, real and imagined, made Truman prepared to leap over a precedent-free gulf and try to put a Chief Justice in the White House.† Vinson, however, was unresponsive. He was 62, not in perfect health, and sensitive about damaging his judicial reputation.

---

* M. Truman, *op. cit.*. p. 257. 'Ready for' was an odd phrase. It is not clear why Truman thought that Choate and Princeton should be premature in 1952 when Groton and Harvard had produced very satisfactory results in 1932, 1936, 1940 and 1944. What he probably meant was that he hoped he had educated the American people away from the need for an Ivy Leaguer. But where did this leave his respected, beloved and much maligned Dean Acheson? Groton and Yale was at least as bad as Choate and Princeton. The answer I think is that Truman had an instinctive view of the shape of an American administration which was the inverse of the old-style view of an English cricket team. Truman thought that the (elected) captain should be a 'pro', assisted by as many competent gentlemen as were qualified to make the team work well. The MCC believed in leadership from a gentleman and technical skill from the professionals.

† Although there was no actual precedent the gulf was not as wide as in most other democracies. William Howard Taft had gone (with a short gap) from the White House to the Chief Justiceship, and Earl Warren's vice-presidential candidature in 1948 was to be considered no bar to his appointment as Chief Justice (after Vinson's death) by Eisenhower in 1953.

By early December he had convinced the President that he was not available.

This left Truman without a satisfactory candidate. Senator Richard Russell of Georgia, Barkley, Harriman and Estes Kefauver all wanted the job, but Truman considered none of them right. Russell was an able Senator but too much a man of the South to be acceptable. Barkley had been 'a great Vice-President', but at 74 he was simply too old. 'It takes him five minutes to sign his name,' which would be a substantial disqualification for dealing with the 600 documents a day which, Truman claimed, the President had to sign.* Harriman, on the other hand, was well capable of doing the job, but Truman thought that his lack of campaign experience and political backing, together with his provenance as the son of one of the great railroad predators of the turn of the century, probably made him unelectable. Kefauver, the anti-crime campaigner in the coonskin hat, he simply regarded as unappetizing. Privately he mostly referred to him as 'Cowfever'.

In these circumstances Truman did two things, neither of which turned out well. First he began to move back towards himself as a candidate, and chose Eisenhower, of all people, as a correspondent to whom to open his mind. Partly because of a certain romantic attachment to the idea of the relationship of the President as Commander-in-Chief to a great commander overseas, and perhaps also to compensate for the MacArthur rupture, he had the habit of writing to Eisenhower in terms closer than that General ever reciprocated, either in thought or word. Certainly on this occasion he wrote to him by hand in a foolishly unbuttoned way:†

'Dera Ike, [Truman wrote on December 18th.]
    'The columnists, the slick magazines and all the political people who like to speculate are saying many things about what is to happen in 1952.
    'As I told you in 1948 and at our luncheon in 1951, do

---

* It might, of course, have led to the earlier introduction of a system to save presidential time, for it is difficult to believe that the two hours which is about the minimum that even a quick signer would need to deal with 600 papers represented a very sensible employment of the Chief Executive's time.

† A large part of Truman's excessive resentment of Eisenhower's politicking in 1952 stemmed from his overestimate of their previous intimacy; Eisenhower was always a conventional domestic conservative, who voted for Dewey in 1948, and had little regard for the policies of the Fair Deal or for Truman's personal style.

what you think best for the country. My own position
is in the balance. If I do what I want to do, I'll go back to
Missouri and *maybe* run for the Senate.★ If you decide to
finish the European job (and I don't know who else can) I
must keep the isolationists out of the White House. I
wish you would let me know what you intend to do. It
will be between us and no one else.

'I have the utmost confidence in your judgment and your
patriotism.

'My best to you and Mrs Ike for a happy holiday season.
     Most sincerely,
          Harry S. Truman.'[2]

Eisenhower took two weeks to reply and then did so at best
guardedly, at worst hypocritically. There was no reciprocation of
esteem let alone affection. Reading between the lines it was clear
that he was open to political angling. But his formal statement of
position, 'you know, far better than I, that the possibility that I
will ever be drawn into political activity is so remote as to be
negligible' was, to say the least, disingenuous. Five days later
Henry Cabot Lodge announced with authority that Eisenhower's
name would be entered in the New Hampshire Republican Primary. Two days after that Eisenhower issued a somewhat unctuous
statement of availability for 'higher duty'.

Truman's name also was entered, by an over-enthusiastic local
supporter, in the New Hampshire Democratic Primary. He tried
but failed to get it withdrawn. He was heavily beaten by Senator
'Cowfever'. Well before that outcome, however, he had made
his second unfortunate move. This was to decide that Governor
Stevenson, even if he carried a little too much ivy, was the most
likely winning candidate, and that he should be summoned to
Washington for a placing of the hands upon the head.

The occasion for this act of consecration was a meeting at Blair
House after dinner on January 22nd. It was the first time they had
attempted to talk intimately. Stevenson had been forewarned by
Murphy what would be proposed. This did not however mean
that he responded with the crisp and grateful acceptance which
Truman expected. Nor, it appears, did he give a clear 'no'. On the
following day Truman reported to Murphy that he had reluctantly

★ No more was ever heard of this idea.

said 'yes'. Stevenson reported to his friends that he had said 'no'. The confusion is probably to be explained by the fact that the two men understood each other about as well as if they had been conversing in a neutral foreign language which neither understood or spoke easily. The reality however was that Stevenson, while flattered by the offer, was genuinely unsure whether he wanted the nomination, partly because of hesitant ambition, partly because of fear of Eisenhower, and certain that he did not want it as Truman's surrogate. He believed that any Democrat with a chance of winning would have to offer a new start in Washington and not a continuation of the Truman régime under a new name.

In the course of a few days Truman came to understand that he had not netted his candidate, but not the reasons for this failure. He believed that Stevenson, like a shy Victorian heroine receiving her first proposal of marriage, had been too overwhelmed by the offer to make a rational reply. A little perseverance would probably do the trick.

On March 4th, when President and Governor met for the second time, Truman was forced to accept defeat, although it seems unlikely that many misunderstandings were cleared away, for the account which Truman wrote on the same day of the interview, while happily friendly towards Stevenson, was frankly incredible:

'Tonight the Governor came to see me at his request to tell me that he had made a commitment to run for re-election in Illinois and that he did not think he could go back on that commitment honorably. I appreciate his view point and I honor him for it . . . His is an honorable man. Wish I could have talked with him before his announcement. He is a modest man too. He seems to think that I am something of a superman which isn't true of course.

'. . . I told him I could get him nominated whether he wanted to be or not. Then I asked what he'd do in that case. He was very much worried and said that no patriot could say no to such a condition [sic].

'Then he argued that only I can beat any Republican be he Taft, Eisenhower, Warren, or anyone else! My wife and daughter had said the same thing to me an hour before. What the hell am I to do? I'll know when the time comes because I am sure God Almighty will guide me.'[3]

Truman in fact turned more for guidance to Chief Justice Vinson, who had the advantage of being resident in Washington. He had him, Charles Murphy and a few others to one of his last dinners in Blair House. They were discouraging. The rest of the story is told vividly, as usual, by his daughter: 'Later, he convened a larger meeting, which included the whole White House staff as well as several congressional leaders. At this meeting he polled the entire room – a dozen or more – and asked each man what he thought. Although they gave varying reasons, not one of them thought he should run again. Mother felt the same way. So did I. Mother's opinion carried a lot more weight than mine, of course. Dad decided that the verdict seemed to be unanimous.'[4]

That settled the question of his own candidature. He went off for another vacation at Key West and on his return used a Jefferson/Jackson Day Washington dinner to make a surprise announcement of unequivocal non-availability. 'I shall not accept a renomination', he said. 'I do not feel that it is my duty to spend another four years in the White House.' It did not, however, settle the question of Stevenson. Truman had switched off him, but public attention had not. Indeed, as soon as Truman made his statement of withdrawal the cameramen rushed to the other end of the same long table where the Governor of Illinois was seated.

Throughout the spring and summer Stevenson played very hard to get. To a large extent his reluctance was genuine. But this did not make it any less irritating to Truman, who had his own troubles during these months. On March 28th his Director of Defense Mobilisation, Charles E. Wilson, the former head of General Electric,* resigned in dudgeon against a policy of profit squeeze on the steel industry and brought a great deal of business and press approbrium upon the head of the administration. On April 3rd McGrath, the delinquent Attorney-General, had to be dismissed for quite separate reasons. On April 8th, almost as though to keep up the interest, Truman seized the steel mills. He had been encouraged to take such action by the private, certainly rash, and doubtfully proper counsel of Chief Justice Vinson. Congress declined to give him power to operate the mills, and a Federal

* Not the same man as the remarkably confusingly named and positioned other Charles E. Wilson, then head of General Motors, who was soon to be Eisenhower's first Secretary of Defense and the author of one of the great business aphorisms of the century: 'What is good for General Motors is good for America.'

Court declared their seizure unconstitutional. The Supreme Court then announced that it would hear the case. This all happened within a week. After that there was an interval until June 2nd, when the Court declared Truman's action unconstitutional by the crushing majority of six to three. Vinson had been overruled in his own Court, and had carried only one, not very notable, Truman appointee (Minton) with him. Much of the indignity lay in the fact that the majority was stuffed with Democrats who were mostly liberals as well. It was quite unlike 1936 when Roosevelt could portray himself as battling against a fossilized Court of 'horse and buggy' reactionaries. In 1952 there was not a single one of the nine justices who was not a Roosevelt or a Truman appointee. Amongst the majority six were Hugo L. Black, who delivered the majority judgment, Felix Frankfurter, Robert H. Jackson, William O. Douglas, and, almost the unkindest cut of all, Tom Clark, the Attorney-General who had been elevated beyond his deserts by Truman a couple of years before.

The immediate result was that Truman allowed the separation of powers to produce the disorganization of government. With the Korean War simmering away, he had a seven week steel strike on his hands. How much harm to national interests it did is open to question. Indeed one of the factors in the adverse judgment was quantitative rather than qualitative: steel stocks were too high to justify presidential high-handedness. But its pressures, leading up to a settlement on July 24th, no doubt increased his feeling that he was grappling with real issues while Stevenson, to quote Joseph Chamberlain's satirical lines on Gladstone, 'left us repining while he is, no doubt, still engaged in refining'.

When, therefore, on that same day of July, Stevenson telephoned the President, the first direct communication between them for several months, and asked Truman whether it would embarrass him after all if he allowed his name to be put forward, he got a fairly rough although favourable reply. That is exactly what I have been trying to urge upon your over-elegant mind for the past six months was the essence of the President's response. In fact this was not wholly true. It had been so, but after the double rebuff of March Truman had switched to Barkley, semi-senile or not, and had sent him out to Chicago with full presidential backing. Barkley, however, in Truman's view mishandled his essential canvassing of labour leaders, and got a turn-down as firm as Byrnes had received in 1944. He then withdrew, in reality in dismay but in form under the happy smokescreen of a splendid valedictory oration, and left Truman once again fancy free when Stevenson telephoned.

The President thereupon threw himself with almost excessive enthusiasm into a campaign of support for the Governor's nomination. He believed that his support was decisive. But the surge towards Stevenson was such that he would almost certainly have been swept in whatever Truman had done. He was the first 'drafted' Democratic candidate since Garfield in 1880, and that had been on the 36th ballot, whereas Stevenson achieved it on the 3rd. Nor did he make much obeisance to Truman. He excused himself from meeting him at the airport or from dining with him on the evening of his arrival in Chicago. He did, however, allow himself to be escorted by the President down the aisle of the convention hall and introduced by him before delivering at 2.00 a.m. his memorable if unusually humourless and somewhat florid acceptance speech. Truman, like most other people, was moved by the speech. He pledged himself 'to take my coat off and do everything I can to help him win'. He wrote him a warm letter at 6.40 the next morning. He invited him to Washington for strategy discussion and policy briefing, and Stevenson, perhaps without much alternative, accepted. It was the brief high point of their relationship.

Truman was quickly offended by Stevenson's replacement of the chairman of the Democratic National Committee, by other campaign appointments, by the setting up of his campaign headquarters in Springfield, Illinois, and not in Washington, and by his generally detached behaviour. By early August Truman was writing one of his famous unsent letters to Stevenson, but the tone was more hurt and complaining and less aggressive than usual:

> 'Dear Governor,
> I have come to the conclusion', he began, 'that you are embarrassed by having the President of the United States in your corner in this campaign. Therefore I shall remain silent and stay in Washington until Nov 4th.'

He retailed all the efforts he had made to get Stevenson the candidature, and continued:

Truman and Stevenson rarely looked in the same direction. Democratic Convention, Chicago, 1952. *(UPI/Bettmann Newsphotos)*

The Truman family free of Office, 1953. *(UPI/Bettmann Newsphotos)*

An early-morning walk at Independence: winter in the 1960s.
(UPI/Bettmann Newsphotos)

'You were nominated and made a grand acceptance speech. Then you proceeded to break up the Democratic Committee, which I had spent years in organizing, you called in the former mayor of Louisville [Wilson Wyatt] as your personal chairman and fired McKinney, the best chairman of the National Committee in my recollection . . . I have tried to make it plain to you that I want you elected – in fact I want you to win this time more than I wanted to win in 1948. But – I can't stand snub after snub from you and Mr Wyatt . . . I shall go to the dedication of the Hungry Horse Dam in Montana (due in late September), make a public power speech, get in a plane and come back to Washington and stay there. You and Wilson can now run your campaign without interference or advice.'[5]

Within a couple of weeks matters got still worse. Stevenson, maybe carelessly allowing an instinctive assumption of his mind to come to the surface, committed Truman's old fault of allowing a questioner to put words into his mouth. It was more reprehensible, however, for it was a written exchange. 'Can Stevenson really clear up the mess in Washington?' the *Oregon Journal* asked him. 'As to whether I can clean up the mess in Washington' he answered, 'I would bespeak the careful scrutiny of what I inherited in Illinois and what has been accomplished in three years.' The reply reverberated around the continent. The Democratic candidate had accepted the validity of one of the main Republican catch phrases of the campaign. Truman was affronted, and returned to the writing table within a few days. On this occasion he started with more raillery and less rancour than before:

'My Dear Governor,
    Your letter to Oregon is a surprising document. It makes the campaign rather ridiculous. It seems to me that the Presidential Nominee and his running mate are trying to beat the Democratic President instead of the Republicans and the General of the Army who heads their ticket. There is no mess in Washington except the sabotage press . . .'

However, he soon jerked himself up on to a sharper note:

'You fired and balled up the Democratic National
Committee Organization that I've been creating over the
last four years.

'I'm telling you to take your crackpots, your high
socialites with their noses in the air, run your campaign
and win if you can. Cowfever could not have treated me
any more shabbily than you have . . .

'Best of luck from a bystander who has become
disinterested.'[6]

It was bitter stuff (again not sent of course) and although it
represented a part of Truman's feelings he gave no public vent to
them and he in no way carried out his threat (which would have
inflicted more deprivation upon himself than upon Stevenson) to
remain silent, stationary and sullen. The Hungry Horse expedition,
for instance, turned into a full-scale campaign trip, with the presidential train, and a pattern of six or eight speeches a day which
was similar to that of 1948, except that the full blast of public
attention was not on the President, who was not a candidate.

He and Stevenson never appeared together, which was perhaps
as well for there was a fairly wide gulf of style and substance
between them. Truman was happy to provide the rough stuff for
which he thought that Stevenson was too mealy-mouthed. Some
of it he did very well. He had a good joke about the initials
GOP really standing not for Grand Old Party but for the Generals'
Own Party. 'The Republicans,' he said, 'have General Motors and
General Electric and General Foods and General MacArthur and
General Martin and General Wedemeyer. And then they have their
own five-star General who is running for President . . . [but]
general welfare is with the corporals and the privates in the Democratic Party.'[7]

On the whole however he made the mistake of striking too
persistent and strident a note of abuse of Eisenhower. From the
beginning he resented his candidature. John Snyder, who was the
closest link between them, was probably right when he said that
Truman thought Eisenhower should have run as a Democrat. It
was Democratic presidents who had given him the opportunity to
build up his reputation.[8] This initial resentment provided the
seed-bed from which there sprouted his violent reactions to any
politickings which Eisenhower indulged in during the campaign.

Some of them were admittedly discreditable, most notably the General's excision of a pro-Marshall section from his speech when he appeared on a platform with McCarthy in Wisconsin. However, Truman treated almost everything the General did, from this craven act to his only mildly demagogic undertaking to go to Korea himself and see if he could dig out the bogged down negotiations, as being intolerable, and denounced him in immoderate terms. His responses to the Wisconsin episode, while strong – Eisenhower had 'betrayed his principles', 'deserted his friends', and amazed Truman by 'stoop[ing] so low', were perhaps justified. But it was clearly a mistake to send a message to the Jewish Welfare Board accusing Eisenhower, on a somewhat convoluted argument about immigration, of having endorsed the practices of the 'master race', and discriminated against Jews and Catholics. Rabbis and cardinals responded by denouncing Truman. He was hit hard by the boomerang which he had thrown. But what was more interesting was that he should have been surprised at Eisenhower's resentment. He had an engagingly innocent belief that Eisenhower should expiate his sin of seeking the Republican nomination by going round the country paying tribute to Roosevelt, Truman, Marshall and Acheson, under or with whom he had served during Democratic administrations, but that his own denunciations of Republicans were the legitimate ammunition of healthy, hard-hitting politics. As a result he drove Eisenhower into muttering that he would break a precedent which had stood since 1801 and refuse to drive down Pennsylvania Avenue with Truman on Inauguration Day. He would meet him at the Capitol steps.

This menace was no more carried out than was Truman's own threat that he would not campaign. But the fissure was never healed. It at least had the advantage that it took Truman's mind off his Stevenson resentments. Strong though these were, he would still have much preferred the Governor to beat the General. He was one of the few major politicians whose commitment to his party was much deeper than any personal dislikes. At least from mid-October onwards there was little doubt that Eisenhower would win. There was no foolish boasting in his talking about what he would do at the inauguration ceremony. The result gave him a majority of about 10% or 6½ million votes over Stevenson. He carried 38 out of 48 states, defeating the Governor in Illinois and leaving him mostly only with a South eroded around the edges.

It was not as overwhelming a victory as those achieved by Roosevelt in 1946, Johnson in 1964, Nixon in 1972, or Reagan in 1984, but it was very substantial. Truman disliked the result but was not surprised by it. He indulged in no public recrimination against the defeated Stevenson. He had a small White House dinner party for him in early December and worked out with him future dispositions in the Democratic Party machine.* In his *Memoirs*, published in 1955, he wrote a detached but not bitter criticism of Stevenson's conduct. 'His was a great campaign and did credit to the party and the nation . . . His ability to put into inspiring words the principles of the Democratic Party earned him fame and world-wide recognition. I hold him in the highest regard for his intellectual courage.'[9] However, he also calmly rehearsed his objections of the time to the shape of Stevenson's candidature and came to the conclusion that, had Stevenson gone straight for the nomination from January 1952 and worked more closely with the traditional Democratic base, he might have won at least 3 million more votes, hardly enough to win but enough to make the result close. As the 1956 election approached, Truman withheld his support from Stevenson and gave it unwaveringly to Harriman, up to and over the Convention, once more in Chicago, at which Stevenson was comfortably re-nominated, but certainly not drafted.

Between the 1952 election and Inauguration Day Eisenhower came once to the White House. It was on November 18th, and was a mutually unsatisfactory meeting. Eisenhower was all buttoned up, and Truman superficially at least, tried a little too easily to let bygones be bygones. He offered Eisenhower some commemorative paintings of local heroes given by Latin American governments, which were refused, a globe which Eisenhower had given to Truman in Germany in 1945, the return of which was 'not very graciously' accepted, and some fairly gratuitous bits of advice about how to run the presidential office, which Truman thought 'went into one ear and out of the other'.[10]

---

* However his diary entry on the day after the dinner struck one ambiguous note. 'The Governor has decided to take a trip around the world, and write a travelogue about it. He is going for his own education. A good thing I think.' (*Off the Record*, p. 279)

After that they did not see each other again until January 20th. That was a spectacularly prickly occasion. Eisenhower declined the supposedly traditional luncheon invitation from the Trumans.* He did, however, resile from his earlier intention to make Truman pick him up at the Statler Hotel. He drove to the White House but did not get out of the car. During the drive the only conversation exchanged seems to have been about Eisenhower not having seen a previous inaugural, for he had not been there in 1948 in order, so he is alleged to have self-regardingly said, not to attract attention away from the re-elected President. 'You were not here in 1948,' Truman emolliently replied, 'because I did not send for you . . . if I had . . . you would have come.'[11] Eisenhower is then said to have complained that the outgoing President had ordered his son, John Eisenhower, home from Korea to attend the ceremony and, no doubt by so doing, embarrass the incoming one. The fact that, three days later, Eisenhower wrote to Truman to thank him for this act of consideration, and indeed for his general courtesy during the handover, does not invalidate the unfortunate picture of two gentlemen in their sixties, both outstanding servants of the greatest democracy in the world, behaving in a way which would have been discreditable to two small boys of eight.

After November 4th the pace of activity began to slow down. Truman was still Chief Executive, but there was no point in trying to execute anything which would not come to fruition in the next few weeks. Already in September he had been told that the incoming mail had fallen below 5,000 pieces a day for the first time during his presidency. This was normal, he was told by the chief clerk (who must have had a long memory for similar circumstances had not occurred since the last days of Hoover) 'when the White House occupant was not coming back'. The lack of pressure did not reduce the length of his days. But it did give him more time for committing rumination to paper. On November 24th at 5.00 a.m., allowing for a few differences of style from Waugh and background from Lord Marchmain, he was

---

* 'Supposedly' because there had previously in this century only been a changeover between Presidents of different parties on three occasions, and on one of them the outgoing President (Wilson) was too ill to do any honours, on another the incoming President (Franklin Roosevelt) was too immobile to go into the White House before the ceremony. Taft, I believe, did provide some pre-ceremony sustenance for Wilson (and no doubt for himself too) but this hardly amounted to a tradition.

almost parodying the deathbed soliloquy in *Brideshead Revisited:*★

'The White House is quiet as a church. I can hear the planes at the airport warming up. As always there is a traffic roar – sounds like wind and rain through the magnolias.

'Bess's mother is dying across the hallway. She was ninety years old August 4th. Vivian's [his brother's] mother-in-law passed on Saturday at eleven thirty. She also was ninety just a month after or before Mrs Wallace. When you are sixty-eight death watches come often . . .

'Since last September Mother Wallace has been dying – even before that, but we've kept doctors and nurses with her night and day and have kept her alive. We had hoped – and still hope – she'll survive until Christmas. Our last as President.

'This old House is a most remarkable one. Started in 1792 by George Washington's laying of the corner stone. Burned in 1814, by the British. Occupied by John and Abigail Adams . . .

'Jefferson receiving diplomats in house slippers and dressing gown. Dolley Madison loading pictures and books and documents into a wagon and escaping just two jumps ahead of the British . . .

'Then Monroe refinishing the rehabilitated old place with his own and some imported French furniture. And catching hell because he sent to Paris to buy things he could not obtain in the primitive U.S.A.!

'Old John Quincy Adams who went swimming in the Chesapeake and Potomac Canal every morning . . . Then old Andy Jackson and his rough, tough backwoodsmen walking on the furniture with muddy boots and eating a 300 pound cheese, grinding it into the lovely Adams and Monroe carpets!'[12]

Mrs Wallace died on December 5th, the day after a rather grand farewell dinner with wives for the Cabinet, the senior White House staff and, almost inevitably, the Chief Justice. In spite of her thirty-three years of determined co-habitation, Truman seems genuinely to have mourned her. 'She was a great lady,' he wrote. 'When I hear these mother-in-law jokes, I don't laugh.'[13]

★ The novel had been seven years published, but not, I think, read by Truman.

The family took her out to Missouri to be buried, and then came back to Washington for a White House Christmas which could hardly be regarded as the end of a tradition, for it was only the second which they had spent in what Margaret Truman liked referring to as 'the great white gaol'.

In early January, when life might have been expected to be getting a little flat, there was a Churchill visitation. Truman had come to adore Churchill. He ought (not in a moral but in a matching sense) to have preferred Attlee, but he did not. Churchill, for Truman, represented greatness without Roosevelt's pretension. The thought of the Hudson Valley always rather oppressed him. Blenheim and Chartwell were too remote to have any such effect. And Churchill reciprocated, with a mixture of flattery and foresight, by treating Truman as a world statesman. He, in turn, almost certainly preferred Truman to Roosevelt, with whom his relationship was much more a necessary and beneficial alliance of occasion than it was a partnership of affection. Roosevelt, in the early 1940s, accentuated the power of the United States by being mildly patronizing, even to Churchill. Truman, in the early 1950s, when in fact the power discrepancy had grown greater, mitigated it by being respectful, although not subservient.

Churchill, in January 1953, responded by turning his full beam upon the outgoing President. Of course he saw Eisenhower, with whom he would need to work for several years in the future, but he did so almost unobtrusively in New York in Baruch's apartment. In Washington his undiluted attention was reserved for the alive but dying administration. He paid Truman a measured and massive compliment. He confessed to his dismay at the succession when Roosevelt died. 'I misjudged you badly,' Churchill added. 'Since that time, you, more than any other man, have saved Western civilization.'[14]

Truman gave him a dinner at which Acheson, Lovett, Harriman, and Omar Bradley assisted, and which seems almost to have got out of hand. Great jollity was contrived, with imaginary juries of historic figures empanelled to try both President and Prime Minister before an infernal (or maybe heavenly) tribunal. Acheson at least enjoyed himself immensely by presaging his 1960 thrust at Britain and saying to Churchill, in response to his confident growl that, wherever it was, he expected to be tried in accordance with the principles of the English Common Law: 'Is it altogether consistent with your respect for the creator of this and other universes to limit his imagination and judicial procedure to the accomplishment of a minute island, in a tiny world, in one of the smaller of the universes?'[15]

These festivities over, the Trumans were almost out of the White House. On January 15th the President made a farewell broadcast to the nation and – for almost the first time – was televised as well. He delivered what Robert Donovan well described as a 'neighborly' account of his stewardship. He thought that his presidency would be most remembered as the time when the cold war began to overshadow everyone's life. 'I have hardly had a day in office that has not been dominated by this all-embracing struggle . . . and always in the background there has been the atomic bomb.' However, 'starting an atomic war is totally unthinkable for rational men.'[16]

On the 16th he made his last (but not lasting – it was reversed by Congress with Eisenhower's approval) significant decision: he declared that off-shore oil belonged to the nation and not to the states off whose shores it lay. On the morning of the 20th (another sparkling day, as in 1949) he wound up his office from 8.45 to 10.30 a.m., greeted the Cabinet and their wives in the Red Room before his final exit from the mansion for the drive to Capitol Hill with Eisenhower and the ceremony there, leading for him to the complete relinquishment of responsibility. So relieved, he drove with his wife and daughter to Dean Acheson's house in Georgetown where there was a lunch for the outgoing Cabinet and a few other close associates. This was a highly successful occasion, with the ex-President on ebullient form '. . . an absolutely wonderful affair,' it was described by Margaret Truman, 'full of jokes and laughter and a few tears'. Then, typically, Truman slipped off to the apartment of a member of his White House staff 'for a nap'. Thus fortified he proceeded to Union Station, where a crowd of over 5,000 saw him off on his last journey in the presidential Pullman car. He made a little speech from the rear platform, and the train pulled out in the early evening to the swelling chorus of Auld Lang Syne.

It was 8.15 the next evening when (an hour late) they reached Independence. There had been small crowds at most of the stations along the route, even during the night, and big ones at St Louis and Independence itself. Typically again, he had got out and had a haircut at one of the Missouri stations. The journey over and the presidential car dismissed not merely to Washington but to near oblivion, for no subsequent president did much train travel, he drove to North Delaware Street. Here there was another crowd of 5,000. When asked subsequently what was the first thing he did when he got home, he was reported as saying: 'I carried the grips up to the attic.'[17] But he may have exaggerated his own matter of factness. Perhaps his diary entry captured his mood better. Commenting on this last great display of respect and affection and the cumulative effect of them all, he wrote: 'Mrs T and I were overcome. It was the pay-off for thirty years of hell and hard work.'[18]

12

A QUIET END

Truman's retirement was one of the longest in the twentieth-century history of the presidency: just three weeks short of twenty years. Only Hoover survived for longer – 31½ years as an ex-president, and his retirement was by no means as complete; he undertook several important tasks on the fringes of government for the Truman administration.* Truman's own long and tranquil survival was the more remarkable as, at the time of leaving the White House, he was the oldest President but three ever to have exercised executive power.†

Throughout these twenty years Truman neither deluded himself with thoughts of a return to power nor greatly sought to make money. When Churchill agreeably told him in 1956 that 'it would be a great thing for the world if [he] were to become President of the United States again,' Truman realistically replied that there was no chance of that. Nor did he ever pursue his rather wild 1951 idea of trying to return to the Senate. He believed, with some force, that former Presidents should be given honorary Senate seats, but this was more a general constitutional reflection than

---

* Perversely, in view of general demographic trends, there were many more long retirements in the first 70 years of the Republic than in the subsequent 140. John Adams, Martin Van Buren and Millard Fillmore exceeded Truman's post-presidential years. Thomas Jefferson, James Madison, John Quincy Adams (who went back to the Congress for 17 years), and John Tyler all rivalled him. Since the Civil War only Taft (Hoover and Truman apart), survived for much more than a decade.

† The three were Andrew Jackson, William Henry Harrison and James Buchanan, who all ended their terms a bare few months older than was Truman. Since Truman, first Eisenhower and then President Reagan became the only presidents to be in office over the age of 70.

any attempt at personal self-seeking. He spoke out, sometimes over-forthrightly, on internal Democratic Party affairs, but he was notably loath to step in and proffer his advice on matters of national security.

During his first year out of office he received a number of offers of lucrative employment involving only a very small commitment of time. None of them was of very high quality. He was offered nothing comparable with Eisenhower's Presidency of Columbia University, or with the sort of blue chip business appointment which many ex-Secretaries of the Treasury easily acquire. It must of course be remembered that he was aged 69 and pretty firmly Missouri-based. What was forthcoming, however, were manifestly attempts by second rank enterprises to buy his name rather than his wisdom. He rightly refused.

He was not greedy, he was not extravagant, and he was not by this stage without some modest resources of his own. His financial altruism, however, was modified by two considerations. First he was eager, partly for reasons of prestige, to do as well as he could out of his writings, and particularly his memoirs. Second he became resentful about the very considerable sums of personal money which, unless he was to ignore his correspondents and sit at home with nothing to do all day, he felt forced to spend on maintaining an office.

At first he received no support of any sort from the Federal Government: no pension, no secretarial or other assistance, no security protection. His Secret Service guards had been removed even before he left Washington. They simply said goodbye to him as he got aboard the train at Union Station. He had travelled home unprotected through the crowds across half the continent. He was equally unguarded from the sightseers who subsequently came in fairly substantial numbers to stare at 219, North Delaware Street. His only screen was the iron fence which in somewhat un-American fashion, but, he claimed, based on the experience of Thomas Jefferson and the advice of Herbert Hoover, he kept around the house. It was all remarkably different from today's practice.

The fence at least was already there and did not cost money. But the office which he established in the Union Bank building in Kansas City did, although not on a huge scale. He wrote in 1957 that he had spent $153,000 on it over 3½ years. This, he said, he

had been able to do only because the accident of the sale of his
share of the Grandview farm land to the shopping centre developers
had safeguarded him from financial embarrassment. The experience had converted him to the desirability of some government
help for ex-Presidents, a proposition towards which he had earlier
been austerely cool. 'I don't want a pension and do not expect
one', he wrote to John W. McCormack, the Democratic leader in
the House, on January 10th, 1957, 'but I do think 70% of the
expenses or overhead should be paid by the Government – the
30% is what I would ordinarily have been out on my own hook
if I hadn't tried to meet the responsibilities of being a former
President.'[1]

The work of the office was directed to answering a large volume
of mostly friendly mail, sorting his presidential papers, writing his
memoirs, and bringing to fruition his plans for the building of a
Truman Library and Museum. The memoirs were not a great
success, either financially or of esteem. They were punctual, despite
the fact that Truman had a fairly severe illness in 1954, and were
published in two substantial volumes in 1955 and 1956. They gave
a clear, narrative account of the main events with which he had
been concerned. If they were undisfigured by his prejudices or
outrageous remarks, they were equally unadorned by originality
or penetration. They received the slightly bland reception which
their slightly bland style deserved. Coming out at a time when his
reputation still hovered a little uncertainly in the haze of the
Eisenhower afternoon, they did not strengthen the market for his
writing. And the direct return was disappointing. This however,
appears to have been more due to the taxation arrangement than
to the gross payment. The book was sold outright to the same
publisher for the same sum of money that Eisenhower had received
in 1948 for *Crusade in Europe*. Truman, however, claimed that,
owing to a taxation change in the meantime, Eisenhower had been
left with $437,000 net, whereas he was left, after tax and research
and other expenses, with little more than $37,000. There emerges
the strong feeling either that he was not comparing like with like
or that he had a very bad accountant. In either case the contrast
with Eisenhower's 'killing' exacerbated his slight sense of dis-
appointment.

It was however more than outweighed by the remarkable success
of the Truman Library. It was planned, built and opened to the

public within 4½ years of his leaving the White House. This was in spite of some initial hesitancy about the location. There was never any question of its being other than in the Kansas City area. He never contemplated a Washington memorial. He was at first attracted by the idea of building the Library on part of the old farm land at Grandview. However, the temptations of the developers, coinciding with a generous offer from the City of Independence of a good and substantial site adjacent to the public park, barely a mile from North Delaware Street, deflected him from Grandview. Money came in well, from both corporate and private donors. There were 17,000 separate subscriptions. The last million dollars was raised by Truman himself on an intensive lecture tour.

There was no embarrassment in his mind about seeking money for what was in effect a memorial to himself. He did not see it in vainglorious terms. He did not want a Washington obelisk, a Jefferson rotunda or a Lincoln temple. What he did want was a political science teaching workshop which would make vivid the nature of the office of President, admittedly by exhibiting the *memorabilia* of himself as local hero, in a part of the United States which had not previously participated in Federal history in a way that had Virginia, Massachusetts, New York, Ohio or Illinois.

He had a good deal of conceit and a certain vanity at this stage. But the vanity was essentially about the grandeur of the office which he had rather surprisingly managed successfully to occupy. He wanted the people – and particularly schoolchildren – in the mid-West and elsewhere to know about this greatest democratic office in the world and, as he saw it, the five facets of the President's role. If the exploitation of this splendour through a library and museum devoted to his own tenure involved some self-aggrandisement, so be it. But that was genuinely not the primary purpose. He had a passionate desire to instruct about the presidency as an institution, and devoted much of his time to addressing quite small school and college audiences on the subject.

The Library was admirably constructed for such a purpose. It also had the unique attribute at that stage of a resident president. Just as the English National Trust rightly believes that an inhabited country house is more interesting to the public than a dead shell, so Independence had the advantage over Hyde Park or, still more obviously, Mount Vernon or Monticello, of having the man it commemorated on the premises. For the first nine or ten years he was quite liable to descend on any visiting party and give them a quick and vigorous tutorial.

Only after 1966 did the vigour and the immanence begin to recede. Until then the Library was his diurnal home. It solved the problems of the expensive and not very convenient Kansas City office. Once it had been built by private subscription its upkeep was taken over by the National Archives and Records Services, an offshoot of an agency of the Federal Government. This conduit of public money brought good practical office accommodation, separate from the replica of the Oval Office which was rather elaborately constructed in another wing, and other public support for Truman. Thereafter he had no problems on this account. Even the Secret Service men came back after the assassination of President Kennedy.

The Library was not only a most satisfactory convenience for Truman, which, in his daughter's view, became 'one of the great joys of [his] old age'. It was also a place for pilgrimages of reconciliation and tribute. Truman found it very difficult to resist the offer of a visit. What would he have done had MacArthur proposed himself? He received Eisenhower graciously in 1961 and the Nixons without wincing in 1969. (At a Museum dedicated to the institution of the presidency it would of course have been difficult to do otherwise with the incumbent President.) Kennedy, with whom a little intra-party reconciliation was desirable, came between his nomination and the election in 1960. Lyndon Johnson, with whom no reconciliation was necessary (he and Truman always got on fairly well) brought a great entourage for the symbolic signing there of the Medicare Bill in July 1965.

Until the mid-1960s, when he was over eighty, Truman remained active both politically and physically – although he always confined his exercise to brisk urban walks, sometimes interspersed with on the hoof political comment to attendant journalists. He did not think it necessary to show his mature statesmanship by becoming less anti-Republican, and he did not hesitate to express his preferences within the Democratic Party. In August 1969, he was writing in good uninhibited form to Acheson about 'Tricky Dicky and Alibi Ike'.[3] The Republican candidates were always satisfactorily unacceptable to him. The Democratic candidates were less satisfactorily acceptable. He never supported Stevenson after 1952. He wanted Harriman in 1956 and Symington in 1960.

He several times referred to Kennedy as 'this immature boy' and believed that his father had bought him the nomination. However, as an old Democratic 'pro', he rallied to Stevenson in 1956 and to Kennedy in 1960 as soon as the campaigns got underway. Later he responded more strongly to Kennedy's attentions, attended the 1961 inauguration and later went with his wife and daughter to stay a night in the White House. However, Johnson in 1964 was the first Democratic candidate who would have been his first choice. Humphrey in 1968 was probably more or less satisfactory to him unless his memory went back too powerfully to the young Mayor of Minneapolis's support for Eisenhower in July 1948, but he played little part in that 1968 campaign. In 1972 he played no part, and it is not known what he thought of George McGovern or whether he was even able to vote for him. He had already faded far by that November, and was dead before Nixon's second inauguration in January 1973.

In the 1950s and the first half of the 1960s he travelled a fair amount: Washington occasionally, although never to the White House while Eisenhower was there; a good deal of mostly unpaid speaking and lecturing about the country; frequent family visits to New York where his daughter, married in 1955 to Clifton Daniels, high in the hierarchy of the *New York Times*, produced four grandsons for him to treat with respect and enjoyment rather than excessive domestic intimacy (he mostly installed himself firmly in the Carlyle Hotel); and on three occasions to Europe, but never, except for Hawaii, not then a state, elsewhere outside his own country.

The first European visit in 1956 was something of a stately progress, and deservedly so. The Trumans were away for seven weeks, in Italy, Austria, France and the Netherlands. They finished in Britain, where Truman (at the age of 72) saw London for the first and last time, received, without opposition, an Oxford honorary degree* and lunched with the Churchills at Chartwell. The second European journey was only two years later, but a much quieter, purely holiday visit to Italy and France. The third was to Athens in March 1964, where he represented President

---

* It had been offered in 1953, but had to be twice postponed. Truman valued the honour, laughed at the hat, and made an odd comment on the university: 'A most colorful, solemn and dignified educational institution.' (*Off the Record*, p. 336)

Johnson at the funeral of King Paul. He was alone (that is without Mrs Truman) on that trip and played poker all night on the aeroplane. Such a reversion to indiscipline showed no sign of exhausting him before his eightieth birthday celebrations, which came later that spring and included numerous luncheons, dinners and even breakfasts, as well as a speech to the Senate.

His reputation at that stage was strongly in the ascendant. In July 1962, for example, the *New York Times* magazine had amused itself by getting Arthur M. Schlesinger Snr to repeat the poll of seventy-five historians which he had first conducted in 1948. They were asked to arrange presidents in order of 'greatness' or 'near-greatness'. The 'greats' came out as Lincoln, Washington, Franklin D. Roosevelt, Wilson and Jefferson. The 'near-greats', also in order, were Jackson, Theodore Roosevelt, Polk, Truman, John Adams, and Cleveland.* It was a far cry from 1946 or even 1952. He reacted to this calmly but with pleasure. 'I don't know how they came to put me so high up on the list', he wrote to a Congressman who had somewhat supererogatively sent him the article, 'but I appreciate it nevertheless. If I had been arranging the first five in the row of the great, I would have put Washington first, Jefferson second, Woodrow Wilson third, Lincoln fourth and Franklin Roosevelt fifth. I, in all probability, would have moved Andrew Jackson into that row and made six of them, but I didn't have anything to do with making it up.'[4]

In his early eighties his powers, not so much of mind as of body, began noticeably to fail. He had a bad bathroom fall in the autumn of 1964. He lost a lot of weight and became a very emaciated old man. He also lost his mobility and for his last six or seven years was more or less confined to his house. Suddenly, over a weekend in the summer of 1966, he ceased to go regularly to the Library (the Nixon visit was a rare subsequent exception) and ceased also to walk briskly about the town in the early mornings, or at any other time of day. When a prominent Independence citizen who was the ex-President's lawyer was asked by an interviewer what Truman thought of some major developments which took place in the town square around 1970 he in effect replied that he had few thoughts about them because he never saw them. Bess Truman,

---

* In 1948 the results had been nearly the same. Jackson was given last place among the 'greats' instead of first place among the 'near-greats'. The 'near-great' list then read: T. Roosevelt, Cleveland, J. Adams, Polk.

who had never taxed herself very heavily, remained much more active, and even after 29 years of courtship and 53 years of marriage still managed 10 years of widowhood before dying at the age of 97.

Truman's agility, although non-athletic, was an essential part of his personality. When it went a good part of his mental zest went with it. His daughter insists that he continued to read two newspapers a day and to keep abreast of events well into the last year of his life. But he lost his desire to comment upon these events or to communicate outside the small family circle. After 1970 his life, which had already gone into a lower gear in 1966, quietly subsided. He died in a Kansas City hospital on December 26th, 1972. He was buried in the courtyard of the Library.

The commemorative stone, while not elaborate, is neither eloquent nor sparse. It lists with equal prominence each office which he had held, from Eastern Judge to President of the United States. This flatness was in a sense appropriate, for he had treated all the offices with equal respect, and behaved in each of them with equal determination to do his best, and equal equanimity about the comments of most others when he had done it. It so happened that the first offices led to the building of some good roads and the last to the building of a Western world which enjoyed unprecedented prosperity and freedom from major war for a generation. In each case he built well, honestly, and without pretension.

REFERENCES

The reference sources most frequently quoted are referred to by title as listed below.

Sketches from Life by Dean Acheson (New York: Harper & Row, 1961; London: Hamish Hamilton, 1961)

Present at the Creation: My Years in the State Department by Dean Acheson (New York: W. W. Norton, 1969; London: Hamish Hamilton, 1970). Extracts reprinted by permission of Hamish Hamilton Ltd.

Roosevelt, the Soldier of Freedom by James Macgregor Burns (New York: Harcourt Brace Jovanovich, 1970; London: Weidenfeld & Nicolson, 1971)

The Man of Independence by Jonathan Daniels (New York: J. P. Lippincott, 1950)

Conflict and Crisis by Robert Donovan (New York and London: W. W. Norton, 1977). Extracts reprinted by permission of the Sterling Lord Agency. Copyright © 1977 by Robert Donovan.

Tumultuous Years by Robert Donovan (New York and London: W. W. Norton, 1982). Extracts reprinted by permission of W. W. Norton Company, Inc.

Plain Speaking, an Oral Biography of Harry S. Truman by Merle Miller (New York: G. P. Putnam, 1973; London: Victor Gollancz, 1974)

Off the Record, The Private Papers of Harry S. Truman edited by Robert H. Ferrell (New York: Harper & Row, 1980)

Dear Bess: the Letters of Harry to Bess Truman 1910–1959 edited by Robert H. Ferrell (New York and London: W. W. Norton, 1983). Extracts reprinted by permission of W. W. Norton Company, Inc.

Harry S. Truman by Margaret Truman (New York: William Morrow, 1973; London Hamish Hamilton, 1973). Extracts reprinted by permission of Hamish Hamilton Ltd and William Morrow & Company, Inc. Copyright © 1972 by Margaret Truman Daniels.

1. THE TRANSITION

1. *Off the Record*, p. 16
2. *Plain Speaking* from 'A preparatory note on the Language'
3. *ibid*, p. 34

2. JACKSON COUNTY

1. *Plain Speaking*, p. 67 and *Dear Bess, passim*
2. *Dear Bess*, p. 293
3. *The Man of Independence*, p. 147
4. *Plain Speaking*, p. 137
5. *Harry S. Truman*, p. 82

3. JUNIOR SENATOR FROM MISSOURI

1. *Dear Bess*, p. 396
2. *Dear Bess*, p. 376
3. *ibid*, p. 420
4. *ibid*, p. 414
5. *Harry S. Truman*, p. 117
6. Charles Robbins, *Last of his Kind* (Morrow, 1979), p. 111n
7. *Dear Bess*, p. 39
8. *ibid*, p. 441
9. *The Man of Independence*, p. 211
10. *Dear Bess*, pp. 445–6
11. *Plain Speaking*, p. 158
12. *ibid*, p. 169
13. *Dear Bess*, p. 495

4. HEIR TO A DYING PRESIDENT

1. Joseph Alsop, *The Life and Times of Franklin D. Roosevelt* (Thames & Hudson, 1982), p. 250
2. *Harry S. Truman*, p. 167
3. *ibid*, p. 168
4. *Roosevelt, the Soldier of Freedom*, p. 505
5. *The Man of Independence*, pp. 248–9
6. *Roosevelt, the Soldier of Freedom*, p. 505
7. *Harry S. Truman*, p. 177
8. *ibid*, p. 186
9. *ibid*, p. 199

5. THE NEW PRESIDENT

1. *Off the Record*, pp. 31–2
2. *ibid*, p. 49
3. *Dear Bess*, p. 522
4. *Off the Record*, p. 55
5. *Dear Bess*, p. 517
6. *Off the Record*, p. 59
7. *ibid*, p. 51
8. *Dear Bess*, p. 522
9. Winston S. Churchill, *The Second World War* (Cassell, 1953), Vol. VI, p. 553
10. *Off the Record*, p. 60
11. *ibid*, p. 56
12. *Conflict and Crisis*, p. 97

6. TRUMAN BATTERED

1. *Dear Bess*, p. 523
2. *Conflict and Crisis*, pp. 134–5
3. *ibid*, p. 135
4. *Off the Record*, p. 73 (in a letter to his cousin, Miss Nellie Noland)
5. *Dear Bess*, p. 526
6. *Conflict and Crisis*, p. 122
7. *Off the Record*, p. 64
8. *Conflict and Crisis*, p. 236
9. *Off the Record*, p. 104
10. *ibid*, p. 83
11. *Conflict and Crisis*, p. 236
12. *ibid*, p. 212
13. *ibid*, pp. 216–17 (quoted in)
14. *Diaries of Harold L. Ickes*

(Weidenfeld & Nicolson, 1955).
15. *Dear Bess*, p. 523
16. *Conflict and Crisis*, p. 172
17. *Off the Record*, p. 96
18. *Harry S. Truman*, p. 330
19. *ibid*, p. 324

7. TRUMAN RESURGENT

1. *Harry S. Truman*, p. 148
2. *Sketches from Life*, p. 157
3. *Off the Record*, p. 109
4. *Present at the Creation*, p. 219
5. Alan Bullock: *Ernest Bevin: Foreign Secretary* (Heinemann, 1983), p. 379
6. *Harry S. Truman*, p. 343
7. *Crisis and Conflict*, p. 287
8. *ibid*, pp. 301–2
9. *The Forrestal Diaries* pp. 333–4
10. *Off the Record*, p. 120

8. VICTORY OUT OF THE JAWS OF DEFEAT

1. *Conflict and Crisis*, p. 319
2. *Harry S. Truman*, pp. 384–5
3. *Conflict and Crisis*, p. 374
4. *Harry S. Truman*, p. 388
5. *Conflict and Crisis*, p. 376
6. *Harry S. Truman*, p. 388
7. *Conflict and Crisis*, p. 376
8. *The Man of Independence*, p. 319
9. Donovan, *op. cit.* p. 382, based upon statements by Clark Clifford
10. *Conflict and Crisis*, p. 361
11. *ibid*, p. 389
12. *ibid*, p. 289 (quoted in)
13. *Harry S. Truman*, p. 9
14. *ibid*, p. 11
15. Irwin Ross, *The Loneliest Cam-*

paign (New American Library, 1968), p. 129
16. *Harry S. Truman*, p. 21
17. *The Loneliest Campaign*, pp. 187–8
18. *ibid*, p. 240
19. *Conflict and Crisis*, p. 438

9. THE LIMITATIONS OF VICTORY

1. *Harry S. Truman*, p. 400
2. *Off the Record*, p. 168
3. *Tumultuous Years*, p. 54
4. *Harry S. Truman*, p. 425
5. *Off the Record*, p. 168
6. *Harry S. Truman*, p. 429

10. TRUMAN'S THIRD WAR

1. *Harry S. Truman*, pp. 435–6
2. *Off the Record*, pp. 177–8
3. Margot Asquith, *Autobiography* (Eyre & Spotiswoode, 1985), p. 295
4. *Harry S. Truman*, p. 455
5. *Khrushchev Remembers* (Little, Brown, 1970), pp. 367–73
6. *Dear Bess*, p. 562
7. *Present at the Creation*, p. 406
8. *Harry S. Truman*, p. 457
9. *Dear Bess*, p. 562
10. *Harry S. Truman*, p. 469
11. *Tumultuous Years*, p. 224
12. *Present at the Creation*, p. 415
13. *Harry S. Truman*, p. 484
14. *Present at the Creation*, p. 406
15. *Harry S. Truman*, p. 493 (quoted in)
16. *Tumultuous Years*, p. 289
17. *Harry S. Truman*, p. 493 (quoted in)
18. *Tumultuous Years*, p. 309

19. *Present at the Creation*, p. 475
20. *ibid*, p. 478
21. *ibid*, p. 480
22. K. Harris, *Attlee* (Weidenfeld & Nicolson, 1982), pp. 463–4
23. *Harry S. Truman*, pp. 513
24. *Ibid*, p. 518
25. *Off the Record*, p. 211
26. *Plain Speaking*, p. 301

11. THE LAST PHASE

1. *Tumultuous Years*, p. 335
2. *Off the Record*, p. 220
3. *ibid*, p. 245
4. *Harry S. Truman*, p. 532
5. *Off the Record*, pp. 266–7
6. *ibid*, pp. 268–9
7. *Harry S. Truman*, p. 545
8. *Tumultuous Years*, p. 392

9. *Memoirs of Harry S. Truman* (Doubleday, 1956), Vol. II, pp. 527–30
10. *Harry S. Truman*, p. 557
11. *ibid*, p. 557
12. *Off the Record*, pp. 275–6
13. *ibid*, p. 279
14. *Harry S. Truman*, p. 556
15. *ibid*, p. 555
16. *Tumultuous Years*, p. 407
17. *Plain Speaking*, p. 17
18. *Off the Record*, p. 288

12. A QUIET END

1. *Off the Record*, p. 546
2. *Harry S. Truman*, p. 562
3. *Off the Record*, p. 382
4. *ibid*, pp. 403–4

INDEX